Paranormal
Experience
and
Survival
of Death

❧

Carl B. Becker

State University
of New York Press

Published by
State University of New York Press, Albany

For information, address the State University of New York Press,
State University Plaza, Albany, NY 12246

Production by Bernadine Dawes
Marketing by Dana Yanulavich

Library of Congress Cataloging-in-Publication Data

Becker, Carl B., 1951–
         Paranormal experience and survival of death / Carl B. Becker
                 p. cm. — (SUNY Series in Western esoteric traditions)
         Includes bibliographical references and index.
         ISBN 0-7914-1475-2 (hard : alk. paper) : — ISBN
0-7914-1476-0 (pbk. : alk. paper) :
                 1. Future Life. 2. Spiritualism. 3. Parapsychology and science.

         I. Title. II. Series.
         BF1261.2.B43 1993
         133.9'01'3--dc20   92-37751
                                                                                             CIP

5 6 7 8 9 10

Paranormal
Experience
and
Survival
of Death

SUNY Series in Western Esoteric Traditions
David Appelbaum, Editor

TABLE OF CONTENTS

ACKNOWLEDGMENTS

This book is the product of more than ten years' study: of philosophy, religion, science, and the paranormal. The people who have helped and encouraged me in this venture are far too numerous to mention, but I should like to express my special thanks to those who have contributed most directly to making this research and writing possible. Parts of this research were conducted while on Danforth, Fulbright, and East-West Center grants, for which I am deeply grateful.

Earlier versions of small parts of this book have already been printed. Part of chapter 2 won the Robert Ashby Competition, appearing as "Out of Their Bodies or Out of Their Minds?" in the *Journal of Religion and Psychical Research* 6, nos. 1–2 (January–April 1983). The section of chapter 3 treating Carl Sagan's "amniotic" theory appeared previously as "Why Birth Models Cannot Explain Near-Death Phenomena," in *The Near-Death Experience: Problems, Prospects, Perspectives*, edited by Bruce Greyson and Charles Flynn (Springfield, Ill.: Charles C. Thomas, 1985). Some paragraphs from chapter 4 have appeared in "ESP, Near-Death Studies, and Paradigm Shifts," in the *Journal for Near-Death Studies* 9, no. 1 (Fall 1990).

The encouragement of Arthur Berger, Boyce Batey, Bruce Greyson, Allan Kellehear, Jim McClenon, Karlis Osis, Ken Ring, and the Robert Ashby Award from the Society for Religion and Psychical Research was warmly appreciated for moving this work towards completion. A big thanks also goes to Rosalie Robertson, and all those at SUNY Press who helped. produce this work with speed and quality.

In Japan, Drs. Soji Otani and Hiroshi Motoyama, originally of Tokyo University, Drs. Yasuo Yuasa, Noboru Miyata, and Michio Araki of Tsukuba University, and psychotherapists Nobushige Koori, Tosio Kasahara, and Joy Norton-Van Buren all provided important suggestions and insights. In Honolulu, Drs. Winfield Nagley and Beatrice Yamasaki, and the staff at Hamilton Library provided invaluable materials and critiques.

My most especial thanks go to Joan and Lou Rose for their constructive questions, criticisms, and Aloha. I should like to dedicate this work to Robert J. "Papa" Baer, whose fatherly warmth and wit, intelligence and creativity, have been a constant inspiration, and to Elice and all the family, for their unfailing spiritual and material support over many miles and years.

INTRODUCTION

At least as long ago as the Neanderthals, human beings have expected there to be some kind of life after death. Throughout the centuries, the dead have been entombed with provisions for their journey to the next world. In the vast majority of cultures, for the whole of human history prior to the nineteenth century, humans expected to continue their lives on a different plane of existence, more or less like this one, after their deaths. The ancient literature of the world is filled with accounts of people meeting the ghosts of their ancestors, leaving their bodies, or visiting the next world on their deathbeds.

But the materialism, cynicism, and "scientism" of the modern West have tended to treat life after death as just so much nonsense or superstition. This has exacerbated the debates between science and religion in the West, and it often has led to a crisis of religious consciousness in the developing countries as well. Science and capitalism have made invaluable contributions to making our world healthier, faster, more convenient. On the other hand, they have not yet addressed the ultimate problems of the human spirit, such as love, happiness, beauty, responsibility, or the ultimate fate of humanity. This failure has led to the emergence of countless religious and pseudoscientific movements, a "New Age" counterculture concerned with channeling and divination, pyramids and purple plates, transcendental meditation and crystal power.

A growing awareness of non-Western cultures has led to increasing interest in the ideas of reincarnation and rebirth—of past and future lives. Films such as *Field of Dreams, Ghost,* and *Flatliners,* not to mention the *Ghostbusters* and *Poltergeist* series, reflect the public fascination and even desire to believe in other dimensions and a life after death. However, a flagging economy has led to cuts in research budgets for themes like out-of-body research, which flourished in early decades.

Another unexpected by-product of the recent "scientification" of the dying process is that some patients revive after nearly dying or even after being pronounced dead. Many of them report having had unusual experiences while their minds are "out of their bodies." Of course there are problems in the analysis and interpretation of these near-death experiences (NDEs). But their widespread nature has led Western scholars to begin rethinking the nature of the dying process. Some scholars even believe that such research can enable us to catch a glimpse of the beginning of the "next world," or "afterlife."

This book studies the "survival hypothesis": the theory that some significant part of the human personality continues after the death of the physical body. To do so, we shall ask (and answer) the following questions:

1. What experiences are mistakenly thought to prove survival, and why? (In each chapter, we must eliminate these first.)
2. What would constitute good evidence of survival, and why?
3. Does there exist such good evidence?
4. How else might such cases be interpreted?
5. Is survival the best interpretation of the evidence?

In attempting to verify or falsify survival, we shall look at the data on past lives, out-of-body, and near-death experiences. By pursuing this process of analysis, we shall come to the curious conclusion that people often believe far more or far less than what the evidence suggests is reasonable. Therefore, we shall also want to ask:

6. What is the "science" by which people judge ideas true or false? What is the position of scientists on the survival issue and why?

This discussion will lead us to the point where we can finally come to some tentative conclusions about the meaning of these experiences, and about whether we can make any sense of the idea of survival of death.

We must always walk a tightrope: we are examining data often ignored by the scientific community and embraced by the religious community, but we are using methodology that is advocated by the scientific community and ignored by much of the religious world. Therefore we should expect to be criticized by dogmatists from both sides of the fence. Of course, there will always be newer and better data deserving analysis. But the reasoning behind the discussion of survival will not change. Future data can be plugged into our same schemes of logical reasoning and examined for the conclusions they do or do not support.

All of us will die, many of us at times or in places we do not expect. But until that time, evidence and reasoning such as the material presented here are about the closest we can come to understanding the ultimate mystery in anything resembling rational terms.

1.

Proof of Reincarnation?

The case for "reincarnation" is based on the assumption of the regularity of the universe: if some people now alive have had former lives, then some people in the future will have lives which are now being lived. So in looking for cases indicative of possible reincarnation, we are looking less for evidence of "future lives" than for evidence of "past lives," which in turn suggests that similar reincarnations may occur in the future. The leading American scholar of this field is without question Dr. Ian Stevenson of the University of Virginia Medical School at Charlottesville. As Stevenson has observed, in mediumistic attempts to contact those who have already died, we have the problem of proving that someone who has died is still alive somewhere. On the other hand, "[i]n evaluating apparent memories of former incarnations, the problem consists in judging whether someone clearly living once died. This may prove the easier task, and if pursued with sufficient zeal and success, may contribute decisively to the question of survival."[1]

Some researchers object to the title "reincarnation," even if placed in quotation marks, for it seems to presuppose an explanation for the phenomena encountered and is laden with religious nuances. H. N. Banerjee, director of the Department of Parapsychology at the University of Rajasthan at Jaipur, prefers to call such phenomena cases of "extra-cerebral memory" (i.e., memory that does not seem to have come from the head of the person who reports it).[2] More important than the name we use is the recognition that the phenomena to be considered do not prove reincarnation per se. Its tenability as one hypothesis must be judged after the evidence is carefully weighed and analyzed.

Phenomena Not Considered

To avoid further confusion, let us first itemize several groups of phenomena that are not appropriate evidences of reincarnation or survival, despite their inclusion by some writers: (1) déjà vu, (2) autoprecognition, (3) child prodigies, and (4) seance mediumism and spiritualism.

Déjà vu

At one time or another almost all humans have the uncanny feeling that they have "been in the same situation before," without being able to pinpoint either the experience or the origin of the feeling. This phenomenon is called *déjà vu*, French for "already seen." When déjà vu persists, the percipient has the distinct impression of knowing what will come next in his or her experience and that the entire sequence of events has been repeated at an earlier time. Some people interpret such déjà vu experiences to be intimations of having lived before, or of the myth of the eternal return.[3]

Such interpretations are manifestly illogical and illegitimate. Déjà vu experiences are akin to hallucinations in the sense that (a) they are completely private, and (b) they are false impressions. The feeling of having been in the same place or situation before is likely not due to actually having been there before, but rather to some very minor brain dysfunctions. Déjà vu experiences are most common among people undergoing severe strain, undernourishment, hormonal imbalances, or physical or mental exhaustion.

To put it simply, déjà vu situations could not be hidden memories of past lives, because déjà vu (by definition) is the feeling that everything is exactly identical to the way it was at some former time. But it is impossible that every element of any situation could be repeated identically, for each moment is unique and all things change over time. It is possible that someone could vaguely recognize a place and honestly not remember when or why he or she had been there before. But such a recognition would not be a case of déjà vu, lacking the déjà vu sense of exactness. Thus the very exactness of the illusion in true déjà vu guarantees that it could not be a memory from some previous situation, in this lifetime or in any other.

Similarly, it is entirely conceivable that a person might arrive in a place where he or she had never been before and report a strange familiarity that is entirely unexpected. This person might even recognize foreign idioms or describe correctly some details of the town that had been true of the town in a previous era. It just might be the case that the scene awakened psychometric powers or inspired remembrances that had been suppressed from previous lives. We shall consider some cases of such phenomena a little later. Whatever else these cases may be, they are not cases of déjà vu.[4]

For the sake of rigor, let us also avoid further discussion of such "vague familiarities" with locales not already known from this lifetime, because any number of factors besides former lives might also give rise to false feelings of familiarity with a place.

Autoprecognition

Autoprecognition is the psychic ability to foresee what will happen in one's own life and in no one else's. Parapsychologists have sometimes argued that autoprecognition might be an indication of having been reincarnated.[5]

The reasoning behind this assertion, however, demands postulation of numerous unprovable assumptions: (1) that the course of the present lifetime was already at least partially predetermined prior to birth, (2) that there was an interim state of personal existence between the previous death and the present life, (3) that the consciousness before birth was able to observe major future events in the life it was about to enter, (4) that living human beings sometimes *recall* elements of the lives they foresaw while disembodied before birth, without recalling the disembodied state itself, and (5) that such people cannot distinguish such recalling from predicting (i.e., that it feels more like prediction than recollection, even though it is really recollection).

While there is nothing totally impossible or logically contradictory about such an account in itself, it involves many assumptions that are unsupported even by the descriptions of the people who possess such precognitive faculties. If reincarnation had already been established as fact, then this theory might provide an explanation of some of the cases of apparent autoprecognition now in evidence. However, autoprecognition in itself cannot come close to proving anything like reincarnation.

Child Prodigies

An argument frequently heard in East Indian circles is that child prodigies such as Mozart or Edison must have acquired their talents in previous lifetimes, because such talents are inexplicable simply on the basis of childhood training. Again, it is true that the reincarnation theory might contribute toward an explanation of such phenomena, but in and of themselves child prodigies cannot properly be taken as evidence of reincarnation.

As it stands, most psychologists and psychiatrists feel that the variables of heredity, environment, and "chance" personality development are adequate to explain such prodigies without resort to theories of reincarnation. Mozart, for example, was born into a highly musical family. He was encouraged to listen to, to perform, and to write music by his family and friends, and he was provided with the perfect environment for the cultivation of those talents. Much as we admire his truly unusual abilities, we might attribute them just as reasonably to his family and to circumstances as to a past life.

Of course, if the doctrine of reincarnation were found to be universally true, and if there were a way to determine one's previous lives, then we might gain a better understanding of the origins of children's talents and predilections. The presence of unusual talents or abilities might be a secondary sort of confirmation of cases of people thought to be "reborn" for other reasons. Variations among children, however, can be adequately understood without resort to such hypotheses, and therefore cannot stand alone as evidence adequate to demonstrate reincarnation.[6]

Mediumism and Spiritualism

Mediumistic performances have sometimes been interpreted as the temporary takeover of the body of one person by the discarnate spirit of another, who is "waiting in the wings" for reincarnation, as it were. However, the emotionally charged atmosphere of the dimly lit seance hall lends itself to autosuggestion. Careful guesswork on the part of the medium, abetted by overt or subliminal cues from other participants and dramatized by a charismatic subliminal personality, may account for the majority of mediumistic sittings. Some genuinely sensitive mediums may glean information through telepathy from the other sitters or through psychometry from an object belonging to the deceased, and misrepresent this information as coming from the surviving personality.

The theory that mediums communicate with discarnate intelligences becomes even more suspect in light of experiments in which "mediumistic contact" has been made with living or demonstrably fictional characters. The manifest potential for fraud in this business has cast such suspicion on the profession that few parapsychologists now count mediumistic seances among their sources of evidence. Curiously, mediumistic communications have dramatically declined in the post–World War II period, with a few noteworthy exceptions of channeling in recent years. However, most channeling sources claim to be transcendental or extraterrestrial and therefore do not directly relate to the question of human survival of bodily death.[7]

There is a further logical gap between seances and reincarnation theory. Even if it were to be conceded that spiritualism had proven the existence of discarnate spirits in a few instances, it would not necessarily follow that any or all of such spirits would ever again have human bodies—which is just the claim which the reincarnationists wish to defend. In short, even if the phenomena genuinely involved paranormal contact with the dead, mediumistic seances are amenable to too many interpretations other than reincarnation to serve as good evidence for that hypothesis.

It is not our intention to impugn the integrity of mediums, nor to imply that all are hoaxes. However, the difficulty of sorting the meaningful phrases from the reams of trivia; the problems in identification of raps, voices or accents with real, previously living people; the paucity of high-quality evidence from recent mediums; the logical gap between the mere existence of discarnate spirits and the conclusion that they will again assume human bodies—these are just a few of the reasons why these phenomena cannot be treated as serious evidence for reincarnation.

Phenomena Considered

The major phenomena we shall treat in this chapter are those of spontaneous possession, hypnotic regression, and spontaneous claimed memories of former lives. In each of these cases, we must ascertain that they demonstrate verifiable skills and memories that the agent could not have acquired through normal or even paranormal means in the present lifetime.

Lest it be contended that these three groups of phenomena are of the same caliber as mediumistic possessions, some critical differences between the two must be briefly noted. Most importantly, the typical seance medium has been deliberately hired to produce spirit voices, materializations, or other indications of contact with dead people known to the sitters. Moreover, the typical seance lasts only for an hour or two, while the parts of the medium's discourse that may be used as possible evidence occupy but a few minutes at a time. We must distinguish mediumistic seances from spontaneous cases of possession in which (1) the surrounding people (and often the one possessed) neither desire nor approve of the "intruding consciousness," (2) they have no prior knowledge of the facts related by the possessed, (3) the atmosphere is normal daylight, and (4) the possession lasts over a period of weeks or even years.

Many other distinguishing factors might be identified, but these four are the most crucial in avoiding the objections that may otherwise be raised against paranormal interpretations of possession cases. This distinction also rules out shamanic possession found in many primitive societies. Shamanic experiences share with mediumism the short duration, emotionally charged atmosphere, sympathetic observers, and possible telepathic or subliminal communication of desired information. However interesting as anthropological studies, such cases have little value as experimental evidence. Let us consider cases of spontaneous possession with these distinctions in mind and these fringe cases excluded.

Spontaneous Possession with Verifiable Memories and Skills

Possession is the name for the phenomenon in which persons suddenly and inexplicably lose their normal set of memories, mental dispositions, and skills, and exhibit entirely new and different sets of memories, dispositions, and skills. Cases of possession have been recorded around the globe since ancient times. Many primitive societies have attributed such cases to the occupation of a living body by the spirit of one who had already died, but this presupposes more than has been established. Psychiatrists prefer to consider most cases of possession to be varieties of mental disease, disorientation, and schizophrenia, to be cured by appropriate medical and psychiatric treatment.

The spontaneous cases of particular interest to our study are those in which the new set of suddenly acquired skills and memories is unknown to the person being "possessed" and the secondary personality traits and information are independently verifiable as beyond the ken of the former personality. Several examples of such spontaneous possession with veridical memory should clarify this definition. One of the earliest cases was recorded in detail by Jacob Fromer in 1811. He reported witnessing a Polish Jewess who exhibited the characteristics of a learned German Jewish scholar who had committed suicide:

> I had a good place, from which I could see and hear everything. She sat down, languid and exhausted, with haggard, fearful eyes, and from time to time lamented, begging to be taken back to the house because she was afraid of the wonder-rabbi. Her voice, weak and beseeching, inspired sympathy and compassion. Suddenly, she sprang up and made efforts to remain standing.
>
> "Silentium strictissimum!"
>
> I could not believe my ears. It was a real man's voice, harsh and rough, and the onlookers affirmed that it was exactly the voice of the [scholar suicide]. Not one of us knew the meaning of these words. We only knew that it was a strange language, which the sick woman understood as little as ourselves. . . .
>
> Then she pronounced a long, confused discourse with High-German turns of phrase, of which I understood only that it greeted a festive gathering and wished to draw attention to the meaning of the feast.[8]

The account goes on to describe the interactions of the possessed girl with the "wonder-rabbi" who has come to exorcise the spirit. In the process, the spirit describes animal rebirths prior to this possession, and says that he was permitted to enter the girl's body when she was rapt in lovemaking. The episode concludes in fisticuffs between the rabbi and the girl, who gives up the spirit when she is finally knocked unconscious.

William James, in his *Principles of Psychology,* discusses several prominent cases in America. He cites the case of Mary Reynolds, who awoke one day in 1811 unable to recall anything of her family, surroundings, or even the use of words. Although she still had the body of an adult, she had to be retrained as if a baby. When reeducated in her new personality, her character and disposition were utterly different from her prepossession state. Alternations from one state to the other continued over fifteen or sixteen years, until at the age of thirty-six the second personality completely took over.[9]

The case of Lurancy Vennum/Mary Roff is an even more striking example of possession exhibiting veridical memories. Mary Roff lived from 1847 to 1865, her later years in an asylum. Lurancy Vennum was a girl born to a nearby family in Illinois, in 1864. She exhibited no signs of abnormality until 1877, when she began to suffer spontaneous trances. After one of these trances, she lost all memory of the Vennums (her real family), declared herself to be Mary Roff, and begged to be taken to the Roff's home. When the Vennums finally consented to let her live with the Roffs, she greeted the Roffs emotionally as her own parents. She also exhibited many of the preferences and memories known only to Mary and the Roffs. To quote James's account:

> The girl, now in her new home, seemed perfectly happy and content, knowing every person and everything that Mary knew when in her original body, twelve to twenty-five years ago; recognizing and calling by name those who were friends and neighbors of the family from 1852 to 1865, when Mary died, calling attention to scores, yes, hundreds of incidents that had transpired during her natural life. . . . The so-called Mary whilst at the Roff's would sometimes "go back to heaven," and leave the body in a "quiet trance," i.e., without the original personality of Lurancy returning.[10]

After detailed study and subsequent publicity, this case came to be known as the "Watseka Wonder," after the Illinois town where it occurred. Philosopher C. J. Ducasse, among others, considered the Roff/Vennum case good evidence not only of split personality, but of the survival of memories and character traits after death.[11]

In 1906, a fourteen-year-old schoolboy named Fritz was possessed by a spirit calling itself "Algar," which showed familiarity with Latin and Armenian. It was eventually ascertained that Fritz had seen some texts of Latin and postcards of Armenia. But this minimal exposure to a foreign language would not explain "Algar's" abilities to copy its pronunciation and grammatical structures, although this may have served as a point of departure for possession by an intelligence familiar with those languages.[12]

Among the most dramatic of the many cases on record is that of Iris Farczady, a Hungarian lady who awoke one morning in 1935 with the language and manners of a deceased Spanish charwoman. She showed no knowledge of her family, surroundings, or even of Hungarian, but had a full memory-set and language ability in Spanish.[13]

These cases certainly seem difficult to explain without resort to "spiritual entities," but they are a long way from proving reincarnation. In each case, the person is already an adult when the intruding consciousness, memories, and skills take over. At best, such phenomena might tend to indicate the existence of discarnate consciousnesses temporarily capable of occupying living bodies.[14] On the other hand, it is possible that they may be subsumed under some less exotic explanation. (We shall review these hypotheses below under "Objections.")

Hypnotic Age-Regression

Hypnotic age-regression is a process in which a hypnotist, usually a psychiatrist, asks his patient to recall her childhood, using a hypnotic trance to facilitate exact recall of events which may have caused severe psychological disturbance. On rare occasions, however, the patient has regressed beyond her childhood into prenatal states, and even to the recall of lives prior to the birth of her present body. There is need for verification of the memories reported, but regressions may thus be another source of evidence of rebirth or reincarnation.

The case of Pueblo, Colorado, housewife Virginia Tighe (pseudonym Ruth Simmons) is colorfully depicted in *The Search for Bridey Murphy.*[15] Virginia agreed to participate in hypnotic experiments conducted by a young businessman named Morey Bernstein. After regressing to the age of one year old, she regressed still further to describe a life in Ireland from 1798 to 1864 under the name of "Bridey Murphy." She demonstrated detailed knowledge of Ireland, its language, customs, and physical objects with which she had no acquaintance in her normal waking life. Sensationalist newspapers were quick either to exaggerate her accounts or to allege that her statements were incompatible with the facts of Ireland and had been gained from Irish people she had known in her youth.

Philosopher C. J. Ducasse went to great lengths to studiously investigate this complex case. He concluded that although not all of the information reported by the "Bridey" personality had been conclusively verified, none had been shown to be historically impossible. Moreover, Bridey did correctly describe many items, such as names of old neighborhoods and the stores in them, which could not be explained by normal means of information acquisition.[16] Curiously enough, in her waking state, Virginia neither cared about nor believed in reincarnation, and she was quite baffled as to what to make of the furor that emerged from her hypnotic age-regressions.

More recently, British psychiatrist Arthur Guirdham collected detailed records on an Englishwoman sent to his hospital who was plagued by recurrent neurotic nightmares of battles and massacres. Investigation revealed that the patient had had memories since her youth that corresponded closely to the history of the Cathars (Albigenses), heretic puritans in thirteenth-century France. It is particularly noteworthy that the language recorded in some of the patient's diaries is early French, unknown to her in normal life. Guirdham writes:

> In 1967, I decided to visit the south of France and investigate. I read the manuscripts of the 13th century. These old manuscripts— available only to scholars who have special permission—showed she was accurate to the last detail. There was no way she could have known about them. Even of the songs she wrote as a child, we found four in the archives. They were correct word for word.

. . . When I first wrote to Prof. DuVernoy at Toulouse, he said, "Get in touch with me about anything you want. I'm astonished at your detailed knowledge of Catharism." I couldn't say, "I've got this by copying down the dreams of a woman of 36, . . . "[17]

This case not only roused Dr. Guirdham to extensive travel and study of Catharism, but ultimately convinced him of the truth of reincarnation of at least some people.

Similar cases of true memory of foreign language (xenoglossy) are to be found in the persons of Edward Ryall, who recalled life in seventeenth-century England with appropriate language,[18] and of Robin Hall, a Californian boy who spoke of a former life in Tibet, using Tibetan words.[19] In other cases known as the Jensen,[20] Rosemary,[21] and Gretchen[22] cases, the subjects spoke in Swedish, Egyptian, and German, respectively, supplying both words and grammatical constructions to which they had had no previous exposure in this lifetime. Such cases of xenoglossy are importantly different from the nonlinguistic babblings of people who rearrange the sounds of their own languages to "speak in tongues," as at religious revival meetings. They are better evidence too than those cases of people who can make sense of what is said to them in foreign tongues they have not learned, but who cannot speak grammatically in the language.

Still other studies have polled subjects who have undergone hypnotic regressions about the nature of their immediately prenatal experiences. They have brought to light many strange reports about disembodied persons choosing the wombs into which they were to be born.[23] Since there is no way to verify such accounts, in the way that we can verify statements about human history or test grammatical structures, these reports will not be treated further here. The important point for our purposes is not the frequency of verifiable regression cases, but rather that such cases exist at all. We shall carefully analyze their implications below.

Spontaneous Memories of Former Lives

Belief in reincarnation seems odd to many Europeans but, in fact, it is so widespread among non-Europeans that Schopenhauer could cynically declaim: "Were an Asiatic to ask me for a definition of Europe, I should be forced to answer him: it is that part of the world which is haunted by the incredible delusion that man was created out of nothing, and that his present birth is his first entrance into life."[24]

Schopenhauer may have had strong prejudices in favor of a Buddhist worldview, but he is correct in attributing the idea of former lives to the peoples of Asia. However, he was a little too short with his European compatriots, for ever since Plato and Pythagoras the notion of rebirth has had philosophical respectability as an alternative to the Christian views of survival by resurrection.

We may still wonder, however, *why* peoples from vastly disparate cultures should believe in rebirth at all if there were no experiential basis for it. One theory might attribute the growth of parallel mythologies to Jungian archetypes in a collective unconscious. Another might suggest that the primitive mind, yearning for permanence and unable to face its own mortality, modeled its myths of survival on the cycles of seasons and plant life, leading to a cyclic notion of human life as well. An equally plausible suggestion is that even primitive peoples had encountered situations that they interpreted as indicating the reincarnation of those who had formerly died. The cases that shall be treated in this section are of precisely that nature; they lend prima facie support to the belief in rebirth.

The best examples of apparent "reincarnation" are those of children who discuss their memories of previous lives, with no prompting from those around them. In many cases these reports are supplemented by peculiar habits, speech patterns, or even physical birthmarks characteristic of the person the child claims to have been in a former life. In some cases, too, the memories of the child correspond to those we would expect of the deceased. We shall confine our attention to some intersubjectively verified cases.

The case of Katsugoro was reported by Professor Lafcadio Hearn, who took great interest in Japanese Buddhism. Katsugoro was born to a Japanese family in 1815. While playing with his sister, at age seven, he asked her where she had lived in her former life. Questioned by his parents and grandmother, he responded that he had remembered everything clearly until he became four years old, but he still could recall the central details:

He had been the son of Kyubei and Shidzu in a town of Hodokubo. Kyubei had died when he was five, and his mother had lived with a man named Hanshiro, after which Katsugoro (then named Tozo) had died of smallpox. Katsugoro's grandmother escorted him to Hodokubo to pay respects to the grave of his "previous father." Katsugoro's report tallied completely with that of the family, and he observed correctly that certain shops had not existed when Tozo was still alive.[25]

The case of Alexandrina is quite similar, except that she was reborn into the same Catholic family. According to the well-attested accounts, Alexandrina Samona died at five years of age in 1910. She appeared to her mother in a dream and promised to be born again, although the mother's recent ovarian operation rendered further childbearing unlikely. Nonetheless, when twins were born late that same year, one so closely resembled her dead sister in birthmarks, habits of play, and likes and dislikes, that she too was named Alexandrina. When told of plans for a trip to Monreale, Alexandrina (II) correctly described a trip that Alexandrina (I) had taken before her birth, to the surprise of her parents.[26]

Shanti Devi was born in 1926 in Delhi, and from 1930 she began to relate numerous details of a former life in Mathura, a city some eighty miles away. Out of sheer curiosity, her granduncle and some educated friends began to investigate her statements. Their inquiries brought an unexpected response from one Kedar Nath of Mathura, who confirmed that he had had a wife corresponding to the person Shanti claimed to be. Kedar Nath even came to Delhi to meet Shanti, and she replied correctly to intimate questions about things only his former wife had known. Following this meeting, Shanti asked to be taken to Mathura, where she understood local dialect unintelligible to others from Delhi, identified friends and relations of Kedar Nath without prompting, and pointed out where wells, outhouses, and money caches had formerly been located.[27]

Each of the cases mentioned above strikes the reader by its apparent uniqueness, emerging from local settings in which such inquiries were uncommon and unexpected. More recently, however, scholars have begun to systematically identify and study such cases in which children report memories of former lives. The leading researcher in this field is Dr. Ian

Stevenson of the University of Virginia Medical School at Charlottesville. In the early 1960s, Stevenson began to compile and research cases of claimed memories of previous lives. He devoted particular attention to verifying or falsifying the information provided by the "memories," and to the physical and behavioral similarities between the living child and the departed person with whom the child identified.

Stevenson's findings gave the lie to the popular assumption that reincarnation cases are peculiar to Hindu and Buddhist countries of the Indian subcontinent, which have strongly believed in reincarnation since ancient times. Of 1,300 cases in his files in 1974, the United States led with 324, followed by Burma (139), India (135), Turkey (114), Great Britain (111), and so on—showing a large number of such cases from among the modern Western nations.[28]

In 1966, when Stevenson first published *Twenty Cases Suggestive of Reincarnation*,[29] it became for a time the talk of the psychiatric world and remains today a landmark in the scientific study of an unpopular hypothesis. In each of twenty cases, from India, Sri Lanka, Brazil, Lebanon, and Alaska, Stevenson identified statements by children about their former lives. He then established that the children had no normal means of obtaining such knowledge and compared the children's statements to the facts known to the deceased persons with whom the children identified themselves. In a number of cases, the children also were found to have unusual birthmarks, either close to the peculiarities of the person remembered or corresponding to the wounds by which the person had been murdered.

Stevenson also itemized the children's preferences for certain foods, sports, speech patterns, or other aptitudes untaught by the children's present environment, which corresponded to those of the deceased. Where possible, Stevenson visited the most promising of these children, escorted them to the villages they claimed to remember, and carefully recorded the number of correct and mistaken statements the children made about things they would have known had they in fact lived there previously. In the 1980s, Stevenson continued to collect cases at the rate of nearly one hundred per year, and his work has been widely discussed in medical as well as parapsychological journals and conferences.[30]

Based on Stevenson's pioneering work, other scholars have been emboldened to publish their own similar studies in this field, including H. N. Banerjee of the University of Rajasthan (Jaipur), [31] Hernani Andrade of the Brazilian Society for Psychical Research,[32] Karl Muller of Switzerland, [33] Resat Bayer of the Turkish Parapsychological Society,[34] and the late K. N. Jayatilleke of the University of Sri Lanka.[35] Although not all reports are as detailed as Stevenson's, they do tend to indicate that such cases are a worldwide phenomenon.

The researchers in this new field generally agree that they have not "proven" reincarnation. Some from Eastern backgrounds assume reincarnation as an article of faith requiring no proof or capable of verification through personal meditations. Others, including Stevenson, feel that the evidence has not yet reached conclusive levels, but that the discovery of "perfect" paradigm cases and the amassing of thousands of similar cases will eventually swing scientific opinion towards acceptance of the reincarnation hypothesis in at least some instances. Finally, some serious researchers are of the opinion that reincarnation is the sort of hypothesis that may never be proved by field work, for alternate interpretations of the data are always possible. Nevertheless, this research is accepted as having at least psychiatric value, and it may provide a better basis upon which educated people may base their personal convictions.

Many personal responses are possible to the question, "What would constitute a really convincing case of reincarnation?" It is well to recall here Michael Scriven's criteria of personal identity: (1) bodily appearance, (2) physical abilities, (3) memory of past experiences, (4) similarity of character, and (5) intelligence, including mental and linguistic abilities.[36]

While no single case to date has exhibited all of these characteristics, it is quite conceivable that some case might eventually do so, and each of these criteria have been met in at least some of the cases studied by Stevenson. The physical discontinuity of corpse and fetus will still prove an intractable obstacle to some materialist philosophers. But for anyone who accepts Scriven's criteria, the discovery of cases displaying all five may constitute a compelling argument for identifying the new children with the former persons, particularly when the children themselves treat their experiences as their own "rebirths."

Objections to the Phenomena as Evidence of Survival

For religious as well as philosophical reasons, many people cannot accept the above cases as genuine instances of reincarnation. Their objections include (1) sheer refusal to accept the evidence, (2) theoretical objections to the consequences of the reincarnation theory, (3) the possibility of knowledge-acquisition by other normal means, and (4) explanations of the phenomena through other known but inexplicable psychic powers, not to include reincarnation. Any thoroughgoing interpretation of the data needs to consider each of these possible alternatives. In order for the reincarnation hypothesis to remain the strongest choice, it must be shown that there are at least some cases to which none of the above objections apply. Let us examine the objections and responses to them in the order just outlined.

Refusal to Accept the Evidence

Refusal to accept the evidence for memories of previous lives may assume several guises. It may be claimed, for example, that many of the supposed memories are nothing more than "scattered shots"[37]—a combination of guesswork, imagination, wishful thinking, and a child's desire to please an investigator. By this theory, the similarity of the child's comments to the actual facts later uncovered are pure coincidence, however improbable. For every child whose memory "matches" the facts, it suggests that there must be millions of children claiming memories that do not correspond to any facts at all. (This argument is analogous to the claim that correct guesses in the Duke University telepathy experiments were nothing more than improbable chance coincidences.)

The response to this objection is fairly straightforward. The correspondences produced in the statements of many of the children studied are of the probabilities, not of one in millions, but of one in trillions of trillions. Moreover, the way the children report their memories does not resemble guesswork at all. They do not venture, "Am I right about this? How about that?" but rather assert, "The old schoolhouse used to be here, where I was taught this Japanese song by Mr. Nakano." Most of their statements show the same level of confidence as their statements about other memories of their present lives. In short, guesswork alone is inadequate to account for the specificity, unique correspondence, and accuracy of many of these children. Nor, of course, could it account for birthmarks, habits, and predilections.

A more strident claim is that the investigator, parents, or both have deliberately distorted the facts to perpetrate a hoax in the name of empirical research. Ruth Reyna is one fanatic opponent to reports of natural memories of former lives. She has collected "refutations" of the reincarnation theory from many sources, which unfortunately she cannot always name. One of her nameless sources asserts:

> I was really shocked by the method of questioning. Almost all the questions were leading questions whereby he was trying to elicit the answer he wanted. . . . An impartial probe was made impossible because of the enthusiasm of the boy's father, who had fully tutored everyone around, including the boy. I found it absolutely useless to make any investigation. . . .[38]

Reyna then goes on to say that the most prolific researcher of claims of rebirth is Dr. Ian Stevenson, and that his book *Twenty Cases Suggestive of Reincarnation,* published in 1966, "stands as the most revealing document of both chicanery and naïveté—chicanery on the part of relatives of the claimants, and naïveté on the part of the investigator."[39] Reyna does not say specifically in what respects Stevenson is naïve, but leaves us with just this general ad hominem character blast.

However, attestations to the scrupulous care of the investigators are not lacking on the other side. Banerjee himself (the one accused in Reyna's nameless letters?) rejects the uncritical attitudes of less careful investigators.[40] Many acquaintances of Stevenson, including those who share neither his enthusiasm nor belief in reincarnation, attest to his thoroughness and impeccable integrity. Harold Lief, M.D., who worked with Stevenson on earlier projects, calls him "methodical and thorough in his data collection and lucid in their analyses and presentation."[41] Montague Ullman, M.D., calls Stevenson's studies "models of investigative field work,"[42] and UCLA psychiatrist Thelma Moss praises his "meticulous diligence."[43] Jacobson goes to great length to show that in relation to Stevenson's cases, "the hoax hypothesis is very poorly founded."[44] Stevenson has personally revisited many of his cases during his thirty years of research to observe personality development and check for signs of fraud or collusion. He is the first to admit that some cases may be tainted by the unconscious or conscious desires of his respondents. But it is unthinkable that all fourteen hundred cases now studied by independent researchers are entirely mistaken. Can we imagine that in all these hundreds of cases the local folk deliberately perpetrated a plan to hoodwink dozens of different investigators into accepting bizarre hypotheses?

It must be reemphasized that Stevenson is not the only researcher to arrive with such cases and conclusions. Banerjee has checked some of the very same cases Stevenson had studied, arriving independently at very similar conclusions. Leading doctors and parapsychologists have found strong cases in Turkey, Lebanon, Brazil, and Europe.[45] These are hardly cultures that traditionally favor belief in reincarnation. Each researcher has risked his professional reputation by publishing accounts that contradict the expectations and religious commitments of the scientific community in the West (and of such readers as Ms. Reyna).

There are many cases in which the information reported by the children as memories of past lives was unknown to anyone they knew in their present lives. It could not have been conveyed to them by their families or friends. The alleged desire of the parents for local notoriety is conspicuously lacking in most cases, nor could it constitute a motive for trumping up memories of past lives where none existed.[46]

Finally, there are many instances in which the family and surrounding people disbelieved, rather than encouraged, the children's discussion of past lives, and yet the children persisted in their assertions. Considering the number and care of the researchers and their independent corroborations, the fraud hypothesis must be discarded as inadequate to account for the whole of the data.

Objections to Population Increase and Lack of Memories

Theoretical objections attempt to reject the evidence of reincarnation purely on the grounds of its logical consequences. A review of those objections and answers may be appropriate here in the context of evaluating the results of empirical research.

The claim is often heard that reincarnation is incompatible with the theory of evolution, for the number of humans on the planet is steadily increasing. However, this objection might be answered in any of a number of ways, for example, (1) that nonhumans may be reborn as humans, (2) that disembodied souls have awaited embodiment, (3) that new souls evolve as the number of humans increases, or even (4) that beings are reborn from other solar systems in which the population is decreasing. We need not resolve such questions here, but simply point out that the population question alone is not a sound basis on which to object to rebirth.

Another major theoretical objection in the light of empirical findings asks why so few children remember past lives. If rebirth is a fact, should we not all expect to remember past lives? Here too, several answers are forthcoming:

1. Few people have good memories of events that happened only a few years before, especially if their minds are occupied and their environments stimulating. How much less should we expect people to remember events previous even to their own childhood!

2. Memories of previous lives may have been suppressed and forgotten, either because they themselves were traumatic or because the death and birth processes were traumatic. Discouragement of such talk by parents and companions may also account for the low instance of children reporting on their previous lives in detail.

3. Alternatively, it is possible that we can all remember former lives through yogic or Buddhist meditation and right living. These particular children may have been karmically gifted in such a way as to remember their past lives without such training in this life.

4. Finally, it is logically possible that not all people are reborn—there are many types of experience possible after death, and rebirth might be a relatively rare sort.

Thus the fact that few children remember previous lives does not preclude the possibility that reincarnation may be the correct interpretation of some cases, although not of every one.

The difference between the intellectual structures of dying persons and those of newborn infants does seem to pose a problem in identifying the two, for no newborn babe has begun to speak, write, gesture, or in any other way communicate that it had any more than the most rudimentary consciousness. Jean Piaget, Bruno Bettelheim, and many other psychologists have attempted to trace the mental development of infants. There is widespread agreement that the newborn cannot even distinguish object from object, color from color, or self from other, let alone make the kinds of logical and axiological distinctions most mature people learn to make before they die. How can the infant's mind be anything like a dying person's?

The first and most obvious answer to this query might be that the physical (neural, cortical) apparatus of the newborn infant is simply unable to comprehend or express the full range of psychic energies that are "transmitted" from dying person to fetus. Not only have the muscles of the body not been trained to move, but the greater portion of the brain has not been taught to sort and label experience as its first few years of education will train it to do. This need not imply that a consciousness from a former person did not contact or influence the fetal brain, but only that the former consciousness was unable to function fully through the infantile brain.

Second, it might be argued that the incredible trauma of coming from an essentially submarine fetal environment into a waking, walking world of objects would be enough to virtually obliterate the memories and dispositions of most individuals, as often happens in traumatic accidents. Westerners generally take as evidence against the theory of rebirth the fact that very few children seem to remember their previous lives. On the other hand, even a few documentable cases might indicate the plausibility of the rebirth theory.

What we are seeking is not proof that everyone had former human lives and can remember them, but rather indications that at least some people had previous lives, and evidence which is most plausibly accounted for by such a theory. Then the question of whether rebirth theory in fact accounts for observed data better than other theories becomes an empirically testable one. There may be many psychological reasons for personally adopting or rejecting the theory of karma and rebirth (for example, the oft-cited allegation that it leads to an attitude of resignation and stagnation), but these personal feelings clearly have no bearing on the nature of reality.

Normal but Forgotten Memories?

Yet another objection would suggest that the knowledge reported by children was obtained in some normal but forgotten means. This phenomenon, known as cryptomnesia (hidden memory), must be excluded before accepting any of the above cases as indications of reincarnation. Cryptomnesia is particularly prominent in cases of hypnotism. One famous example is a patient of Dr. Harold Rosen in Toronto, who reproduced a ritual curse in the old Etruscan language while in trance. Although he had never studied Latin, much less its precursors, thorough examination revealed that the patient had once glanced at a page in which that same curse was inscribed in large letters. He had apparently memorized it entirely unknown to himself, and therefore was able to reproduce it in trance.[47]

Critics of Bridey Murphy have claimed that Virginia had known someone of that name as a girl, that she had often spoken to an Irish immigrant, or that her childhood home had similarities with that reported by the trance personality of Bridey.[48] Such allegations have since been shown to be the manifestly false claims of fundamentalist Christian writers who neither met Virginia nor studied her case. They completely fail to explain the many details of names, places, and dates with which the Bridey trance personality showed familiarity.[49]

Although the cryptomnesia objection might hold for certain hypnotic regression cases, it is untenable in most spontaneous cases. It would be impossible for children to produce factual accounts of people and places they had never seen, even in cryptomnesia. Nor is the "hidden memory" hypothesis adequate to explain the strong emotional attachments of such children to members of their "former families," and their persistence in habits or declarations which win them only the censure of their family and peers.[50]

The Super-ESP Hypothesis

The only reasonable approach remaining open to critics of the reincarnation interpretation would be to (1) accept the facts that have been discovered under rigorous controls, (2) admit that normal methods of information-acquisition are inadequate to explain them, and (3) propose that some other paranormal mechanisms should be held responsible. Such critics suggest that extrasensory perception (ESP) might account for the claimed memories of former lives equally as well as the reincarnation theory. However, the mechanisms and explanations behind other ESP faculties are at least as unclear as those that would explain apparently prenatal memories on the reincarnation hypothesis. So this move gains little in explanatory power, but it does allow its adherents to reject a position they find distasteful for religious or cultural reasons.

Any so-called super-ESP hypothesis attributes to humans powers that violate the mechanistic worldviews of analytic philosophers almost as thoroughly as would a reincarnationist approach. Whatever their respective motives or advantages, we may itemize the super-ESP theories purporting to explain possessions and memories of former lives as follows: (1) psychometry, (2) telepathy, (3) precognition, and (4) retrocognition. Let us examine the case made for each of these hypotheses, observing how closely they fit the available evidence and what modifications in our understanding of these paranormal powers would be necessary to make each hypothesis fit.

Psychometry. In the branch of ESP known as psychometry, a sensitive or subject reports information about past events while handling an object that had intimate association with those events. Such objects as pens, wallets, watches, and even building stones are commonly used. In and of themselves, these objects do not appear to provide much information about the people or situations with which they have been associated. In the hands of a skilled psychometrist, however, they appear to provide access to detailed and independently verifiable knowledge of which the sensitive would otherwise be ignorant.[51] Although its mechanisms are inadequately understood, the phenomenon of psychometry gives evidence that memory traces may be attached to (or at least accessed through) material objects other than living human brains.

Advocates of the superpsychometry theory over the reincarnation hypothesis propose that we are dealing with cases of memories surviving in some *invisible* object, "picked up" by children or hypnotized patients and misinterpreted as their own prior experiences.[52] What are the advantages and flaws in this proposal?

First, the phenomena discussed here are different from psychometric cases in important respects. They do not happen when an object is present and cease when it is removed, but rather continue over long periods of time. They are not reported as visions of something happening somewhere else to someone else, as in psychometry; rather they are firsthand accounts in which the children or patients really believe that the events happened to *them.*

Worse yet, the psychometric model loses the very explanatory power it had hoped to provide, because there is no visible object with which the memories are associated. The proponents of this theory might try to extend their model of psychometry by asserting that, in some cases, the carrier of memories is not a visible physical object. But then they are left to postulate an invisible, undetectable something that carries memories over time and distance from the body of a dying person to the body of an infant or to a subject undergoing possession or hypnosis. Insofar as this theory is essentially unfalsifiable, analytic philosophers might well call it meaningless. At best, it offers no substantial improvement over the reincarnationist version.

The only crucial difference remaining between the two theories is that the psychometrist claims that the carrier of memories is an inanimate and unconscious physical (but invisible) object, whereas the reincarnationist holds that it is the surviving mind of the deceased person. The descriptions of some children and hypnotic regression subjects—of memories of states between death and rebirth—give prima facie support to a theory of animate consciousness rather than inanimate memories surviving, although we have no independent means of verifying these claims at present. Given the dissimilarities between these cases of claimed memories and cases of psychometry, and given the overextension of the psychometric model necessary to make sense of the phenomena, the "superpsychometry theory" emerges as less adequate than that of reincarnation.

Telepathy. Telepathy is that branch of ESP in which information known to one person is paranormally conveyed to another through purely mental means. At one time it was believed that this was a matter of one person projecting his or her thoughts to another, and indeed some telepathy appears to work in this way. Recent research has demonstrated that the "sender-receiver model" is not the only one; occasionally information may be telepathically obtained without deliberate attempts at sending or receiving.[53] The claim of the "supertelepathy" theory, then, is that the information reported by the subjects concerned was telepathically derived from the minds of other people, presumably those who knew the subject.

This telepathic model, however, simply fails to fit the evidence presented. People who are possessed, who are under hypnosis, or who claim to remember former lives often exhibit knowledge that is not part of the conscious waking knowledge of anyone known to them. Bridey Murphy's naming of places and markets, Guirdham's subject's knowledge about the Cathars, and the reports of some of Stevenson's child subjects have required extensive digging in obscure historic records to confirm that these accounts were indeed correct.

There is also the question as to whose mind the subject is "tapping," if anyone's, to get the information being reported. Critic Ruth Reyna believes that, in some cases, the parents are projecting ideas through the mouths of their children: "Assisted by parents and older relatives, the hallucination [*sic*] that he is someone else is induced in the child. This flagrant inducing of hallucinations in a child by adults merely to gain an advantage for themselves or for the child is, to my mind, an unconscionable and criminal violation of the child's human dignity."[54]

Contrary to this allegation, it is abundantly clear that in a number of cases the parents were completely surprised at the memories of their children. Some had no knowledge themselves of the facts the children were relating, and many allowed an investigation only reluctantly.[55] Ironically, the alleged motives of "gaining an advantage for themselves or for the child" are contradicted by Reyna herself in a following paragraph, where she says that parents believed that the investigation of their child's retrocognitive memories hurt rather than helped his performance at school.[56]

True parent-child telepathy may indeed be a common phenomenon.[57] It does not apply to the cases we are considering here. For that, we should need a model of telepathy from many obscure and different minds to a child or subject whom many of them did not even know. Alternatively, we should have to grant that the child had the power to telepathically acquire information, and only information that correctly pertained to only one person whom he or she did not know and who was now dead. We must suppose that the child telepathically gathered such information, bit by bit, from all the various unknown people who were presently alive and shared the memories of the deceased in their subconsciousnesses. This clearly stretches the telepathy model to the breaking point.

A last-ditch effort to save the telepathy model might argue that the child or subject were telepathically receiving memories from the surviving consciousness of the deceased, rather than being the embodiment of the deceased's consciousness. First of all, this move substantially concedes the survival question, admitting that only the continuation of a single human consciousness would enable telepathy to explain such phenomena. (As we saw above, telepathy might well account for some information gleaned from mediumistic seances, where the apparent possession or communication is only temporary and fragmentary.)

The crucial difference between telepathy from a surviving spirit and the rebirth of that spirit into a new body is the question of perspective. When people receive messages or ideas by telepathy, they report seeing pictures, hearing sounds, or having other impressions, more or less clearly, which correspond to those in the mind of another person. But they do not say that the images are "theirs," that they remember them, nor that they feel any intuitive familiarity with, or affection for, those images.

By contrast, the subjects in our study feel that the images they "see" are really *their* memories. They identify themselves with pictures and actions of a former person rather than simply feeling that they have had impressions of those pictures or actions once before. Thus, even when the telepathy hypothesis is modified to admit discarnate survival, it is still not as appropriate to the evidence as is the straightforward hypothesis of rebirth.

Precognition. Precognition is the ability to accurately foresee events in the future. It is one of the least understood of paranormal abilities, as it seems either to violate commonsense notions of the unidirectional passage of time or else to suggest a large measure of predeterminism in the universe. Applied to the cases of our inquiry, the "superprecognition" theory would assert that the subjects obtained knowledge of other people's previous lives, abilities in foreign languages, etc., by precognition of the very facts that the investigator was later to reveal.

For example, it would suggest that Guirdham's subject did not really remember that Cathar priests' robes were blue (a fact not public until some time later), but rather that she *precognized* that her psychiatrist would someday uncover the fact that Cathar priests' robes were blue, and that she misinterpreted the precognition as a memory.[58] This is analogous to saying that I answered as I did on the examination not because I recalled the answers from previous study but because I foresaw the way I would answer, through precognition of my completed test in the future.

The appalling circularity of this argument renders it difficult to discuss and impossible to falsify. As long as a case is uninvestigated, believers in this theory can also claim that the subject's memories have not been shown to be correct, and therefore that the subject does not remember any past life. As soon as the case is investigated and the subject's statements are shown to be in accord with historic fact, "superprecognition" theorists can claim that the subject does not remember any past life because it is a case of precognition of the findings of the investigation.

If the prima facie absurdity of this suggestion does not immediately rule the theory out of court, then certainly the logical illegitimacy of switching interpretations (as above) to fit the particular case should rule it out; for thousands of children make true but uninvestigated statements. According to the superprecognition theory, all such statements are groundless and probably false. But then a curious thing happens: as soon as someone demonstrates a correspondence between previous events and the child's statements, the statement is reinterpreted. It becomes not only true (which it was not held to be before), but precognitive of the discovery of its truth, which it could not be if not investigated.

In short, the precognition theorist ascribes different logical status to the very same statement depending on its state of investigation. Moreover, it is strange that subjects should assert to be true from memory some items they should foreknow would be proven false in the future, if they were truly precognitive. Further differences may be shown between the nature of precognitive experiences, like fuzzy hunches or dreamy flashes, and the feeling of the subject that these are his or her memories, like any other memories. If psychic at all, these are less likely to be examples of precognition than of a special case of retrocognition. Surely it is unnecessary to take this proposal seriously.

Retrocognition. Retrocognition is knowledge of the past. Parapsychologists occasionally find cases where people have clairvoyant visions of things that have happened before their time. Such reports are particularly common from psychically sensitive people visiting old battlefields, the pyramids, Versailles, or other historic spots. On this model, the claim is made that the subjects of our study are not really remembering events in their own lives, but "are glimpsing someone else's life through retrocognitive clairvoyance."[59]

In a sense, all memory is retrocognitive. The crucial question to be posed is this: How are memory-type retrocognitions different from non-memory retrocognition, necessary to the super-ESP theory? The answer again is simple. People who are capable of clairvoyant retrocognition generally catch glimpses of scenes in the past, but they are unable to identify, to date, or to place themselves within them. The memories of the subjects we have considered, by contrast, include their subjects as the central actors and perceivers of the scene, which they can identify, date, and place. They "feel like" other normal memories too, and may frequently be placed within a sequence of other memories in time and space by the subject. Thus, the title of genuine memory of a former life seems more appropriate than that of retrocognitive clairvoyance. There are still other considerations that militate for the rejection of not only these but of all possible super-ESP hypotheses.

Objections to All Super-ESP Hypotheses

Even if the mechanisms of ESP were well enough understood to make ESP an aesthetically or scientifically preferable theory to that of reincarnation, fundamental dissimilarities between cases of ESP and the cases we have cited require either immense modification of our understanding of ESP or the admission that these are not cases of ESP at all. First, as we have illustrated throughout previous arguments, there are the testimonies of the subjects, even in the face of family opposition, that what they are describing are *their* experiences, *their* old families, *their* past lives, with all the natural emotion attendant thereupon.

Second, as Stevenson explains, the super-ESP hypothesis

> does not adequately account for the fact that the subjects of cases of the reincarnation type show no evidence of having powers of ESP apart from the claimed memories of a previous life. It may reasonably be asked why a child with paranormal powers of this sort that would be required to obtain all the correct information that many of these children show would not manifest such powers in other situations or with regard to other persons besides the single deceased person whose life the subject claims to remember.[60]

His question is rhetorical, its implication clear: other theories cannot explain this focus of interest and memory on a single dead person otherwise unknown to the subject and his family.

Third, psychiatrists such as Michael Polanyi hold that, even if memories were transferable or facts obtained clairvoyantly, habits, attitudes, dispositions, and skills (linguistic as well as physical) are not obtainable except by repeated practice. Above all, skills are essentially nontransferable and incommunicable.[61] Michael Scriven, among others, considers skills an essential element in the identification of persons—more fundamental than even appearance.[62] So when there emerge cases of people who not only claim to be the reincarnation of someone who died previously but who also exhibit their same innate skills in swimming, mathematics, or languages from childhood and without training, there is some warrant to identify them with the former person rather than stretching an already inadequate ESP theory.

We have already noted the important matter of birthmarks. Children frequently show warts, wounds, or scratches corresponding to the wounds by which the person with whom they identify was killed. There are many reasons to reject Reyna's farfetched supposition that these may be superimposed on the fetus by a mother who desires to have her relative born again:[63]

1. There is no evidence that mothers' desires affect the birthmarks of babies.

2. Many mothers were displeased by, rather than desirous of, the marks and deformities of their babies.

3. Many mothers were unaware of the existence, much less the manner of death, of the people their children claimed to have been.

4. Even if it were shown that mothers' desires could somehow influence fetus development, this would not rule out the possibility that the mind of the deceased deliberately chose that body in which to be reborn.

Taken together, the display—of memories that correspond to those we should expect if the deceased were still living; of habits, preferences, and skills, linguistic and physical; and of birthmarks like those of the deceased —makes up a stronger case for the identification of the mind of the subject with the mind of the deceased than for any of the so-called super-ESP hypotheses proposed in the literature. This is far from saying that reincarnation has been proved. As research continues, however, we are able to offer some generalizations about the ways in which people seem to be reborn. Already a few such rules have been suggested.

Although our empirical studies are still in their infancy, the past twenty years of research have led to some further generalizations about the nature of rebirth, worthy of summarizing here:

1. Story's Law suggests that persons are usually reborn within a few hundred miles of their deaths, although not necessarily in territory known to the dying person.[64] This may be due in part, however, to the difficulty in studying cases that are further removed—particularly if the parents ignore their children's coherent statements in foreign languages as mere "baby talk."

2. Evans-Wentz's Law says that persons will reincarnate in ways they believe possible; if a person is raised to believe that sex-change is impossible in rebirth, he or she will be reborn in a body of the same sex, and vice versa.[65]

3. Parker's Law sees violent death and/or unfulfilled cravings or desires for things in this life as the primary causes of reincarnation, and

this agrees with the Buddhist teachings on the subject.[66] Both Stevenson and Banerjee have found that many of the reincarnation cases reported were those of people who had died violent deaths.

4. Martinus's Law would assert that people are reborn relatively quickly when they die in childhood, but adults who die must spend a longer period in some intermediate state.[67] In fact, Stevenson's data suggest that periods of several years are not at all uncommon between remembered incarnations.[68] However, we have no validated cases of people who report seeing their way into a new body at the moment of death. The rebirth process, whether of days or of years, is not immediately apparent to dying persons as they depart from this world.

We must stress that all of these "laws" or hypotheses are inductive generalizations open to empirical verification, in the same way that generalizations about meteorites or earthquakes can be better confirmed or rejected as more and more examples are found and examined. As empirical accounts have stressed, it is the element of conscious continuity that is necessary to make sense of identity between rebirths.

Cases of remembered past lives are reported more frequently in developing nations than in developed ones. These are often the countries that believe most in reincarnation. Certainly children remembering past lives are less likely to be discovered or reported in societies that consider such notions to be nonsense or heresy, for the parents will discourage and disbelieve their child in such a cultural context. On the other hand, children born into societies that accept reincarnation may find more receptive ears for their strange tales of past experiences.[69] Moreover, underdeveloped nations tend to have fewer stimuli (TV, films, electronic games) and obligations (school, YMCA, scouts, *juku*) to occupy the time and mind of the child.

Particularly in semiliterate areas, the memories of adults tend to be much better developed than those of literate industrial Europeans. It is just possible that all the stimuli and obligations of industrialized societies contribute to clouding the memory and focusing on present rather than past experiences, which might also help to explain this variation. Even today, many exceptions have been found to the "underdeveloped/believers" rule of reincarnation, like the hundreds of rebirth cases reported from Catholic Brazil and Protestant England. If such research breaks down societal tabus, further studies might demonstrate approximately equal frequencies of rebirth cases in developed and less developed nations, irrespective of cultural expectations.

On the other hand, it may be the case that some people are reborn into human bodies and some people are not. If we take all subjects' accounts literally, some claim to remember equine or simian births between their human incarnations; others remember heavenly lands with nostalgia. Such language is anything but conclusive. At the same time, by simple calculations we can reach some conclusions about the interval between the death of one person and the birth of another who claims to be the same person. The minimum period on record seems to be that of the Alexandrina case cited above, in which slightly less than nine months passed between the death and purported rebirth. The maximum period may be hundreds or even thousands of years, if we accept cases like the Rosemary case as philosopher Ducasse does.[70] It is common for a period of several years to elapse between the death of one party and the birth of someone who remembers parts of his or her life.

This time gap has important philosophical implications. It means, first of all, that rebirth is not an immediate experience simultaneous with death. If the early Buddhist theory were correct, we might expect an instantaneous transfer, a lightning-like flash rushing from a corpse to a fetus in a womb, with less than a year elapsing before rebirth. But the evidence seems to require a longer intermediate state. Whether we accept the testimonies about animal incarnations and heavenly realms or look for more sophisticated theories, the evidence requires the postulation of some other form of continuity between embodiments. Thus, although the theory of reincarnation presupposes survival, it does not answer the question of what form consciousness takes, if any, immediately after the death of the physical body.

In overview, a growing body of data suggests that at least a small number of dying people are reborn later in other human bodies, but that such reincarnation is seldom if ever immediate upon death. We must seek other evidence concerning the nature of a disembodied state, if there is one, after the death of the material body—at least to provide continuity and identity between death and rebirth—and at best to make sense of survival, with or without a future rebirth on this earth.[71]

2.

Invisible Bodies?

In the previous chapter we saw that the reincarnation hypothesis is the most plausible of several alternative theories to explain certain phenomena of possession and claimed memories of former lives. We also noted that even the reincarnation hypothesis requires some other invisible entity to maintain the identity and continuity of the person between incarnations.

This chapter will consider paranormal events that seem to point to the possibility of conscious personality outside of the normal physical body. Such a conscious personality would in turn provide the continuity and identity required in the above arguments. In particular, the phenomena of most importance and interest to us are those of apparitions and out-of-body experiences (OBEs).

Loosely speaking, apparitions are popularly known as ghosts and wraiths—visible spirits of dead and living persons apart from their bodies. An OBE, on the other hand, is an "astral projection" in which the soul or center of consciousness and perception travels to another place while the body remains inactive. No matter how dispassionate, such discussions invariably call to mind certain similar terms, such as phantoms and haunts, or they raise the accusations that all such phenomena are merely some type of subjective hallucination.

This chapter will reject both these popular names and the misconceptions that surround them. We shall deal instead with the verifiable experimental data, and then with the various possible interpretations of them, to most rigorously evaluate their relevance to the survival hypothesis.

Phenomena Not Considered

To clarify the nature of apparitions and OBEs, we need to narrowly define our domain from the outset. We shall do so by excluding certain similar-sounding but radically different phenomena, particularly hallucinations, phantom limbs, poltergeists, and hauntings of place.

Hallucinations

The literature of psychiatry and parapsychology frequently confuses the terms *hallucination* and *apparition*. Clarity and logic demand that we distinguish between them and use these terms in a more precise and technical manner. There are at least three crucial differences between hallucinations on the one hand and apparitions (and OBEs) on the other, namely, intersubjectivity, causal conditions, and continuity.

Intersubjectivity. An apparition is someone or something temporarily perceived, which is found not to have been physically present where it was perceived to be. Similarly, an OBE is an experience of feeling oneself absent from one's body and present in some other location apart from the body, having the perceptions appropriate to being in that other place. Of course it is possible that either of these experiences might be delusions, with no correspondence to reality.

In this study, the term *hallucination* refers solely to appearances which are purely subjective. On the other hand, those that possess intersubjectivity, can be independently verified, or possess other characteristics of physicality, will be termed *apparitions*. This is not to deny that there may be many cases where the subjectivity or objectivity of the perception is very difficult to establish. (We shall soon review some of the experiments constructed to assist in doing just that.) It does mean, at least, that the pink elephants of the drunk, the stars seen by a boy knocked out in a street fight, and the dreamer's common feeling that she is not in her bed but is awake in some other place will not be treated as cases of apparitions or OBEs.

A skeptic who believes neither in veridical apparitions nor OBEs might incline to suggest a priori that all apparitions and OBEs are hallucinations. Conversely, a subjective idealist might incline to the view that all hallucinations are as real as any other phenomenal experience. However, both of these views ignore certain stubborn facts.

There is a knowable difference between hallucinating and perceiving an apparition or having an OBE. As a simple illustration, let us imagine a case in which I "see" a ghost walking through my parlor. If other people are present and see it too, or if I can detect it on film, and if our accounts or tests yield completely compatible reports, then we have some reason to call it an apparition. If no one else can detect the images I "see," however, then it is quite probable that I am hallucinating.

Similarly, if I feel myself drifting out of my body into another room and can correctly describe all the details I would be expected to perceive if I were physically present in that room—or if my "presence" in that room can be observed by other persons or machines, while my body lies dormant in bed—then this experience may indeed be an OBE. On the other hand, if what I experience when I feel "outside my body," has no correlation to a real place or to real events, then we must classify the experience as another dream or hallucination, however psychologically interesting. This study shall concern itself only with apparitions and OBEs that fit this description. Additional criteria may be useful to help distinguish between hallucinations and genuine apparitions or OBEs.

Causal conditions. Hallucinations (i.e., purely private visual imagery as defined above) are generally produced by mental diseases such as schizophrenia, by high fever and delirium, by hypnotism, alcohol, or hallucinogenic drugs.[1] These abnormal conditions produce physicochemical changes in the brain that cause people to vividly imagine perceiving something that has no real external existence. Similarly, the vivid images produced by probing the brains of epileptic patients with electrodes should also be classified as hallucinations, since they sound or appear external only to the patients and are inaccessible to anyone but the patients themselves.[2]

On the other hand, apparitions and OBEs can take place when the perceivers are in perfect health and free from alcohol and hallucinogenic drugs. Of course, there are cases in which the perceiver may have been imbibing, or the OBE is triggered by drugs. It is not possible to say that all hallucinations are drug or disease related, and that no apparitions or OBEs are. In such borderline cases, we must take double care to assure that other criteria such as intersubjectivity are met before accepting a case as genuine. For the purposes of this study, we shall restrict ourselves wherever possible to the experiences of people in normal health and free of drugs or alcohol to reduce the likelihood of including hallucinations among apparitions and OBEs.

Continuity. Neither hallucinations nor apparitions and OBEs tend to last very long; both types of experiences usually last but a few minutes, followed by restoration of normal consciousness and experiences. On the whole, however, apparitions and OBEs seem to be shorter than hallucinations, which may recur or continue for hours. More diagnostically, hallucinations tend to persist regardless of whether the eyes are open or closed. Apparitions cannot be seen with the eyes closed, and OBE's tend to terminate when the eyes are opened.[3]

Thus, I can test the objectivity of the ghost in my parlor in part by closing my eyes. If it continues to appear before me, I may be assured that it is a hallucination of my own brain and not likely to be visible to anyone else. On the other hand, if it disappears along with my parlor and reappears when I open my eyes, I have one indication that it may be an apparition. Here, too, there may be cases whose precise status is difficult to determine. While we cannot guarantee that all images seen with open eyes are apparitions, we can at least agree to restrict our discussion to those experienced perceptions that do not continue in spite of changes in the visual mechanism and that do not recur or persist for many hours. Thus, we may rule out another source of hallucinations.

Phantom Limbs

There is almost nothing in common between phantom limbs and "phantoms" of the sort which deserve to be called apparitions. But word-association and the mistaken belief that phantom limbs are "astral" limbs persisting after amputation sometimes give rise to this confusion. *Phantom limb* is the name applied to the sensation or impression that one still has a limb that has been amputated. Claims of itches or twinges in amputated arms or legs are almost universal among people whose amputations took place after the age of five (but are rare among younger children); cases of phantom breasts or genitals are also not uncommon.[4]

The phantom limb is primarily a tactile hallucination, unlike apparitions and OBEs which are primarily visual images. The tactile impressions generally do not correspond to any external condition other than the state of the limb stump. Feelings of phantom limbs may be intensified or decreased by stimulating or anaesthetizing the stump; they are sometimes also eliminable by cranial or spinal operations.[5] The evidence thus seems to point to the conclusion that phantom limbs are a purely neurophysiological event, the result of excitation of nerves the brain had formerly learned to associate with a particular body part. The fact that young children with amputated limbs do not experience phantom limbs also points to the fact that their brains had not yet formed strong or indelible connections between specific nerves and brain areas and their bodily self-image.[6] Since phantom limbs are tactile and not visual, illusory in the sense of not providing true information, and completely explainable on a neurophysiological model, they need not be treated further in this chapter on paranormal apparitions and OBEs.

Poltergeists

Poltergeist phenomena (from the German for "noisy spirit") are technically known as RSPK: recurrent spontaneous psychokinesis. Manifestations include rappings, spontaneous breakage or movement of objects, and spontaneous fires not attributable to any known agent. Poltergeists are particularly common in homes at the moment of someone's death, as in the oft-cited cases where "the clock stopped short, never to go again, when the old man died."[7] The reason for not including poltergeists in this study is not that they are amenable to other physiological explanations as are hallucinations and phantom limbs, but that they are so difficult to categorize and study at all. As a result, they do not provide fruitful insights on the survival question.

The best available modern studies of poltergeists indicate that they are generally associated with human teenagers with severe psychological disturbances. This is not to say that the youths deliberately rap walls or throw furniture, but rather that noises and movements of objects can often be associated with para-epileptic brain states of such people in the same room at the same time.[8]

The argument may then be put forward that poltergeists are the result of the exercise of psychokinetic powers and that, in cases where no living agent is present, poltergeists may demonstrate the psychokinetic powers of the discarnate mind of a deceased person. While the hypothesis is quite intriguing, it obviously embodies too many presuppositions to accept at face value.

It remains open to question whether these para-epileptic brain states are actually the causes or rather merely the concomitants of the RSPK. Postulation of "spirit" agencies by no means clarifies most poltergeist cases. There are obvious problems in interpreting or attributing intelligibility to nonverbal noises. It is unclear why a particular discarnate agency would go about moving furniture or throwing dishes. What's worse, any theory of discarnate agency would attribute more powers to dead disembodied people than it does to the same people before their deaths—PK powers like moving objects against the laws of gravity, friction, and trajectory, without physical contact! In sum, we know too little about the way RSPK works, and it is too uncommon and uncontrollable for careful study. Moreover, its implications for survival are too tenuous at this stage to make this a fruitful avenue of inquiry.

Hauntings of Place

Hauntings of place constitute a subset of genuine apparitions. They are frequently intersubjective in the overt sense, that is, their images are seen by more than one person at a time or by many different visitors to the same place at different times. They differ from other apparitions in being apparently purposeless, recurrent, and obsessed with a particular place rather than a person or idea. Most of the "ghosts" in so-called "haunted houses" presumably fall into this category.

Hauntings of place are particularly open to psychometric explanations of the sort we found inappropriate to explaining possession or memories in the previous chapter. Rauscher asks:

> Now, keeping in mind this notion of memories adhering to an object, such as a watch, a pen, or a wedding ring, can you see how they might adhere to a house? Such place memories . . . could manifest to the occupants of the house as visions, sounds, or in the Collinses' case, smells. . . . Memories of anguish are most commonly associated with sinister or malevolent hauntings. In such cases, the house is pervaded by the distilled terror of every tragedy that transpired in it.[9]

Professor H. H. Price, who personally inspected the Borley Rectory and a number of other "haunted houses" in England,[10] also concluded that there was a significant difference between hauntings of place and other apparitions. The former seemed to exhibit no consciousness; the latter often expressed conscious purpose.[11] Hart cites the "Six Theories of Apparitions" study, which found that "apparitions of persons dead twelve hours or longer differ significantly from other apparitions, in that they much oftener are reported as having an emotional bond with the *location* and as being seen *repeatedly,* [and not] as having an emotional bond with the percipient or as being recognized."[12]

The further implications of these differences will become clearer as the nature of nonhaunting apparitions is detailed below. We must bear in mind these differences and not jump to the conclusion that the psychometric explanations that work quite well for hauntings of place apply equally well to all manner of apparitions (which is not the case).

We shall not ignore the evidence to be gleaned from hauntings of place altogether. In fact, they are particularly amenable to scientific inquiry precisely because they do stay in one place and are reasonably predictable. Moreover, they share certain similarities with other apparitions, such as their manner of appearing and disappearing, passing through physical objects, etc. Thus, their careful study may eventually shed light on the physical or paraphysical composition of such phenomena. In this context alone, we may have occasion to refer to them again below.

Phenomena Considered

With these qualifications in mind, we are now ready to examine the phenomena of apparitions and OBEs. These phenomena are like two sides of the same coin: in apparitions, people see someone who is not there; in OBEs, someone who is not really there sees things as if he or she were. Further inverse correspondences will be noted during the course of this chapter. For the time being, we shall treat them as two separate phenomena, briefly reviewing the history, characteristics, and experimental findings relevant to apparitions and OBEs respectively.

Apparitions

Apparitions have captured the imagination and fear of peoples ranging from those of the most primal cultures to the most modern of physicists and philosophers. Sometimes people perceive their deceased loved ones, as does Hamlet; more often they encounter unknown and unexpected figures, as does Ebenezer Scrooge. Significantly, like Scrooge, many people who perceive apparitions are those who least expect or believe in apparitions prior to their first encounters. Such examples in literature are legion, but let us turn our attention to some of the better documented historical examples.

History. Ancient mythologies and early literature from almost every major culture contain references to apparitions of the dead, which appear as if alive and relate to their living descendants. It seems that the earliest methodical attempt to collect, document, and discuss apparitions was a Latin treatise, published in 1573, entitled *Ghostes and Spirites Walking by Nyght*.[13] Although publishing in George III's England was less common than today, David Simpson of Macclesfield unveiled his "Discourse on Dreams and Night Visions" in 1791—this time reporting seventy-seven cases of apparitions believed authentic.[14] A century later, this number had more than doubled, and Gurney, Myers, and Podmore brought forth their ground-breaking tome *Phantoms of the Living*—still a standard reference work today.[15]

In 1889, the young Society for Psychical Research sent out a survey to nearly 17,000 people on the subject. Of those who returned the survey,

353 reported having seen apparitions of living people, and another 163 of dead people. In the society's "Report on Census of Hallucinations," Sidgwick observed several important correlations borne out by subsequent studies: that most apparitions of the dead are seen within an hour of death, and most apparitions of the living are seen at the time and place when the living person was dreaming about being there.[16]

The voluntary creation of apparitions has been practiced by Tibetan lamas, and claimed by Alexandra David-Neel in the 1930s.[17] World War II brought another flood of stories relating that apparitions of dying soldiers were perceived at the moments of their deaths by their loved ones.[18] Stimulated by discussions at the First International Conference of Parapsychological Studies (Utrecht, 1953), a team of forty-eight collaborators from twelve countries compiled a report called "Six Theories About Apparitions."[19] Almost simultaneously, D. J. West's *Psychical Research Today* devoted substantial space to apparition research,[20] and G. N. M. Tyrrell's classic study entitled *Apparitions* reemerged into public prominence.[21] The "Six Theories" study concluded strongly in favor of survival:

> Since full-fledged ESP projections [apparitions] have been shown to be genuine occurrences, and since these conscious projections of living persons are in most respects essentially indistinguishable from most types of apparitions of the dead, it follows that some of the most frequent types of apparitions of the dead presumably carry with them the memories and purposes of the personalities which they represent, and that they thus constitute evidence of survival of personality beyond bodily death.[22]

We shall have to reexamine the presumption, as well as the evidence behind this assertion, before concurring with the verdict of the international commission.

Since the 1950s, apparition research has continued at a less sensational pace. Teams from UCLA visited haunted houses to collect features of apparitions of place,[23] while Duke University quietly collected a data bank of eight thousand cases of apparitions. In dozens of such cases, only the fact that the person perceived as an apparition was actually in another place at the same time (sometimes a grave!) allowed the perceivers to distinguish between the apparition and the real person.[24] The *British*

Medical Journal reported that 14 percent of Welsh widows and widowers had "distinct visual hallucinations of their departed spouses,"[25] but more corroborative studies are needed.

Objectivity. An essential feature of apparitions is their objectivity. That is, they appear to follow the laws of perspective and parallax as we would expect of solid bodies in three-dimensional space. They are visible inter-subjectively, meaning that they may be seen by many people from their respective perspectives. Countering the claim that ghosts are usually perceived only when the perceiver is alone, Walter Prince's studies concluded that "the percipient at the moment of the apparition was with one or more persons in slightly more than 30% of them."[26]

In colonial times, nearly one hundred people saw, spoke to, and marched around with the apparition of Lydia Blaisdell.[27] Hart diagrams a case in which an apparition was correctly perceived in a mirror while another person saw it directly.[28] Tyrrell claimed to have collected as many as 130 collectively perceived cases by 1953.[29] The "Six Theories" study indicated that of forty-six cases where more than one person was in the room when the apparition was perceived, twenty-six (56 percent) were perceived simultaneously by more than one person.[30]

Such considerations lead philosopher C. E. M. Joad to assert that those who see ghosts "have actually seen something." "By using the word 'seen,'" he says, "I mean to imply that the retina of their eyes and their optical nerves were stimulated by events which were independent of the seer . . . in a word, what they saw was an objective occurrence and not a subjective projection."[31] Joad also mentions that animals often respond to apparitions even before they are noticed by humans—a fact to which we shall have future reference.

There remains the awkward fact that some people do not see apparitions when others do. This seems to be related to the degree of belief and "psychic receptivity" of the perceivers.[32] Studies of other psychic abilities have frequently observed this coincidence; in fact, it is so common that it has become a "law" called the "Sheep-Goats Effect."[33] This law suggests that, all other things being equal, people who believe in psychic abilities are more likely to manifest them than those who are skeptical of them. The Sheep-Goats Effect has been experimentally checked in numerous instances and has been found to hold true in far greater measure than would be expected merely by experimental error or bias. For whatever reasons, the Sheep-Goats Effect seems to be a valid generalization about paranormal phenomena, and perceptions of apparitions also seem to follow this rule.[34]

It has been hypothesized that the skepticism of our culture has led to a reduction in the collective annual number of apparition sightings.[35] But among the sighters of apparitions are a number of military officers, M.D.s, and clergymen—so it is not the case that apparitions are sighted only by uneducated rustics.[36]

For all their intersubjectivity, however, apparitions appear to pass through solid objects, and they tend to appear and disappear in closed rooms. So we must distinguish apparitions from the materializations of mediums, which occupy space, can be felt, and of which wax molds can be made before they dematerialize.[37] This might also account for their silence; if the "stuff" of which apparitions consist meets no resistance from physical objects, it is unable to create the vibrations of the air which we hear as sound. (Less than one in ten apparitions makes any sound at all, although some seem to try to speak.)[38]

In temporal distribution, it has been calculated that over 40 percent of apparitions appear in daylight hours, and another 10–20 percent in good artificial illumination. Thus darkness does not seem to be a prerequisite for apparitions, despite popular superstitions.[39]

Content. As for content and appearance, apparitions tend to be colored rather than the sheeted white of the traditional ghost story, and their coloring resembles that of living persons.[40] Apparitions are almost invariably clothed, and may carry hats, canes, swords, watches, books, or other such paraphernalia.[41] These possessions and clothes tend to correspond to those last worn or best loved by the person appearing—but not necessarily to those the percipient would have expected. Thus, there are numerous cases of apparitions wearing the clothes in which the people to whom they correspond had died. In one famous case, the apparition even bore a scar on her cheek corresponding to one the mother had accidentally caused while dressing the corpse, unknown to the percipient.[42] The fact that apparitions are clad and accoutered is of great importance because it indicates that they are not dependent upon the biological body as much as on a self-image or mental projection.

On other occasions, there have been apparitions of pets, with or without their masters, or of draft animals and their wagons.[43] There is inadequate evidence to establish whether apparitions of pets are, like clothing, a projection of some human mind, or whether they possess the same psychic capacities to manifest themselves volitionally as do humans —or both. Murphy went so far as to argue that animal apparitions weaken the case that apparitions demonstrate survival—because of the inherent improbability of survival of things which lack both souls and intellects.[44]

One need not be an animal lover to remark on the gross assumptions implicit in this argument. Murphy is assuming that animals could not survive death and arguing that, since human and animal apparitions are essentially similar, neither animal nor human apparitions indicate survival. However, this same evidence might be equally interpretable as an indication that both animals and humans do survive—and perhaps that animals have certain mental abilities that Murphy is unable to concede to them.

Hauntings of place agree with other apparitions in their intersubjectivity, appearance, and disappearance. Moreover, they are far more accessible to study, since their location and even timing may be predicted, unlike those of apparitions. Apparatus set up in haunted houses to detect "ghosts" has produced such results as time-lapse photos of a "blob of light" crossing a hallway,[45] tape recordings of strange, inexplicable sounds, and sudden drops of temperature in only certain parts of the room.[46]

It has become fairly standard practice to give floor plans of "haunted houses" to psychic "sensitives," who are then asked to inspect the house individually, describing the apparition and marking its location as specifically as possible. Their descriptions and positions coincide so precisely with accounts given by the other percipients (often ± 1 foot) that these abilities can no longer be doubted.[47]

It is precisely their ability that leads to explanations of such hauntings as place-centered psychometry; such methods are usually fruitless in spontaneous nonrecurrent apparition cases. The evidence from haunting cases is valuable, however, in showing that apparitions may be objectively perceived by recording devices and that they are not merely the projections of the perceivers.

Purpose. With the exception of hauntings of place, apparitions tend to demonstrate intention or purposefulness in manifesting themselves in the ways, at the times, and to the persons they do. One study found that 90 percent of apparitions manifested "agent motivation" (attributable to the personality making the appearance) and only 10 percent of apparitions could be attributable to motivations on the parts of the percipients.[48] E. P. Gibson also determined that apparitions are largely teleological in nature.[49] This purpose may consist in comforting or encouraging the perceiver, in revealing some "unfinished business," or in informing the percipient of some personal tragedy elsewhere.

Examples run into the hundreds, but it is worth noting a few of the better-studied paradigm cases to illustrate the point. One famous collectively perceived purposeful apparition was that of S. R. Wilmot, who sailed from Liverpool for New York on the *City of Limerick* on 3 October 1863. His wife was at home in Connecticut, but he later reported that about 4 A.M. on Wednesday, 13 Oct.,

[h]e saw his wife come to the door of his stateroom wearing her nightgown. At the door she hesitated. Above her husband's bed was an upper berth, set farther back, in which another man was lying. Mrs. Wilmot's apparition looked for a moment at this strange man. Then she advanced to her husband's side, stooped down, kissed him, and after caressing him for a few moments, quietly withdrew. In the morning it developed that Wilmot's fellow passenger in the upper berth . . . had seen a figure enter and act in a manner corresponding exactly.[50]

When they reached Connecticut, they learned that Mrs. Wilmot had in fact been worried for his safety because another ship had run aground. About the same time they had seen her apparition, she had been imagining herself crossing the ocean to seek him. She described his ship and stateroom correctly in every particular, and also the man looking at her from the upper berth. Her motive, of expressing concern and affection for her husband, was unmistakable in the actions of her apparition, which corresponded to what she "imagined" herself to be doing at just that time.

Apparitions often seem to want to announce their deaths to loved ones, particularly in wartime. A typical and well-corroborated case is that of Capt. Eldred Bowyer-Boyer, who was shot down over France early on 19 March 1917. At that same time, his sister-in-law (who did not know that he was in combat) saw his apparition approach her in her room at the Grand Hotel in Calcutta, India. At first he appeared so real that she thought he had come to visit. Then, when he suddenly disappeared, she felt something must have happened to him, and a terrible fear came over her.[51] At the time he was shot down, his sister was still in bed at home in England. Her daughter (his niece) came upstairs and announced that uncle Eldred was downstairs! Both sisters were so struck by the occurrence that they wrote to their mother of it, who confirmed the time and date of his fatal flight.

The Harford case demonstrates intention some years after the death of the agent. John Harford was a Wesleyan lay preacher; on his deathbed, he asked his good friend C. Happerfield to care for his wife. Happerfield readily agreed, and saw that Harford's widow was cared for, first by friends, and then by her grandson. After that, he lost touch with both of them for some time. But then, he said,

> one night as I lay in bed wakeful, towards morning . . . I suddenly became conscious that someone was in the room. Then the curtain of my bed was drawn, and there stood my departed friend, gazing upon me with a sorrowful and troubled look. I felt no fear, but surprise and astonishment kept me silent. He spoke to me distinctly and audibly in his own familiar voice, and said, "Friend Happerfield, I have come to you because you have not kept your promise to see my wife. She is in trouble and in want."[52]

Happerfield promised to look into the matter, the apparition vanished, and he roused his wife. They learned that the grandson had lost his job and the grandmother (widow Harford) was about to be sent away. Promptly they sent them money, asked the widow to visit them, and provided her again with a comfortable home. This particular apparition is noteworthy not only for its conveyance of information to which Happerfield had no normal access, but also for its drawing aside his bed curtain and speaking audibly. Similar cases of dead friends asking others to care for their widows or children are not uncommon. The apparition is particularly impressive when it coincides with or describes the time of death, which is unknown to the percipient through normal means.[53]

G. N. M. Tyrrell, in his landmark study *Apparitions* divided apparitions into four types: experiential (those of living people), crisis (including death and near-death), postmortem purposeful contact, and hauntings of place.[54] The Wilmot, Bowyer-Boyer, and Harford cases just cited give examples of the first three types. If we exclude the psychometrically explicable hauntings of place, we can see a wide agreement in the apparent "purposefulness" of apparitions of the living, dying, and long dead. These three categories also bear striking witness to one other phenomenon: their timing in relation to critical events.

Timing. Eleven major studies of apparitions conducted in the past century have been impressed by certain correspondences in timing. As early as the 1894 "Census of Hallucinations," it was discovered that when a living person's apparition was perceived, that very person was thinking or dreaming of doing exactly what (and being where) his apparition was.[55] Later studies have supported this observation: the location and actions of apparitions correspond to the time, place, and action of a dream or daydream of a living agent.[56] The evidence is so clear in this connection that many scholars suggest that vivid dreams may actually be the cause of apparitions of the living, although the mechanism is not yet understood.[57]

Most apparitions, however, are not of the dreaming, but of those who are on the brink of death or have just died. Again there is a close correspondence in timing. Sidgwick found that in close to two hundred cases where the apparition of a dead or dying person was seen, over 60 percent of these apparitions were confirmed as having been within an hour of the actual death somewhere else.[58] In another study, Prince found that "out of 135 cases of death coincidence, where it was found that the ghost was clearly recognized at the moment, [there were] 107 where the percipient in some way expressed his or her conviction [that the apparition meant the death of the person] prior to knowledge of the actual death."[59]

Reports of such apparitions were particularly common during the World Wars, when an unusually large number of violent deaths was occurring every day.[60] In some cases, the apparition did or said exactly what the dying person was doing at the same time on his deathbed.[61] In others, the dying person had on the same garb or displayed the same symptoms and appearance as his apparition did.[62]

Apparitions of the living tend to occur when the living person is thinking deeply of the place where his apparition is perceived. Apparitions of the dying most often appear, frequently with the clothing or language of the dying person, to those for whom the dying person has strong emotional attachments. Without speculating on the ontological nature of apparitions, we may at least observe that there seems to be a sense in which they are produced by the dreamer or dying person, thinking of his loved ones, and not by the percipient.

But what of apparitions of those long dead, whose physical brains could not possibly be producing anything? If apparitions of the long dead are essentially similar to those of the living, does their occurrence point to a consciousness surviving somewhere, thinking of loved places or people and communicating about "unfinished business," as in the Harford case? Hornell Hart carefully compared numerous apparitions of the dead with apparitions of the living, in respect to forty-five different characteristic qualities and behaviors. Hart concluded:

> With respect to the 45 traits most frequently mentioned in 165 apparitional cases, apparitions of the dead and dying are so closely similar to the 25 conscious apparitions of the living persons that the two types must be regarded as belonging to the same basic kind of phenomena. . . . A similarity as close as that thus demonstrated between apparitions of the living and apparitions of the dead would not occur by mere chance once in 10 to the 150th power.[63]

Hart goes on to qualify this statement, however, by adding that hauntings of place should not be included in these conclusions, for their characteristics vary from those of other apparitions, particularly in regard to the quality of purposefulness. (We have also observed above that hauntings may be amenable to psychometric explanations not appropriate to other apparitions, so there are several good grounds for their exclusion here.)

Slightly simplified, then, the logic of the argument runs as follows:

1. Apparitions of living (and dying) people correspond to conscious processes in the minds of those whose apparitions are perceived.

2. There are no significant differences between apparitions of living (and dying) people, and apparitions of people already dead.

Therefore, by analogical inference:

3. Apparitions of those already dead correspond to conscious processes in the minds of those whose apparitions are perceived.

From which we may deduce

4. The minds of some dead people still have conscious processes, and at least in that sense, survive bodily death.

Several cautions must be appended here in regard to each part of the above syllogism. The truth of the premises, however plausible from the evidence adduced above, needs to be carefully checked. In regard to premise (1), we use the words *correspond to* rather than *are caused by*, because there are many cases in which the person whose apparition is seen does not realize that he is "causing" such an appearance to others. In premise (2), it might be argued that there is a substantial difference between apparitions of the living mind and of the dead. In the former case, the person is still thinking with his brain; in the latter, he is dead and this is impossible. The possibility of thought apart from the body is the crucial issue here. The objector assumes that this is impossible, on neurophysiological grounds; the proponent of survival considers it an open question that needs further study. To critically evaluate this possibility is the burden of the following discussion, on the phenomenon of "out-of-body experiences."

Out-of-Body Experiences (OBEs)

If apparitions are the forms of people perceived by another party where they are not, then OBEs are cases where people feel themselves to be where their bodies are not. Like apparitions, OBEs have been reported in many cultures from ancient times.

History. The Indo-Tibetan cultures, in which yoga and meditation have been practiced for millennia, are most profuse in these reports.[64] In the classical world, it seems that Plato may have believed in OBEs.[65] Further west, Native American peyote cults and drug-based religious initiations were apparently designed to foster OBEs and incorporate them into legitimate religious experience.[66]

More recently, the OBE of Alfonso de Liguori is well documented; while he was starving in a prison cell at Arezzo in 1774, his apparition was simultaneously seen by many at the bedside of the dying Pope Clement XIV.[67] In the nineteenth century, spiritualists Stainton Moses and D. D. Home both reported OBEs.[68] Robert Dale Owen published the first collection of similar cases in 1860.[69] From November of 1881 to April of 1884, S. H. Beard conducted a series of OBE experiments in which he successfully projected himself into the bedroom of his fiancée, observing the conditions of her room, while she simultaneously (and unexpectedly) saw his apparition in her room.[70] F. W. H. Myers's 1906 survey cited several cases of OBEs,[71] and theosophist C. W. Leadbeater devoted a whole book to the subject in 1912.[72]

An average American youth,[73] Sylvan Muldoon (b. 1902) had so many spontaneous OBEs that he began studying the subject and came across a book by the British psychical researcher Hereward Carrington. He wrote to Carrington, and their correspondence led to the publication of several books on the subject, now considered classics in the field, which described Muldoon's firsthand experiences.[74] About the same time, Oliver Fox also published a lengthy description of his own OBEs.[75] Muldoon's adoption of the peculiar term *astral projection* for his OBEs unfortunately conjures up irrelevant images and presuppositions, but it was applied to many later works by his publishers.[76] The name, of course, neither adds nor detracts from the veridicality of the experiences, but we shall avoid it in our discussion here.

Since World War II, English geologist Robert Crookall has published numerous books documenting close to four hundred such OBEs and seeking their common features.[77] In India, even well-educated skeptics have recently reported the apparitions of religious leaders Dadaji and Sai Baba at the same times and places where these gurus claimed to have projected themselves.[78] Even more remarkable were European psychic Ingo Swann's attempted OBEs to Mercury and Jupiter. The scientific world was astounded when all of his observations were confirmed by subsequent NASA space probes to these planets.[79]

With the increase of drug use and meditation among American youth in the 1970s, reports of OBEs proliferated. At the same time, laboratory tests for studying OBEs and scientific criteria for verifying them have been largely perfected.[80] In addition, rating scales for the reliability of OBE evidence have demonstrated it to be "statistically incredible" that all of such reports should be spurious.[81] Granting that such experiences may be real, however, there still remains the problem of interpreting their content and nature.

Separation of consciousness. The definitive characteristic of OBEs is that people feel their minds—specifically, the central loci of their visual, auditory, and mental activities—separating from their physical bodies and occupying a position where they can observe things or events their physical bodies are not in a position to observe. As in the case of apparitions, we must again distinguish between true OBEs and hallucinations of "leaving the body." It is expected that events witnessed by a person in an OBE will be corroborated by independent witnesses. If the account of the OBE describes only subjective impressions and has no bearing on intersubjective reality, we may have an interesting hallucination, but we do not have an OBE.

Typically, subjects feel their "selves" (again, their loci of perception and consciousness) drifting up and out of their reclining physical body.[82] To their surprise, they note their body from a spatially detached standpoint, and they sometimes observe a "cord of light" connecting their cataleptic physical body with the location of their consciousness.[83] They find that, by merely willing, they can travel great distances or pass unimpeded through physical objects.[84] After a short period of such travel and observation, they feel drawn back into their bodies, in which they awake with a start.[85]

The "Six Theories" study itemized some of the major features found in OBEs, in part as follows:

- seeing one's physical body from a point completely outside it
- having a projected body with parts like one's physical body
- directing one's attention towards persons of emotional ties
- traveling swiftly by the mere direction of one's attention
- observing physical objects in the location to which one traveled
- observing the person to whom one's attention is directed.[86]

(Of course, this is not to say that all OBE's have such features.)

Yet another commonly observed feeling is one of complete emotional detachment from the fate of the material body. For example, a woman having an OBE looking down at her body on the operating table felt herself unconcerned about the outcome, "which," she said, "was absurd, for I was young, with a husband and two small children."[87] Or again, mountaineer F. S. Smythe had an OBE when his body fell from a precipice. His consciousness felt detached from his plummeting physical body, "and not in the least concerned with what was befalling it."[88]

Crookall's summaries emphasize that the "double" (conscious locus of the OBE) seems to emerge from the head, hovering horizontally over the dormant physical body at a distance from one to six feet.[89] Crookall interprets such features, together with the appearance of an "umbilical" cord, as showing an analogy between physical birth and the birth of a new body in death or OBE—but we need not debate that analogy here.

How frequent is this phenomenon of "exteriorization," as it is sometimes called? Conservative psychologists have estimated that one person in one hundred may have had an OBE at least once.[90] Hart's surveys at Duke University showed that almost 30 percent of the students claimed to have had OBE's.[91] Green's studies of Oxford and Southampton Universities discovered 34 percent and 19 percent, respectively.[92] My own surveys at

Tsukuba University (Japan) also found that 3 out of 130 students had naturally experienced OBEs. Of course, it is difficult to confirm such memories of past experiences, and to confirm that they were indeed OBEs and not dreams (in which all people sometimes feel disembodied, subjectively). It is therefore essential to test the objectivity of claimed OBEs.

Third-party observation. OBEs are often occasioned by severe illness or accident, so it is not uncommon that friends, relatives, or medics are gathered around the body of the patient. Some observers have reported seeing a "mist," "haze," or "phosphorescence" emerging from the body of the patient who is having an OBE, which the patient will describe upon waking.[93] Observers at deathbeds have frequently reported similar "violet mists," "shadowy forms," or "luminous clouds" hovering above the body of the dying person.[94] When Carl Jung had an OBE during a heart attack, his nurse later told him that he had been surrounded "by a bright glow."[95]

It is important not to *assume* that such accounts of dying people (whom we cannot often interview afterwards) are the same as accounts of those having OBEs—but the observations are at least very similar. Moreover, the distances and positions of the "mists" observed correspond very closely to the distances and positions described by OBE subjects in recalling their "detached bodies" (e.g., horizontal, one to three feet above the body).[96]

Photographs of such a haze rising from a corpse were first published by the French doctor Baraduc in 1908, but later efforts failed to duplicate his results.[97] Similar localized mists have been photographed at seances,[98] and in haunted houses where "ghosts" have been seen.[99] Taken alone, some of these results might be thought to be as freaks of lighting or mechanical failures, but they correspond significantly to what has also been observed in locations were someone is having an OBE. In one case, a misty form of an OBE subject was recorded on a television monitoring the room to which he later claimed to have gone in his OBE.[100] In another, a ghostly haze was seen hovering over the sleeping body of a person having an OBE, and again over the medical recording apparatus he later described as having hovered over in his OBE.[101] It has already been mentioned that animals seem sensitive to apparitions even before people in the same room perceive them. In a series of experiments in which talented OBE subjects "sent themselves" into other rooms, mammals seemed to respond to an invisible presence. Whenever the subject "visited" the animal in his OBE, the animal which had previously been actively roaming around suddenly quieted or cowered.[102]

Much remains to be done in the detection of OBEs. The unrepeatability of some of these experiments is a major source of skepticism. But the fact that some people or cameras see something and other people or cameras do not does not in itself invalidate the perceptions of the first group—particularly when the accounts of those who perceive things independently at different times and places sound so similar. Rather, it should cause us to seek the variables or factors that might lead to these differences in personal perception (just as the element of confidence and belief has proven to be a significant variable in telepathy).

The challenges, then, are to prove that OBEs produce verifiable information and are not simply hallucinations, and that the subjects were genuinely "out-of-body" and not merely clairvoyant at the time that this information was gained. The accounts above strongly suggest that something is actually perceivable outside the patient's body when he or she is having an OBE. Further recent experiments bolster this claim.

Experimental reproducibility. Repeated experiments have helped to distinguish between genuinely out-of-body OBEs and hallucinations. Some of these have been conducted by individuals who had had OBEs and wanted to test their ability to reproduce them, and to check their nature by the confirmation of friends. The experiments of Beard are an early example of this sort.[103] William James also reported incidents where reputable professor acquaintances of his had had similar experiences.[104] Like Beard, Fox and Landau both reported successful experimental projections into the presence of their fiancées under "evidential conditions."[105] In 1934, psychic Eileen Garrett projected herself to Reykjavik at a specified time, observed a complex set of operations performed by the Icelandic chief of mental health, and reported correctly on them.[106] In 1954, Hart listed forty-seven experimental cases, some assisted by hypnosis, many of which reported verifiable details of the scenes to which they had "transported" them-selves.[107] Ducasse cited yet further examples, attested to by highly educated people.[108]

Hindu yogins and Buddhist *siddhas* have long claimed the ability to travel at will outside of their bodies; certain talented subjects in America have also learned how to repeat and control their OBEs.[109] Subjects with many OBEs show the ability to distinguish between evidential OBEs on the one hand and lucid dreams or false hallucinations on the other.[110] Early experiments to verify the ecsomaticity (literally, out-of-body-ness) of OBEs involved placing a number or figure on a shelf above the sleeping body of an experimental subject in a laboratory. Despite the subjects' difficulties in falling asleep while wearing numerous electrodes and monitoring equip-ment, correct reports of the shelved numbers accompanied the subjects' descriptions of their rising out of their bodies to the shelf where the figure was placed.[111]

These early experiments were faulted on two grounds: (1) that uncon-scious perceptions of subliminal reflections from windows, clocks, etc., might have aided the subject in perceiving the figures without being out of body,[112] and (2) that the number may have been obtained telepathically from the experimenter, because it is known that sleeping people are particularly receptive to the thoughts of agents trying to influence them.[113]

To avoid these dangers, Karlis Osis designed various experiments using "displacement boxes" which measure the ecsomaticity of OBEs.[114] These boxes may be placed at great distances from the sleeping subjects so the chance for subliminal reflection is eliminated.[115] Some involve the use of lenses and mirrors so arranged as to distort the image to an external observer. If the image were seen correctly (undistortedly), it might indicate direct clairvoyance on the part of the subject, whereas if it appeared distorted as it would to a human eye at a certain location, then we should have some indication that perception of light rays from a particular place (out-of-body) was involved.[116] Other boxes may have numbers projected into them by random number generators to assure that no human being knows what the correct target is until after the OBE is finished.[117]

Osis believes that healthy living people have "less complete" OBEs than those on the brink of death.[118] Palmer's failures to enable normal people to OBE by showing them white ganzfelds and playing white noise to them may also support this claim that healthy people have more difficulty having OBEs.[119]

Physical correlates. Physical and physiological correlates of OBEs are so wide-ranging that experimenters have been unable to exclusively isolate the variables or conditions that make people susceptible to them. Some OBEs occur in normal, healthy sleep or even in waking moments, while the body continues to walk or write.[120] More common are cases where the locus of consciousness separates at the moment of a serious accident, explosion, or shock.[121] Ether anaesthesia, chloroform, and other narcotics such as peyote, LSD, and even marijuana may assist in dissociating the perceptual locus from the physical organism (and also in creating numerous false hallucinations).[122] Meditation, hypnosis, and other forms of consciousness-altering may also have similar effects.[123] Walker covers the field as follows:

> Asceticism, bodily austerities, starvation, enforced solitude, sexual and sensory deprivation, shock, stress, have frequently been known to result in exteriorization of the double. Long periods of meditation, autohypnotic suggestion, religious rituals including such methods as the prolonged chanting of spells, and whirling dances, can have the same effect.[123] Psychosis, insanity, and "possession" are believed to result from [this] pathological loosening.[124]

To say that OBEs are one form of "altered states of consciousness" is little more than a tautology, but it does not limit the wide variety of conditions under which people have them. Laboratory experiments have attempted to relate OBEs to specific brain activities through the use of electroencephalographs (EEGs). Tart reported that "OBEs were accompanied by a flattened EEG record that showed prominent alphoid activity but no rapid eye movements. This also appeared to represent a stage one sleep or drowsiness [hypnogogic] period."[125] Mitchell's electroencephalograph observations showed relatively flat EEGs with alpha frequency but less *amount* of alpha.[126] Still other studies show slow alpha waves, reduced skin resistance, and a drowsy state on the edge of sleep,[127] or theta spikes amid a slow alpha state in sleep level two, to be the commonest states of people having OBEs in laboratory conditions.[128]

On the other hand, this is far from proof that these brain states are necessary to having OBEs. Some people continue their normal waking activity, which would be impossible in alpha or sleep levels. Others with no detectable brain activity have even been pronounced dead, only to revive and report having had OBEs.[129] So EEG studies have been unsuccessful in correlating OBEs to any one particular brain state, although drowsy slow alpha occurs in the majority of laboratory cases.

These EEG reports are important in another way, however, because they indicate that people can have OBEs when they are neither dreaming nor perceiving anything in their normal bodies. They awake to report having had experiences for which we have been able to detect no parallel physiological functions. This may be corollary evidence to indicate that the consciousness is not "in" or associated with the body in the way that it is in normal waking or dreaming experience. More important than the physiological state of the body seems to be the psychological state of the experiencer.[130]

The aura. It has sometimes been suggested that research on the human aura might provide another criterion of the ecsomaticity of OBEs. If it were found that the aura indeed left the body during an OBE or that it corresponded to that ethereal haze or light perceived by some observers and cameras, we might speculate that the aura was in some way associated with the locus of consciousness and perception.

Auras were first studied seriously by Dr. Walter Kilner, of St. Thomas's Hospital, London, who observed the auras of his naked patients through screens of dicyanin dye. These auras appeared to surround the bodies of his patients to an extent of several inches, and varied according to the health of the patients.[131] The Chicago physician O'Donnell claimed to have duplicated Kilner's findings some years later, but some others have had difficulty in replicating his experiments.[132] It is interesting that Kilner's findings correspond closely to occult literature about auras, but neither his work nor such literature proves the truth of the other.[133]

More sophisticated procedures for viewing and photographing auras were developed by Soviet scientists Semyon and Valentina Kirlian (after whom the images are often named) at the University of Alma Ata.[134] UCLA professor Thelma Ross and student Ken Johnson developed and improved their techniques for taking photographs of objects within high-frequency electrical fields. These photos show halos of varying size and color, depending primarily upon the emotional state of the person or the state of health of the plant being photographed.[135] Their experiments have provoked heated controversy, since others have both succeeded and failed in reproducing their results. Phantom photos (of parts of organisms that had been amputated) proved hard to reproduce, whereas "false auras" around reheated dead material were also proven possible.[136]

The debate continues. While it has been shown that some kind of images are produced, it remains in question whether these correspond to the auras perceived by psychics or by some normal people undergoing OBEs.[137] It would be extremely valuable to photograph the auras of the sleeping bodies of people having OBEs in laboratory conditions and to photograph, using Kirlian methods, the targeted ecsomaticity boxes when subjects were attempting to OBE to that spot. But such research remains to be conducted, and at present aura research yields no conclusive evidence as far as OBEs are concerned.

We concluded our discussion of apparitions with the question of whether consciousness could exist apart from the physical body. We have seen that there are cases, however rare, in which (1) subjects claim that their consciousnesses were not within their bodies; (2) people, cameras, or animals observe something ("mists") at places outside of the subjects' bodies, where the subjects will later report having "been"; (3) subjects report correctly on facts or events which they could not have known if they were not in those places, distant from their physical bodies; and (4) although subjects later report having had conscious perceptual experience, neither their bodies nor their brains exhibit the electroencephalographic evidence we should expect for such conscious perceptual experience, either waking or dreaming. From such cases, we have strong prima facie evidence against the identity of mind and brain. C. D. Broad suggests that OBEs are indeed among the strongest possible evidence for the nonidentity of mind and body.[138]

Of course, even true OBEs would not prove survival in and of themselves, unless the body were dead at that time and later revived. Taken together with our information on apparitions, however, they indicate that we can at least make sense of the notion of a diaphanous, ethereal body, outside of the physical, which nonetheless can serve as a locus of consciousness at least temporarily. The apparitional projection of consciousness outside of the physical body gives further credibility to the hypothesis that apparitions of the dead may also be visible projections of disembodied consciousnesses, especially after the trauma of approaching death, which on this theory leads to OBEs.[139]

Objections to the Phenomena as Evidence of Survival

As seen in our discussion of the reincarnation evidence above, there are several avenues open to those who would like to reject either the evidence for apparitions and OBEs or the conclusions favoring the survival hypothesis from such evidence. Here, too, we shall examine each of four possible objections to the evidence and its survivalist interpretations: (1) refusal to accept the existence of such evidence, (2) theoretical objections to consequences of the theory, (3) attempts to explain the phenomena through normal means, and (4) the "super-ESP" theory applied to apparitions and OBEs. We have already suggested responses to some of these objections, but for the sake of organizational clarity and thoroughness, we shall review them in order.

Refusal to Accept the Existence of the Evidence

Refusal to credit the evidence for OBEs is virtually impossible now that they have been demonstrably repeated and measured in laboratory settings by independent investigators. A few voices have still been raised against the veridicality of spontaneous apparitions, for which the evidence is largely from surveys, censuses, and collected anecdotes. Famous antisurvivalist D. J. West has suggested that the most striking apparitions are those that occurred long ago, embellished by legend and elaboration: "It amounts to almost invariable law in spontaneous cases that the more remarkable the alleged coincidence, the worse the supporting evidence, and conversely, the better the evidence, the weaker is the coincidence. There can be only one conclusion. . . . Most cases are spurious."[140]

Along the same lines are the arguments that apparitions are seen only by the feeble-minded, the sick and dying, or the rustic, conforming to the superstitious expectations or projections of those people; in short, that nothing at all was seen.[141] Strong as these objections may sound, they are based on ignorance of the facts.

Evidence not outdated. It is true that some of the more striking cases of apparitions were collected in the late 1800s by the Society for Psychical Research (S.P.R.) Census. However, the passage of time since that census neither invalidates nor embellishes the signed affidavits of its contributors. On the contrary, it has subjected them to repeated scrutiny and has led to the discarding of cases whose evidentiality is open to question. On the other hand, if a similarly sweeping survey of thousands of people were made today, an equally large and impressive collection of recent apparition-sightings might emerge. The absence of such a recent census does not in itself prove the absence of such cases. Moreover, it is peculiar that West should have leveled his criticisms in 1954, for large numbers of apparition cases corresponding in time and appearance to war casualties had just been reported within the previous decade. Reports of apparitions continue to be collected today by an office at Duke University. So the claim that old stories are most distorted and new sightings do not occur is simply mistaken.

Witnesses not incompetent. The contention that ghosts are sighted primarily by men who are senile, rustic, superstitious, or "poor observers" imagining things is refuted in careful detail by Walter Prince, who devotes thirty-five pages of fine print and footnotes in the chapter entitled "Old Dogma and Later Statistics" in his *Enchanted Boundary* to laying to rest traditional ghost theories. In particular, he illustrates the responsibility, modern critical attitudes, and calm states of mind of apparition-perceivers in dozens of cases.[142] Hornell Hart cites the following facts as indicative of the veracity of the reports:

1. There is widespread agreement among many OBE subjects about the nature of their experiences, although they had not communicated with each other.

2. Most persons had their first OBEs before they were aware of the possibility of such experiences, much less read anything about them.

3. OBEs are producible experimentally and have been confirmed by independent testing agencies.[143]

As yet another indication of the quality of the apparitional evidence, 165 cases were rated on "scales of evidentiality," to test their consistency, clearheadedness, and tendencies to report unsubstantiated claims. Hart says that "when modern statistical checks were applied to determine whether the low-evidentiality cases show any tendency whatever to report more of the marvelous, the impressive, and the striking traits than did the high-evidentiality cases, the conclusion was clear-cut: . . . The differences in characteristics between the two groups are practically negligible."[144]

In sum, there is no proof that reports of the more remarkable cases are less well-authorized than the less striking cases. So it is inappropriate to throw out all the information-bearing cases as trumped-up illusions and retain the less evidential cases as mere hallucinations.

Theoretical Objections about Animals and Doppelgängers

Outside of outright refusal to accept the evidence on apparitions, some scholars have preferred to attack their possibility from more theoretical or logical grounds. Foremost in these attempts are the objection based on the appearance of animals and inanimate objects, and the objection which would equate apparitions with doppelgängers.

Animal souls and apparitions. We have already considered Gardner Murphy's argument related to apparitions of animals and clothing. Simplified, it says that apparitions cannot be produced by minds or souls because (1) neither animals nor clothes have minds or souls, and (2) even so, apparitions of animals and clothes are still perceived.[145] Murphy deduced from this that apparitions are not evidence of surviving consciousnesses.

The first flaw in this argument is that it may well be the case that animals do have minds or "souls" like ours. Even if they do not, this still does not mean that apparitions of horses and carriages must be produced by the minds of horses and carriages. It is admitted that apparitions are perceived, and therefore that they may be at least hallucinated by the mind of the percipient. Then they might equally well be projected by the minds of dreamers or dead persons accustomed to clothes and animals or even using them to help convey a presence and message.

The apparition of clothing, carriages, and animals may be just as much an objective projection of the mind of the deceased as any subjective hallucination. Nothing inherent in the shape or soullessness of a hat or shoe makes its apparition less real. We know that even apparitions of the living are clad, and sometimes accompanied by animals, when their apparitions correspond to their own conscious mental projection. If considered as a purposeful projection of the conscious mind doing the "appearing," the appearances of inanimate objects and animals cannot constitute an argument against the survivalist interpretation of apparitions.

Doppelgängers. Cases involving doppelgängers are cases in which persons perceive their *own* bodies as apparitions, in a place where they are not (as opposed to OBEs, in which they perceive their bodies correctly from loci outside them). Doppelgängers are often taken to be indications of coming death, although not always so. Tymms cites the famous example in which Goethe saw himself riding on horseback in the opposite direction, just as he was actually to do many years later.[146]

Murphy also argues that doppelgängers and hauntings show the survival interpretation to be invalid. Doppelgängers appear to be apparitions that are not the product of any conscious projection on the part of the person who appears. Similarly, hauntings seem to be merely obsessive repetitions of small actions, and not the embodiment of anything like a full, human, conscious projection. Doppelgängers and haunts are not projections of consciousness, but in other respects they seem similar to other apparitions. On this basis, Murphy concludes that other apparitions of the dead need not be projections of surviving consciousnesses either.

In the first place, not enough research has been done on doppelgängers to show whether they are indeed apparitions or should more properly be classed with hallucinations—in other words, whether they are perceived by all present or only by the hallucinator. Well-known examples seem to be classified better in the category of hallucinations.[147] Second, even if doppelgängers were of the status of hauntings, and demonstrated objective apparitional characteristics without consciousness, this would not disprove that some apparitions are still the "embodiments" of individuals' loci of conscious perception or "projections" of them onto someone else.

There remain two distinct classes of phenomena: those that show conscious purpose and correspond to conscious processes, and those that do not. The problem becomes this: Into which category should we group apparitions of the dead that seem to exhibit purpose and reveal information unknown except through the apparition? We must recall the distinction made between purpose (seen in most apparitions except for doppelgängers and haunts) and purposelessness (characteristic of haunts and doppelgängers). As Hart has said, "Apparitions of the dead and dying are so closely similar to the conscious apparitions of living persons that the two types must be regarded as belonging to the same basic kind of phenomena."[148]

In short, it is better to group apparitions of the dead with those of the living, rather than with doppelgängers and haunts. Although there remains ample room for further study, if this line of reasoning holds, then the fact that doppelgängers are not consciously produced has no direct relevance to the question of whether apparitions of the dead are consciously produced. The fact that some hallucinations of the living may be unconsciously produced cannot constitute a valid argument that all apparitions of the dead are unconsciously produced.

Normal or Physiological Explanations

Doppelgängers resemble hallucinations in the sense that both are perceptions of bodies perceived as distant from the perceiver. The similarity appears even closer in the case of heautoscopic hallucinations, in which perceivers hallucinate their own body-images as if in an external location. But whereas doppelgängers are purportedly external and unrelated to the consciousness of the percipient, hallucinations, including heautoscopy, are defined as nonreferential projections of the percipients' consciousnesses. The argument from doppelgängers, which we reviewed above, holds that apparitions are like doppelgängers, and hence both are unrelated to consciousness. The arguments from hallucination, by contrast, argue that apparitions are consciousness-produced but hallucinatory—that both are nonreferential delusions produced by the minds of the perceivers, rather than projections of other surviving consciousnesses.

Antisurvivalists among both parapsychologists and physiologists have attempted to explain away all apparitions and OBEs as varieties of hallucinations. They suggest that nothing objective has really been perceived, but that all these experiences were taking place within the mind of the (clinically abnormal) perceiver. Louisa Rhine, for example, argued that her studies showed " . . . the percipient, often if not always producing his experience according to his own interpretation. . . . The percipient generates the hallucination, agent and all, and the nature of his projection depends on his knowledge of the expectation of the agent [the person seen as an apparition] at the time."[149]

In regard to heautoscopy, or the seeing of oneself during an OBE, prominent medical doctors make pronouncements that "[t]he autistic reduplication of himself 'out there' may support the schizophrenic in his attempts to find some proof that he is not about to lose body-identity." [150]

Or similarly, according to Dewhurst and Todd, "Archaic modes of thinking are released in the process of the accompanying dissolution of the personality at death. As a result, bizarre hallucinatory delusional themes invade consciousness. Visual hallucinations originating in this way may assume any form, but man's ancient preoccupation with his reflection and shadow particularly favors the appearance of his autoscopic double."[151]

These arguments are straightforward; let us approach each in order.

Hallucination. Louisa Rhine's objection is that all apparitions are merely perceiver-generated hallucinations. She came to this conclusion after experiments in telepathy in which she had been forced to revise her earlier "sender-receiver" model to one that attributed more power to clairvoyance on the part of the perceiver, reducing the importance of the sender in these tests. Indeed this may be an important discovery in the mechanism of knowledge of Zener cards or dice faces. However, Rhine shows regrettable ignorance and unfamiliarity with the facts in her zeal to apply this reversal of traditional theory to all aspects of the paranormal, including survival evidence.

In many of the cases which have been shown to be of the highest standards of evidentiality, the percipient had neither knowledge nor expectation of the apparition whatsoever at the time (as in the Harford case). Also, the percipient's attention was absorbed in unrelated activity. In many instances, the apparition provided knowledge (e.g., of a death or dire need) at a time when the percipient could not have anticipated it, and at times the apparition was seen simultaneously by several percipients in appropriate parallax and perspective. Finally, in most of these cases the percipients were in good health, lacking any history of hallucinations or the symptoms usually productive of hallucinations.

Certainly, many more people project hallucinations than experience apparitions. But the presence of hallucinations in other cases does not in any way invalidate the perceptions of apparitions treated here. However appropriate to card-guessing experiments, Rhine's theory simply fails to fit the characteristics of apparitions as studied.

Autoscopy. Seeing the apparition of oneself somewhere else is called *autoscopy* or *heautoscopy*. It is a hallucination common to autistic schizophrenics. In fact, perception of one's double autoscopically may be produced by other measures, such as sensory deprivation and LSD.[152] But such an account of these apparitions is inappropriate because none of the subjects whose OBEs have been studied and verified have been found to be either autistic or schizophrenic, despite thorough psychological examinations in some cases. Many subjects have OBEs when there is no great threat at all to their body-identity, real or imagined, so this motivation to project or dissociate also is not present.

Furthermore, if neurological and psychiatric causes are to blame, we should expect a higher incidence of autoscopy among brain lesion patients. While other hallucinations are common, however, autoscopy is almost never found in this class of patients.[153] And finally, even if it were the case that false OBEs or autoscopy were triggered by such mental problems, this would not indicate that our other evidence of genuine OBEs is any less valid.

Preoccupations. There are also many responses to Dewhurst's claims that hallucinations of oneself at death are due to preoccupation with the shadow or double. First, it has not been shown that OBEs or autoscopic hallucinations are any more common at death than at any other time. Studies cited above indicated that OBEs occur at many times not specifically related to death, such as during sleep or even relaxed waking moments. It also has not been shown that OBE or autoscopy is the most common form of vision at death. On the contrary, true OBEs occur in only a small percentage of all observed deathbeds, as we shall document below. But even if it were the case that OBEs are distinctly linked with death, this should not be an argument against survival. On the contrary, it might lend credence to the claim that postmortem experience is an OBE. Furthermore, even if OBEs were connected to neurophysiological correlates, or if OBEs could be predicted by observing a certain series of systems, this would in no way deny the fact that OBEs do occur. The evidence that they are genuinely ecsomatic also would not be denied. Nor would the regular correlation of certain brain states with OBEs, if discovered, deny the possibility that OBEs might occur without physical bodies present.

A final problem with Dewhurst's claim is that he treats reversion to archetypes and "preoccupation with reflections and shadows" as if they were confirmed facts by which he might confirm his findings. In fact, however, they are nothing more than ad hoc conjectures and hypotheses.

There is no inherent reason people should be more preoccupied on their deathbeds with their shadows than with their mothers, or with their food, or with phallic symbols, or with anything else. So if autoscopic doubles are genuinely more common than visions of other things, we should like more evidence on this point. Regardless of their frequency, their causal relation to archaic modes of thinking is far from demonstrated.

Although he favors a materialistic interpretation, even Dewhurst himself eventually concedes this issue. He begins by admitting that nearly all who see their doubles on account of disease seem to know that the vision is a hallucination, an unreal aspect of their illness. This is in marked contrast to the cases of OBE subjects, who almost universally insist on the *reality* of their experiences even before they can be verified. Ultimately

Dewhurst concludes, "Strictly neurological hypotheses fail to explain fully individual variations in the degree of complexity of hallucinations in general, and the occurrence of autoscopy in particular."[154]

OBEs are not the same as autoscopy, nor should the two be grouped together. Yet even if they were, medical testimony admits itself incapable of explaining the occurrence of perceptions of oneself from an objective perspective.

All of the above objections fail in the attempt to explain how apparitions or OBEs could be any more than random hallucinations. Yet in hundreds of cases studied, the apparition or OBE yields true information unavailable through normal means. The only other avenue to explain such coincidences is through further extension of the "super-ESP" theory.

Super-ESP Theories

As noted in the previous chapter on interpreting claimed memories of former lives, the super-ESP theory is not a major theoretical improvement; it does not really replace an unknown theory with a better-known theory, for we still know extremely little about the mechanisms of non-OBE ESP. And it concedes that there are human powers which violate a simple, mechanical, three-dimensional, Newtonian worldview.

Admittedly, a "superpsychometry" theory might explain certain incidences of hauntings, in which particular memories seem attached to a particular place—but we have already excluded such hauntings from our consideration. Otherwise, neither superpsychometry nor superretrocognition has any direct applicability to most apparition and OBE cases, in which no past time or object association is involved. If it were found that doppelgängers predicted the percipient's own death, then the superprecognition theory might be applicable in some way to doppelgängers. But the evidence on doppelgängers is still too scanty to warrant this conclusion. Since they seem to lack conscious purpose, we have excluded them also from our consideration of veridical apparitions and OBEs. Outside of such doppelgänger cases, the superprecognition theory falls subject to the same logical circularity that led to its rejection in the previous chapter.

Thus, the only real candidate that remains is the supertelepathy/superclairvoyance theory, which would suggest that apparitions and OBEs are hallucinations of the percipients in which the veridical material is supplied by subconscious clairvoyance or telepathy.

Formulation of the supertelepathy/superclairvoyance theory. The supertelepathy/superclairvoyance theory admits the existence of apparitions and OBEs which produce verifiable information through no normal human means. What it denies is that apparitions are real and external and that OBEs might continue after bodily death. It suggests that both are particular types of hallucinations which supply veridical information through ESP, completely within the minds of the perceivers.

This theory was espoused by many leaders in the field of ESP and apparition research from the 1920s to the 1950s. Claude Richet was among the first to formulate the hypothesis, emphatically embellished in 1934 by E. R. Dodds's famous article, "Why I Do Not Believe in Survival."[155] F. W. H. Myers had called his studies of apparitions a "Census of Hallucinations," and this terminology continued to be used in the 1950s by scholars like Hereward Carrington, who referred to apparitions as veridical hallucinations.[156] Their arguments were very similar: the dramatizing powers of the unconscious, so often observed in action in seance rooms, were responsible for creating apparitions of the dead. In Hart's words, "Telepathy, clairvoyance, retrocognition, and even precognition operate in ways which can gather pertinent information from anywhere in the world. And they have come to believe that the information thus comprehensively gathered is organized into plausible form by the dramatizing capacity of the . . . mind."[157]

Such faculties are invoked to explain apparitions without recourse to a survival hypothesis. The earliest and most often-heard objection to this theory is that the perceiver could not possibly have known how or where to search through the whole world for the particular bits of information necessary to compile such a model and dramatize it. Antisurvivalist Gardner Murphy turned this objection on its head: he proposed that apparitions proved mind's special capacities.

Space is utterly irrelevant to the issue. The mind makes contact with that which is relevant to its purpose. If a cluster of ideas relevant to a given central theme exists, . . . [these] ideas which are related tend to function as a unit. . . . It must again be stressed, lest the point be regarded as sheerly hypothetical, that we have *direct evidence* that this process of filching and sifting among the minds of the living does actually occur.[158]

Murphy's point is quite appropriate to the interpretation of the evidence provided by certain seance mediums—particularly when sitters already knew the evidence or characteristics which were to be looked for. It is less clear that apparitions are "direct evidence of filching and sifting" in the minds of unexpected perceivers who are certainly unaware of the process, if it occurs at all.

As of 1950, the evidence seemed to say merely that some people experienced apparitions or hallucinations with information provided by telepathic assistance. Survivalists felt that this was explainable in terms of the projection of disembodied minds. Antisurvivalists held that the "searchlight and assembler" capacities of the human mind provided a better hypothesis. Neither had other examples of the existence of the phenomena they took as paradigmatic—except for a few scattered references to OBEs on the side of the survivalists, and a few indications of "searchlight" abilities of seance mediums on the materialists' side.

The question then became: to which phenomenon was the seeing of apparitions more closely related, to OBEs or to mediumistic information acquisition? J. B. Rhine, impressed by the growing range of ESP powers in his labs, agreed with Murphy that survival was less probable; both deprecated the OBE data.[159] With the increases in the use of hallucinogens and reporting of OBEs in the late 1960s, and with laboratory studies of OBEs in the 1970s, the picture changed substantially. Today there remain arguments favoring the survivalist theory which the antisurvivalists seem unable to counter.

The failure of supertelepathy. With regard to apparitions, there is not only the question of how the percipient received the information provided, which might be theoretically accessible through telepathy or clairvoyance. There are also the issues of timing, purpose, and multiple perceivers. We have seen that in many apparition cases, the perceiver was not expecting the apparition, and had never seen one before or since. Why should he or she perceive one at that particular time? In most cases, the purpose of the apparition is explicable only in terms of the projector, or the person whose apparition was seen. There are many cases in which more than one person beheld the apparition, and instances where the "projector" (person seen) did not want to be seen by others but was seen (e.g., the Wilmot case). This sheds serious doubt on the claim that apparitions are merely telepathically implanted hallucinations in the minds of the people who receive them.

Second, the defenders of supertelepathy face a dilemma in explaining purposeful apparitions of the dead. They understand the purposefulness and information communicated in apparitions of the living on the basis of the supertelepathy by which their "projectors" influenced the hallucinations of the percipients. But if they retain the same model for apparitions of the dead, they admit that there exist telepathic projectors among the dead, who influence correctly the hallucinations of those who perceive their apparitions. They save their horse but lose the battle; they preserve the notion that apparitions are really subjective hallucinations at the cost of conceding the survival issue.

The other option is to suggest that what is involved is not telepathy, but some form of clairvoyance, which does not require a communicator or sender. But surely we do not want a model in which telepathy is used before death and clairvoyance after death to explain what is clearly the same phenomenon. And if clairvoyance is adopted in place of telepathy as the universal explanation for all apparitions, then the purposefulness of unexpected apparitions is even more baffling and incongruous.

Neither the telepathic nor the clairvoyant models do justice to the cases in which an apparition is perceived as being in the same place, as dressed in the same garb, and as performing the same activity as the projectors who feel themselves to be having OBEs. Even if supertelepathy were able to account for some of the cases presently mistakenly classified as apparitions or OBEs, these accounts where projectors' agree with perceivers' descriptions cannot be written off so smugly (cf. Beard and Garrett cases, supra). They testify beyond doubt to the identity of apparitions and OBEs, at least when the subject is living. The remaining question is whether this mutual OBE/apparition is something objective or a mutual subjective hallucination. The laboratory studies of OBEs have helped us to answer this question, for they tend to indicate that apparitions and OBEs are no more subjective than cameras and recording devices.

The failure of superclairvoyance. Some features of OBEs are similar to clairvoyance, in that the person is aware of things happening somewhere else. But there the similarity ends, and the differences are important in analyzing the superclairvoyance theory of OBEs. First of all, we have the firsthand reports of the OBE subjects themselves to compare with those of clairvoyants. When Swedenborg told his friends and the governor at a party that there had been a fire in Stockholm, he may have perceived the scene clearly and correctly from a distance—clairvoyantly.[160] But Swedenborg never imagined that his consciousness had left his physical body, flown to Stockholm, appraised the scene, and then flown back to arouse his body. In genuine OBE cases, however, we have the testimony of the subjects that they felt themselves to be leaving their physical bodies and moving through walls and against gravity to other places. This alone does not prove that OBEs are not a species of clairvoyance, but coupled with other factors it helps us make important distinctions.

We also have the testimony of witnesses, cameras, and animal experiments that something was happening at the place where the OBE subject claimed to be having an OBE, coupled to the sounds and temperature changes detected in some apparitions cases. Surely it is easier to suggest that something, however unusual, is "out there" (in the sense that any matter is phenomenally "out there") affecting all these instruments and people in similar ways. The alternative would be to argue that the perceiver was hallucinating a veridical presence or scene which was not there *and* simultaneously psychokinetically affecting photographic film, magnetic tape, or thermocouples—a far more complex and improbable construct![161]

If this evidence were not enough, we have the results of experiments using Karlis Osis and Janet Mitchell's ecsomaticity boxes. These boxes preclude telepathic transmission of the knowledge obtained because no human knows it until the OBE subject perceives it. They also preclude clairvoyance in its traditional sense because, in clairvoyance, objects or scenes are "seen" directly and not through a series of mirrors and lenses in a process of optical distortions. It is possible that some OBEs are mere hallucinations in which the subject imagines himself somewhere but no other evidence is obtained. But in some of our studies we have cases where (1) the subjects feels themselves to be outside of their bodies, (2) other witnesses or equipment detect something in the place where they claim to have been, and (c) they return with information which they only could have obtained by optical perception from a particular point in space. In these conditions, real ecsomaticity seems a far more straightforward theory than one of telepathy and clairvoyance with psychokinetic assists.

Conclusions

We may conclude, then, that the super-ESP theory cannot explain the facts of apparitions/OBEs as adequately as the theory that a genuine exterior-ization of the locus of perceptual consciousness occasionally takes place. In some cases, this locus of consciousness may be completely invisible; in others, it appears like a haze or localized mist. In yet other cases, it may appear to either the experiencers or the perceivers (or both) like a "double" of the physical body, and then disappear as the mind drifts elsewhere. We know very little about this diaphanous body outside of the physical body, or the mechanisms of how and when it appears or disappears, and to whom. This ethereal body corresponds to concepts common to Hinduism, Buddhism, and Theosophy. It provides evidence of a possible vehicle for memory and consciousness between incarnations, if reincarnation occurs. And it gives flesh to the suggestions of philosophers like Wheatley that life after death might be conceptualized as a continuing OBE.[162]

3.

The Heart of
Near-Death Experiences

Possession, memories of past lives, apparitions and OBEs are apparently confined to a small segment of the population—enough to compare various accounts and propose tests for verifiability, but not enough for large-scale statistical comparisons. By contrast, the study of people's deathbed experiences provides a broad base for understanding the nature of death and possibly of what comes thereafter. The notion that some people can see to the "other side" (the next world) on their deathbeds is widespread in non-Western and developing countries. Many cultures' descriptions of life after death appear to be based upon reports of the dying or those revived from death. The scientific study of near-death experiences (NDEs) is by far the most recent of the attempts to approach an answer to the question of survival.

With recent advances in technology, the number of cases in which people are resuscitated from clinical death is increasing every year. Moreover, the availability of modern computerized information storage and comparison enables the study of thousands of such cases in ways previously thought impossible. With a few exceptions, it is only since the late 1970s that researchers have begun to publish their studies of NDEs, and public receptivity is gradually following such publicity.

In cases where people previously pronounced dead revive to report having had various experiences while clinically dead, we have prima facie evidence that some people survive death. Such cases need careful scrutiny and should not necessarily be accepted at face value. The determination of death constitutes a very sticky issue. NDEs may occur in any of several states: waking, sleeping, delirious, coma, or dead. In the majority of cases, the patients have not yet died, but are simply on the brink of death, when they have experiences of a sort which they have never encountered before. There is a very wide range in the experiences reported by the dying and resuscitated—although not as wide as the range of their personalities, beliefs, and manners of death.

The leading survivalist scholars have classified these phenomena into as many as ten discrete categories, from which they have attempted to construct a single model of which any dying person may experience some part. Thus, Raymond Moody discusses phases of ineffability and peace, "the tunnel," OBEs, meeting others, "the being of light," and reaching a heavenly border.[1] Kenneth Ring similarly constructs a model with euphoric, OBE, darkness, light, and otherworldly phases.[2] Unfortunately, many investigators have tried to treat such descriptions as a unified package and to confirm or deny the entire package at one fell swoop. Such assertions are patently premature, as it is rare that anyone experiences more than one or two of these phenomena. We have far too little evidence to place these stages in any cut-and-dried continuum. Rather, at this stage it is far more prudent to treat each individual phenomenon for its own worth.

Phenomena Not Considered

Rather than accepting or rejecting a whole theory as to the nature of death, we shall examine each discrete type of experience in turn to see what its evidential value is. Some of the experiences classified above are clearly not unique to dying situations but have perfectly good neurophysiological explanations. Therefore, we shall first delimit the range of evidence by a review of the phenomena we shall *not* discuss in detail, and the reasons for this discrimination. Most important of these items are (1) OBEs, (2) "the life-review," and (3) sound effects and visualizations, as of a tunnel, a void, or geometric patterns, which have good physiological origins and explanations.

OBEs

OBEs are indeed important phenomena at death, particularly common as products of violent accidents. Many subjects do report their experiences on the battlefield, in automobile accidents, or during surgery, describing veridical OBEs during such events. This tends to reinforce the suggestion of some scholars that life after death may be conceived of as a continuing OBE. It is important to remember that OBEs are often reported by those resuscitated from death or coma. These people report having OBEs when their bodies are dormant or even dead to all examination.[3] As previously discussed, however, OBEs are not unique to deathbed situations.

The Life-Review

Many NDEs include the dying person's loss of consciousness of surroundings, followed by a mental "life-review" in which the memories of previous experiences recur vividly in the mind of the subject. Some people feel surprised or nostalgic at this unexpected jarring of memory. Others interpret it as a substitute for a religious judgment in which their review of their own lives is designed to teach them the moral value of life. However, there are several reasons why this life-review phenomenon does not apply directly to the issue of survival of consciousness after death.

First, the life-review is a somewhat rare phenomenon. Moody describes 6 out of 150 cases reporting a life-review; Karlis Osis found it in 7–9 percent of his sample.[4] Ring found it in 24 percent of his sample, Russell Noyes in 29 percent. This may be because their studies had high incidence of violent and unexpected deaths, with which life-review is most commonly associated.[5]

Within this narrow segment of people who experience a life-review, there is little agreement about its nature. Some people see their lives from their own perspectives, as they remembered it happening from their own eyes. Others see themselves from a detached, OBE-like perspective, as if watching a movie of their younger selves from a distance.[6] Some describe it as moving like a motion picture in fast motion; others call it a series of still images, like slides.[7] Some see only the highlights of their earlier years, whereas others claim to see "everything" or every single episode in their entire lives.[8] Presumably, this is made possible by a psychological distortion of the patients' subjective sense of time, so that what is in fact a few minutes seems to the patients like many years.

This variation in life-reviews is quite interesting. If the life-review were based purely on memories recorded in the brain, we should expect people to remember past situations from the body-centered perspective from which their senses recorded the experience. But many people see themselves from a third-party perspective, as if in a movie or OBE. This seems to indicate that more than mere reactivation of old memories is going on here, and perhaps that a "self" other than the brain is involved in this life-review.

Whereas most patients report memories only of their present lifetimes, some report previous lifetimes, with or without verifiable evidence.[9] Reincarnationists naturally seize upon such evidence as further fuel for their arguments that people will not only continue to live after death, but also that they already have lived in other bodies in the past. However, the small size of the available sample combined with the wide variations of types within the sample casts doubt upon the universality of the life-review and its causes.

Neurophysiological explanations of the life-review are readily available. Experiments by Wilder Penfield, Herbert Jasper, Maitland Baldwin, and others have demonstrated that remarkably vivid replay of prior memories could be brought about by probing the temporal cortex and stimulating it with a mild electrical shock of short duration.[10] Noyes and Kletti trace the life-review to seizure-like firings of neurons in the temporal lobes of the brain.[11] The experience of condensation of time also points to disturbances of the temporal lobes as the locus of this phenomenon. Minor seizures of the temporal lobes may be caused by a gradual depletion of oxygen, which we might expect near death. Side effects of temporal lobe seizures might include the regurgitation of numerous memories thought forgotten by the subject. Variations in the life-review experience might be due to variations either in the seizures or in memory-storage mechanisms.

This is all quite speculative, but the possibility of such neurophysiological explanations for these experiences tends to depreciate their evidentiality as indications of a future life. Nor is there any proof that such life-reviews may continue more than a few minutes in any case. Thus, they do not seem to be a particularly fruitful line of research for an inquiry primarily concerned with life after death.

Physiologically Explicable Sounds and Lights

Other feelings common to dying people include hearing annoying buzzing or whooshing sounds, seeing geometric nets of flashing light, and feeling drawn through a long dark tunnel, black void, or domed/vaulted empty space. However, each of these states may be explained as purely physiological repercussions of the lack of oxygen and/or minor seizure of the temporal lobe.[12] On the other hand, research has failed to uncover many cases in which such phenomena were reported by people already pronounced dead. Most of the people who experience buzzing, geometric, or tunnel phenomena agree that it is but a short-lived phase. Therefore, it seems of little importance to the issue of survival of human personality after death. The possibility that there are physiological reasons for these states does not rule out the patient's experiencing them as if they were objective and external.

Phenomena Considered

In this study, we shall confine our attention to three aspects of NDE, all of which fall within the description of deathbed visions: (1) visions of one's departed friends or relatives, (2) visions of a "spiritual guide" or religious saint, and (3) visions of another world, with heavenly or otherworldly images. The nature of the person's disease or decease might have an influence on the content of such visions, but the evidence indicates that these three types of visions are widespread among dying people and those thought dead in a wide variety of circumstances.

Accounts of "returning from the dead" are perhaps the most impressive and convincing to the popular mind. But such cases are relatively infrequent, so these cases alone do not provide an adequate basis for study. Moreover, the exact status of such patients is open to question, as we shall detail below. If it is found that the visions of those approaching death are similar to those temporarily pronounced dead, then we have a broader base for observation and stronger basis for comparison. In this study, we shall refer to both accounts of those resuscitated from death and of those in their last moments. We cannot simply assume that these visions prove afterlife or depict a future world. First, we must review the evidence about the nature of these NDEs, and subsequently consider the alternative interpretations available.

Deathbed Visions Down Through History

Tales of those who have returned from the dead come from many ages and cultures. Er's trip to the Plain of Oblivion and River of Forgetfulness in Plato may well be an allegory, but stories of resuscitation in the Bible more likely contain some truth. In the Old Testament, there is the report of Elisha resuscitating the Shunammite widow's son.[13] Jesus' raising of Jairus's daughter is reported by two synoptic gospels, while John says that the raising of Lazarus after four days was one of the direct causes of the priests' plan to do away with Jesus.[14] Peter brought the weaver Dorcas back to life, and Paul resuscitated Eutychus, who had fallen from a loft.[15] Unfortunately, Jairus's daughter, Lazarus, Dorcas, and Eutychus failed to record their experiences for posterity, if indeed they experienced anything while they were dead.

In A.D. 731, the Venerable Bede recounted the "noteworthy miracle" of the revival of a Northumbrian named Cunningham, who thereupon entered the monastery of Melrose.[16] Many Chinese and Japanese Buddhist saints of the first millennium had life-changing NDEs, and their disciples described figures of light and heavenly scenery at their demise.[17] Outside the pale of the major religions, E. B. Tylor recounts the case in New Zealand of a Maori's death, burial, and revival, surprisingly similar to Western accounts that could hardly have influenced it.[18] Resuscitation of plague victims (even in their coffins) was so common that it led to the invention of caskets with life-support systems and bells operable from the inside—and to embalming laws that would surely prevent revival![19]

As biographies of famous people came into wider circulation in recent centuries, testimonies of NDEs were better preserved. Numerous biographies record Friedrich Schiller's deathbed vision (8 May 1805), in which he exclaimed, "Is this your Heaven? Is this your Hell?" Apparently his close friend Johann Wolfgang von Goethe was psychically aware of Schiller's state, for he was heard crying in his room that night, and the following morning he asked, "Schiller is very ill, is he not?" Goethe himself recalled Schiller on his deathbed, although there is some debate about whether this was a vision or merely a memory.[20] Thomas de Quincey described an NDE (of his mother or aunt) in his *Suspiria de Profundis;*[21] Laurence Oliphant's celebrated "Christ touched me, He held me!" followed an NDE two days before his death on 23 December 1888.

Among NDEs in which the dying person sees a dead relative appear at his deathbed, William Wordsworth's vision of his wife Dora (23 April 1850), and actress Rachel Felix's greeting of her deceased sister Rebecca one day before her death (2 January 1858) are well-documented cases. Perhaps because they are most in the news, cases of actors and singers having NDEs continue to be common even today. Singers Charles Aznavour and Serge Lama, actors Daniel Gelin and Curt Jurgens, dancer Janine Charrat, and even King Paul of Greece (d. 4 March 1964) reported otherworldly visions while on the brink of death.[22]

Cases of lesser-known individuals may be less widely reported, but they emerge in surveys such as those made by Sir William Barrett, who was prompted to publish a study of deathbed visions by a striking NDE his wife (a nurse) had observed.[23] Recent studies have been much broader in scale, funded by sources ranging from Arizona prospector James Kidd[24] to Xerox inventor Chester Carlson.[25]

The first major recent studies were conducted independently by two doctors who published their studies of deathbed experiences in 1975 with little knowledge of each others' projects: Elisabeth Kübler-Ross at the University of Chicago, and Raymond Moody, Jr., at the University of North Carolina.[26] Their methods were to solicit information from doctors who had witnessed NDEs and from patients who themselves volunteered such information. More statistical approaches were employed by Karlis Osis and Erlundur Haraldsson, who collected hundreds of such cases in both India and America, and by Kenneth Ring, who applied computer analyses to numerous variables in his New England survey.[27] Since 1977, books and articles reporting NDE research have multiplied.

There is still little agreement on the percentage of people who have significant NDEs while approaching death—nor is it always clear just what kind of NDEs the percentages should reflect. Robert Kastenbaum conservatively suggests that the vast majority of patients near death simply black out, with no memory nor experience during that period.[28] Hackett and Carlson also pin the figure at a low 5 percent, but the same article suggests figures of 40 percent in Sabom's survey and 60 percent in Schoonmaker's.[29] These figures are modified by others who cite Sabom's ratio at 20 percent and Schoonmaker's at 70 percent.[30]

There are several possibilities here. Many of the people who have NDEs may hesitate to report them for fear of being ridiculed. Charles A. Garfield attributes the low 21 percent (of those people near death having NDEs) to their reluctance to report such experiences for fear of being considered strange.[31] W. Dewi Rees's study tends to bear out these findings, in discovering that 72 percent of the population would fear ridicule if they reported such experiences.[32] Or it may be that everyone has NDEs, but the majority of people simply do not remember them, just as the majority of us do not remember the dreams we dream every night. In fact, there is some evidence to indicate that those who do not remember their dreams are also unlikely to remember their NDEs. Or, for reasons we do not yet understand, it may be that some people have NDEs, and others simply do not. Perhaps the clearest figures are again provided by Ring's study. Ring found as many as 48 percent had some part of a "core NDE," but only 10 percent reported the most significant types of visionary/ heavenly experiences.[33]

Visions of Departed Relatives or Friends

It is quite common for people having deathbed visions to "see" the face or figure of departed friends and relatives in their NDE. Visions of mothers and spouses are apparently commonest, comprising about half of the cases in which nonreligious figures are "seen."[34] These are followed by visions of siblings, children and, in American studies (but not Indian), friends.

> The doctor gave me up, and told my relatives that I was dying. However, I was quite alert through the whole thing, and even as I heard him saying this, I felt myself coming to. As I did, I realized that all these people were there . . . who had passed on before. I recognized my grandmother and a girl I had known when I was in school, and many other relatives

and friends. It seems that I mainly saw their faces and felt their presence. They all seemed pleased. It was happy.[35]

Such appearances sometimes lead to dramatic changes in the character of the percipient, as in the case of a seven-year-old boy dying of mastoid infection. He had been rebellious, refusing medicine and fighting the nurses. Then he had an NDE:

> The boy insisted that Uncle Charlie [a doctor] came, sat beside him, and told him to take his medicine. He also told the boy that he would get well. The boy was very sure that Uncle Charlie had sat in the chair and told him these things. After this experience, the patient was cooperative. He was not excited, and he took the deceased doctor's "visit" as a matter of course. The next morning, the boy was much better—a dramatic change had occurred in his condition.[36]

Aside from the conviction on the part of the perceiver that the person seen was "really there" and the fact that apparitions of dead relatives drastically outnumber those of living relatives,[37] there is nothing in these NDEs that would in itself indicate survival. It would be very easy to suggest that the dying persons simply thought about other people who had died as they lay dying, and this concentration on dead friends led to their visualization.

There is an immediate answer to this skeptical hypothesis. It is clear in many cases that the dying patient had not been thinking about nor expecting to see such friends or relatives. Even more important, however, are the many instances in which the dying patient "sees" deceased persons whom the patient had not known to be dead (called "Peak in Darien" cases). An early, well-documented example is the case of Doris Clark B____, who saw her sister Vida as she was dying on 12 January 1924. Vida had died the previous Christmas day, but the fact had been carefully kept from her sister Doris, so as not to affect her condition.[38]

In other cases, the dying persons have provided information that was unknown to any of the people present—such as the death of relatives in India, Italy, Paris, or other distant locations.[39] Such dying persons' declarations that they saw dead friends and knew that they were dead were often taken as indications that they were hallucinating, until later information confirmed that they had been correct about the prior death of their friend or relative.[40]

Purpose. Another curious commonality of the figures seen, aside from the fact that they are deceased, is that they generally exhibit an interest in "guiding" or "taking away" the patient.[41] Typical of this phenomenon are instances like those of David and Harry:

> Harry died at Abbot's Langley on November 2, fourteen miles from my vicarage at Aspley, David the following day at Aspley. About one hour before the death of the latter child, he sat up in bed, and pointing to the bottom of the bed, said distinctly, "There is little Harry calling to me." Or again, the dying words of tenor James Moore, "There is Mother. Why, Mother, have you come to see me? No, no, I'm coming to see you. Just wait, Mother, I am almost over. I can jump it. Wait, Mother."[42]

The apparent purposefulness of these bedside visions reminds us of the apparent purposefulness observed in other apparitions of the dead, and is an important difference from other hallucinations, which tend to lack this characteristic quality.

Intersubjectivity. Most impressive of the NDEs, however, are the cases in which other people present in the room are also able to witness the presence of the departed relatives with their "take-away purpose." Nurse Joy Snell described her friend Laura Stirman's NDE as follows:

> A short time before she expired, I became aware that two spirit forms were standing by the bedside, one on either side of it. I did not see them enter the room. . . . I recognized their faces as those of two girls who had been the closest friends of the girl who was dying. They had passed away a year before and were then about her own age. Just before they appeared, the dying girl exclaimed, "It has grown suddenly dark; I cannot see anything!" But she recognized them immediately. A smile, beautiful to see, lit up her face. She stretched forth her hands and in joyous tones exclaimed, "Oh, you have come to take me away! I am glad, for I am

very tired." As she stretched forth her hands, the two "angels" each extended a hand.[43]

Laubscher relates that, in his medical practice, he has met many nurses who have "actually seen the joyous faces of the relatives of the deceased who were dead, as if they gathered round with happy welcome to receive him."[44] Florence Marryat Lean attested that she saw the spirits of a patient's father and grandmother at a girl's passing.[45] In yet another instance, Colonel Cosgrave reported that he had seen an apparition of Walt Whitman (d. 1892) hovering over the bed of his dying friend Horace Traubel (d. 1919), who stared at the apparition of his long-gone friend and said, "There is Walt!"[46] Dr. Crookall also cites a number of such cases, which add yet another note of verification to the idea that these NDEs are closer to the objective apparitions of our previous chapter than to the subjective hallucinations of someone in delirium.[47]

Visions of Religious Figures

Next in frequency to visions of departed loved ones are visions of religious figures, sometimes called "beings of light." Preliminary cross-cultural studies comparing Indian and American deathbed visions indicate that religious figures are "seen" far more commonly on Indian deathbeds than American. In the West, religious figures are usually identified as God, Jesus, Mary, Moses, or Saint Peter. In India, Yamaraj [the god of death] is most commonly reported, followed by Rama, Krishna, and other such mythological figures.[48] Since no one has actually met God, Jesus, or Krishna as a fellow human in the twentieth century, the identification of these figures is usually a superimposition of the perceiver.

One girl, for example, had a throat implant and had been told that she would not be able to receive Holy Communion. She said of her vision,

> I can see that form now: It had blond-gold hair and it had a beard, a very light beard and a moustache. It had a white garment on. And from this white garment there was all this gold shining. There was a red spot here [she points to her chest], on his gown, there was a chalice in his hand, and it said to me, "You will receive my body within the week." And he went. And I thought to myself, "Well that's funny."[49]

The identification of the figure of light with Christ or God is often explicit, as in the now-famous case of Private George Ritchie. Ritchie died temporarily on 20 December 1943, and later testified, "The light which entered that room was Christ: I know because the thought was put deep within me, 'You are in the presence of the Son of God.' I have called Him 'light,' but I could also have said 'love,' for that room was flooded, illuminated, pierced, by the most total compassion I have ever felt."[50]

On the other hand, there are many less religious people who have very similar experiences, but feel no need to label the apparitions with any particular name, referring merely to "a bearded man against a golden light."[51] It might be argued that these too are merely the final projections of the minds of the dying persons, who expect such religious comfort at death. But any such expectations must be very subliminal, for no correlation has been found between the religiosity of the percipients and the content of their visions or the frequency of this type of religious vision. Rather, religious patients more often give specific religious names to the "being of light." Moody relates, "In quite a few instances, reports have come from persons who had no religious beliefs or training at all prior to their experiences, and their descriptions do not seem to differ in content from [those of] people who had quite strong religious beliefs."[52]

Even more surprisingly, Ring's detailed statistical surveys found that those most familiar with the literature of NDEs had the *fewest* visions, and those least expecting them had the most![53] Even in cases where the patient was highly religious, the percipient sometimes hesitated to identify the figure with a religious character.[54] A more striking case is that of a woman who thought she saw her patron saint, Gerard. She had long prayed to him, imagining him to be handsome and garbed in velvet finery like the pope. But in her NDE, he appeared to her dressed like a medieval monk with sandals.[55] So her desire to meet her patron saint was played out in her NDE, but his appearance utterly contradicted all her expectations. Such examples suggest that NDE visions are not merely dependent on the desires of the perceivers.

Purpose. These religious "figures of light" seem to exhibit a purpose of guiding or conducting the dying person, as do apparitions of friends and relatives discussed above. While this comforts the majority of dying people, a large minority of the Indian subjects identified the apparitional figure as the god of death and were reluctant to "go with him." An Indian college graduate, for example, about to be discharged from the hospital, suddenly shouted, "Someone is here dressed in white. . . . I will not go with you!" He died ten minutes later.[56] But such cases seem rather the exception than the rule. In most cases there is a distinct mood elevation, a serenity or even joy gained by the patient through this vision. Regardless of whether or not the percipient is pleased or afraid of this apparent intention, the purposefulness of such visionary figures seems clear.

Intersubjectivity. As in the cases of visions of deceased relatives, there are some instances in which third-person observers in the sick chamber also witness the alleged visitor. In 1918, the Society for Psychical Research published the case of one Mr. G____, who saw, "standing at the head of my dying wife, a woman's figure, seeming to express a welcome. A famous doctor of nervous and mental disease who was present did not witness the figure, but attested that there was no natural explanation for G____'s vision, and that it could not be attributed to temporary hallucination."[57]

Others have reported observing "two white figures,"[58] or "white-robed figures, a man and a woman, [who] wrapped their robes around her. . . . They floated away."[59] In an earlier section we noted that animals in laboratory experiments sometimes are able to sense the presence of one having an OBE when humans cannot. A recent case where animals seemed to sense something was reported by an experienced nurse:

> The patient, a Hindu policeman in his forties, was suffering from pulmonary tuberculosis. . . . Suddenly he said, "Yamdoot is coming to take me away. Take me down from the bed so that Yamdoot does not find me." He pointed upwards and outwards. "There he is!" . . . There was a large tree with a great number of crows sitting on its branches. Just as the patient had his vision, all the crows suddenly flew away from the tree with much noise, as if someone had fired a gun. We were very surprised by this and ran outside through an open door in the room, but we saw nothing that might have disturbed the crows. . . . It was as if

they, too, had become aware of something terrible. As this happened, the patient fell into a coma, and expired a few minutes later.[60]

While such cases are not conclusive, they provide further evidence that NDEs share certain characteristics with OBEs; they are occasionally perceived by animals, psychics, and observers. Could it be that people become more psychically sensitive to such apparitions at death?

Visions of Another World

Next let us consider NDEs in which dead or dying people report seeing heaven, or "traveling through another world." Some patients explicitly identify the place as "heaven"; a majority, who find the experience pleasant enough, simply say, "So that's what it will be like," or "Now I know there is life after death."[61] Such subjective experiences by no means prove the truth of their impressions, but these NDEs do deserve to be analyzed for their major features and conditions before we can go on to generalize upon them.

The commonest imagery among visions of "other realms" is description of fields of flowers, gardens, or hills.[62] While temporarily left for dead, Commander A. B. Campbell saw "a wide moor, with a well-worn track . . . to the brow of a hill."[63] Dr. Wiltse, whose case of temporary death was published in the *St. Louis Medical and Surgical Journal* also saw scenes of trees and sky, and a path leading to a barrier of rocks.[64] Such visions of paths or roads and barriers seem almost as frequent as those of fields and flower gardens.

Some people feel themselves to be on a vessel on a large body of water, recognizing relatives on the far shore. Many see colorful sunrises or sunsets, or hear music during their NDEs of other worlds.[65] Gates, some of rough-hewn stone, others of golden palaces or castles, are also very commonly reported, reminding us of the visions so widespread in ancient Chinese and Japanese literature of those who had been to heaven and back.[66] Intellectuals and students sometimes have visions of a realm of "sculptors and philosophers, composers and inventors."[67] In almost all cases, the imagery seen is imbued with a radiance of its own, glowing or emitting a warm, intense light.[68]

Content similarity. There appears to be some "archetypical" similarity in the content of these visions, which is not significantly affected by the religious hopes or expectations of the dying patients. After detailed statistical analyses, Osis and Haraldsson concluded:

> Belief in life after death doubled the frequency of visions symbolizing death as a gratifying transition (p = .003), and responses with religious emotions (p = .006). Belief did *not* significantly change the frequency of experiences of beauty and peace and the frequency of images of another world. Apparently the belief in life after death changes very little of the afterlife images themselves, but rules the religious emotions and sharply increases positive valuation of death.[69]

Moreover, the frequency and content of these visions seemed closely similar among reports from both Indians and Americans, Hindus, Christians, and Jews.[70]

Paranormal insights. Visions of "other worlds" also occasionally include paranormal knowledge which can later be verified. Sometimes it is of the "Peak in Darien" variety: sighting relatives not yet known to be dead, in this realm where many other dead people are perceived.[71] Janine Charrat, thought dead on 18 December 1961, saw visions of future events in her life, extremely contrary to both the laws of probability and to her own waking thoughts, but her life indeed evolved as she had foreseen in these visions.[72] Serge Lama, by contrast, had visions of past lives, from which he apparently gained correct information about buildings and events which he could not have known normally.[73] Many people dead or on the brink of death have visions in which they are told exactly when they will die, and their deaths follow these predictions even though their doctors have very different expectations.[74]

In one case, a girl who thought that she was bound by messengers of Yama actually exhibited rope marks on her legs after the experience.[75] This may remind us of hypnotic phenomena in which the patient exhibits symptoms for which no physical cause is present. Therefore, our question becomes not whether there were invisible ropes actually binding her legs but rather, what so altered her mind as to make her believe that she was

bound by ropes, to the extent that they affected her body psychosomatical-
ly. Apparently the unexpected vision of heaven and its messengers had an
intense, hypnotic-like effect on the subject's mind and body.

Deathbed visions of other worlds are not only interesting; they also are
important indications of survival to the extent that they are intersubjective,
not in the sense of being perceived by many people in the same room, but
in their similarities that cut across cultural and religious boundaries. In
addition, such visions produce verifiable information paranormally that is
not otherwise known to the subject. And finally, deathbed visions
frequently occur after the patient has been pronounced dead, after which
the patient again revives. The subjects' feelings that they still have unfinished business to do on earth seems important for their revival in such
conditions.[76]

To be sure, there are exceptions to this general picture. Some people
hallucinate; a few have visions of monsters, hell, or blackness.[77] The point
is not so much *what* other worlds they experience as *that* they experience
other realms at death. Now we must critically analyze these claims.

Objections to the Phenomena as Evidence of Survival

In the face of the thousands of cases amassed and studied in the past two
decades by doctors and scholars, not even the most skeptical of readers can
deny that NDEs are experienced as described. Nor can we assert that they
have been produced by collusion and fraud between subjects and doctors.
If anything, the medical profession itself has tended to downplay the
importance of such experiences, but outright rejection of NDEs as nonexistent or fraudulent simply does not occur.[78]

The countersurvivalist argument to "explain away" NDEs must include
at least the following three claims: (1) that the subjects were not really
dead when they had NDEs, (2) that the subjects were hallucinating and not
"seeing" anything at all, and (3) that information gained during NDEs and
later verified may be ascribed to ESP knowledge-acquisition, but that all
other parts of the vision are again hallucination. If any one of these antisurvivalists' objections fails, then the survivalists' case is left in a strong

position, for it may assert (1) that people really return from death, and thus sometimes survive death, at least for a short time; (2) that people really see into "the next world," something objective and not hallucinatory; or (3) information was indeed gained through contact with the dead or with religious figures at the moment of death. The rest of this chapter will be devoted to evaluating the relative strengths and weaknesses of the arguments surrounding these three important objections.

Patients Pronounced Dead Were Not Really Dead

One frequent argument against the data of resuscitation cases claims that the person pronounced dead and resuscitated could not have *really* been dead. There are several ways of approaching this question. In short, doctors can say one of two things:

1. The fact that the patients revived proves that they weren't really dead and therefore we don't really know how to define death medically, or

2. Our medical criteria for defining death are adequate; (from which it follows that) some people really do return from death.

Naïve materialism. Naïve materialists say that the fact that persons revived in itself proves that they could not have been dead. But this is specious question-begging because it assumes as a fact the premise that no one ever revives once truly dead, which is precisely the issue in question. Whenever a case of resuscitation from death is adduced, it is simply attributed to a mistaken pronouncement, for "the person could not have been dead if he revived." This very circularity renders meaningless the concept and definition of medical and physical death.

We now have a broad spectrum of medical criteria, ranging from pulse and breath to reflex checks, pupil dilation, body temperature and stiffness, and EEGs. While no single test adequately defines death, taken together they exhaust the functions we should expect in a living human body. If these tests are called inadequate to determine when a body has died (because people pronounced dead by these criteria sometimes are still really alive and will revive), then we are left with no way of distinguishing living from dead people, which is as absurd as it is inconvenient. We might await putrefaction or demand embalming to guarantee death, but these are further undesirable consequences of inherently fallacious logic and assumptions. The only alternative is the second one, that is, accepting medical criteria for death and admitting that, on very rare occasions, people do come back from "the other side."

Parabiosis. On a somewhat more logical and scientific line, it might be seriously argued that the people who were pronounced dead were not really dead, because life lingers on even in a human corpse in the sense that parts of the body die at different rates. Not surprisingly, this was the line taken by Russian doctors who were ideologically committed to explaining everything on purely materialistic grounds.[79] By this analysis, mere cessation of breath and heartbeat—which the Soviets considered the primary indicators of death—by no means implies that the organism cannot be revived and regain consciousness. In fact, the Russians performed numerous experiments in which decapitated animal heads *showed* every sign of life when reinfused with oxygenated blood some minutes after severance.[80] To deny that patients who later revive were ever dead, while admitting that they showed no signs of life, required the Russian invention of a new term for a state that is neither life nor death:

> In the corpse, protected from the processes of decay, the life of its separate cells, tissues, and organs continues to glimmer for a long time. True death comes to the body's cells only after their inherent physiological functions have ceased finally and irreversibly. Prior to the arrival of this moment, every dying cell passes through a unique state, which cannot be characterized as life [since its vital functions have stopped] nor recognized as death [since, under certain conditions, its lost functions may be restored]. The noted physiologist N. E. Vvedensky named this transitional, intermediate state between life and death *parabiosis.*[81]

There are several points to notice among these fancy phrases. In the first place, Leonid Vasiliev qualifies his statement with the phrase "protected from the processes of decay," and then goes on to speak of refrigerated corpses of the sort he had been working with. But the vast majority of our corpses are not refrigerated at death—least of all those of the people reporting the NDEs discussed here.

Second, Vasiliev's grouping of cells with organs is inappropriate. It may be true that certain cells (e.g., hair follicles) continue to function for several days after brain and heart functions cease. But it would be absurd to suggest that human beings should be identified with their hair follicles or that someone is not dead because follicles continue to live for a while. Even Vasiliev admits that the critical elements in determining human life or death are the heart, lungs, and brain:

> If the organ of the psyche ceases to function immediately after the stoppage of the heart and breathing, this means that the soul, which is tied to cerebral activity . . . cannot in any way exist after the death of the body. On the contrary, success has been achieved in demonstrating the possibility of temporary bodily vital activity with complete exclusion of the brain.[82]

Here again, however, we find more a circular development of Vasiliev's own assumptions than a persuasive logical argument. Vasiliev assumes that the psyche has an organ (the brain) and that the soul is "tied to cerebral activity." He then deduces that when the brain stops, the soul must stop existing. It is hard to see what this soul might be, except another name for brain functions. If Vasiliev uses the word "soul" to mean brain functions, then he is trivially correct that, when the brain stops functioning, the soul ceases to exist. On the other hand, if he means something like "the conscious locus of thought and perception," then he is premature in asserting that it is "tied to cerebral activity," and his "conclusion" that it cannot survive bodily death does no more than reiterate his a priori convictions.

It is also curious that Vasiliev asserts the independence of the body and the brain. He uses his findings to document the idea that bodily activity can continue without mental activity, but he is completely opaque to the notion that mental activity might continue without bodily activity. It may or may not be the case that mental activity can continue independently.

This is a question empirical studies are in the process of answering. But Vasiliev's Marxist-materialist assumptions do not get us very far toward an impartial answer.

Vvedensky's notion of parabiosis was modeled on the concept of "anabiosis," the suspended animation seen in some seeds, eggs, and even insects that possess the potential for full life but cannot really be called living while yet undeveloped. His suggestion is essentially that, just as seeds or eggs may exist for years before exhibiting life, so humans near death may exist (for minutes) before again exhibiting life. Although they appear dead, Vvedensky would say that such humans should be called parabiotic. In facing this claim, we must first ascertain that it is not circular in the sense of the arguments used above; that other criteria than the fact that the person later revived are used to determine whether he is parabiotic.

By the admission of Russian as well as American scientists, this parabiotic state, if it exists at all, can endure for at most ten or twenty minutes without artificial resuscitative measures.[83] By contrast, among the cases of NDEs of people revived from the dead are a number of cases of those dead for several hours.[84] Other cases involved deep coma and tetany (rigor mortis) for a number of days, or comas of several weeks.[85] In short, they simply do not fit the parabiosis model. Elisabeth Kübler-Ross testifies, "I have investigated similar cases from Australia to California, involving patients from age 2 to 96—I have hundreds of very clear-cut cases from all over the world, both religious and nonreligious people. One had been dead 12½ hours. All experienced the same thing."[86]

In short, these parabiotic stages, if we choose to call them such, lasted longer than medical science should expect to be possible. So we return to the original dilemma: either we must admit that science does not know how to define death (or parabiosis) because there are many exceptions to these definitions, or we may admit that certain people in fact die and revive to report having had unusual experiences prior to their revivals. Given the first option, the only way to know whether someone is dead is to wait and see whether he or she revives. Regarding the second option, the Russian arguments have not been very successful. Many Western neurophysiologists also incline to materialism, however; the best of their arguments deserve some attention.

Brain death. An improved version of the antisurvivalist interpretation might run as follows. We need to define death unambiguously according to medical criteria rather than in post facto declarations. There is no question that the human physical body survives its death. The crucial question is, rather, whether consciousness survives bodily death. The brain is the part of the body to which consciousness is most closely related. Therefore, the condition of the brain should be more important than the condition of the heart, lungs, pulse, etc., in determining death in relation to consciousness.

We know that it is possible for the heart and lungs to function without brain functions (with artificial support systems). We have less knowledge about the ability of a brain to continue to act (think) after a body has ceased to function. Cessation of breathing is normally taken as an indication that the brain has ceased to control the autonomic functions of the lungs, but even this does not guarantee that consciousness is absent. What we need, therefore, is clear determination that brain activity has ceased by brain-scan or EEG measurement—so-called "brain death" criteria.[87]

Except in rare cases of hypothermia or drug overdose, it is thought impossible for the body to revive after brain death occurs. For all material purposes, if the brain is dead, we expect no continuation of consciousness. Therefore, we should predict that the people who report visions of relatives, saints, or other worlds are not flatliners (brain isoelectric) at the time they have such visions. The key empirical question is not whether people have been pronounced dead and later revived; we must accept the data on such cases. Rather it is more useful to ask whether anyone has had mental activity, hallucinatory or otherwise, when his or her brain was electrically inactive.

Survivalists agree on the importance of this question. It is a question capable of empirical verification and one deserving of more study. If there are clear-cut cases where there is no brain activity but patients report having had experiences, this is an outstanding refutation of the mind-brain identity theory. If we define death in terms of brain activity, and someone has no brain activity but later reports experiences during that period, we have proof that conscious experience is possible after death, at least temporarily. Preliminary investigations suggest that this is indeed possible: "Flat EEG tracings have been obtained in persons who were later resuscitated. Overdoses of drugs which are depressants of the CNS [central nervous system] as well as hypothermia [overcooling] have both resulted in this phenomenon."[88]

One fruitful line of inquiry might be to study victims of drug overdose and hypothermia in order to try to identify their NDEs during brain death. But Ring, who has studied this relationship, found an inverse correspondence between drugs and NDEs; the more drugs patients ingest, the less likely they are to have true NDEs.[89] So the fact that drugged or hypothermic people may be revived after hours of no brain activity is not likely to prove helpful in NDE research. (It does mean that these conditions must be carefully watched in order to determine whether the brain death is irreversible!)[90]

There are some reports, however, of people having NDEs when they were brain dead without being drugged or hypothermic. Kübler-Ross has reported a case in which brain activity ceased and the heart stopped but, afterwards, the patient was able to correctly describe the resuscitation procedures used on his own body from the perspective of observing them in an OBE.[91] Similarly, Tom Clack, killed in battle in Vietnam, had an OBE in which he felt he met and conversed with his other dead comrades while surrounded by light. The doctors told him after he was resuscitated that he had had neither heartbeat nor brain waves.[92] Denver cardiologist Fred Schoonmaker has encountered cases in which brain waves were nonexistent for several hours, after which his patients revived and reported having had realistic experiences during that time.[93] Further study of such cases is essential, for if people indeed have NDEs while brain-dead, then it will be established fact that consciousness can temporarily survive the brain.

Patients' Visions were Hallucinations

Revival of brain-dead people is a truly rare phenomenon. But visions of relatives, saints, or other worlds by people on their deathbeds are not uncommon and are, therefore, much easier to study quantitatively. The anti-survivalist argues that such visions are neither perceptions nor do they have any real referents, but are rather the fantasies of diseased or dying brains.

Before we look at the specific attempts of antisurvivalists to explain away the NDE evidence, let us make a few observations on their logic.

The arguments we shall confront below are either reductionistic or nonreductionist. Reductionists claim that NDEs are reducible to, and nothing more than, certain brain states which we already understand in other terms. Nonreductionists claim that NDEs resemble certain other conditions, but are not necessarily exhaustively described by them. Thus, the reductionist may say that NDEs are exhaustively explained as brain malfunctions, and there is nothing more to concern ourselves with. Nonreductionists might say, in the same circumstances, that brain malfunctions may give rise to certain abilities or experiences—but this does not itself deny the reality of the images perceived nor invalidate the need for further study. Since the nonreductionist position does not negate the validity of NDEs as potential materials for the study of survival, it need not trouble us any further at this point.

Reductionists, on the other hand, must demonstrate at least two subclaims. First, they must claim that NDEs are similar to or belong to a legitimate subclass of phenomena whose explanation is already understood. Second, they must show that these phenomena are hallucinatory or delusory, giving us no information about reality, but only (perhaps) about mental malfunctions. For example, it is argued that NDEs are like mental disease, that such mental disease gives us no understanding of reality, and that therefore NDEs give us no understanding of reality.

Most of the arguments depend upon the first claim, that "NDEs are like (or are a subclass of) *X*." Even if this were admitted as a first premise, however, the second premise would not yet be demonstrated, and the conclusion would still be unreachable. For it might still be the case that, although NDEs are *like* experiences of diseases, drugs, or OBEs, *both* sets of similar experiences tell us something about another level of reality rather than both being delusory.

This is precisely what meditating yogins and drug-tripping Native Americans would say: that there are essential similarities between meditation or drug trips and death. They would add that *both* sets of experiences have important external referents, and both tell us important truths to which we are blind in our normal mundane consciousness. In fact, it is hard to imagine how we could ever tell with certainty that the visions of meditators were totally delusory, although popular opinion believes them so.[94] Thus, even if NDEs were reducible to a subclass of some other phenomena, it would not follow that their content would be nonreferential or that survival would be invalidated.

So much for this less-approachable of our two reductionist premises. Now let us concentrate on understanding the arguments that all NDEs are reducible to (1) chemical changes in the brain, (2) psychological defense mechanisms or schizophrenia, or (3) a mental replay of the birth experience. After examining each of these arguments in turn, we shall conclude with more counterarguments relevant to all three of these classes en bloc.

The argument. The argument that NDEs are mere hallucinations with a chemical or neurophysiological basis is among the commonest tacks reductionists may take. Six major proponents of this view have each proposed slightly different theories to "explain away" NDEs, each based, however, on physicochemical changes in the brain.

British psychiatrist James McHarg has suggested that NDEs are due to anoxia (lack of oxygen) in the dying brain, and are analogous to seizures of the temporal lobe, which are also presumably inducible by anoxia.[95] These suggestions have been picked up and elaborated on by D. B. Carr and by doctors at the University of Chile.[96] Detroit physician Ernst Rodin, by contrast, has proposed that NDEs may be produced either by anoxia or hypoxia (an overabundance of oxygen!), which he says leads to feelings of well-being and the acceptance of false judgments as true, particularly where persons' hopes, fears, or preoccupations are involved.[97]

R. S. Blacker has noted the similarities of seeing lights and having OBEs to experiences of ether anaesthesia, but he regards "hearing pronouncement of one's own death" to be analytically impossible.[98] UCLA psychiatrist Ron Siegel has emphasized the similarities between NDEs and drug hallucinations, especially with respect to four features: tunnels, cities, lights, and memory images.[99] Polish physicist Janusz Slawinski has proposed that the "death flash" of bioelectric light radiation which can be observed at the death of living organisms may account for NDEs visions of intense light.[100] Let us examine the applicability of any of these arguments to our NDE evidence and the conclusions drawn from it.

NDEs are not hallucinations. Most people undergoing NDEs are not demonstrably anoxic, hypoxic, nor drugged. Ernst Rodin's article in particular brought forth a stream of responses to this effect. M. A. O'Roark has cited evidence that NDEs may occur in the absence of cerebral anoxia.[101] Ring adduces evidence to demonstrate that ether reduces the frequency of NDEs, and that the NDEs reported to him were not of anaesthetized patients.[102] Also Ian Stevenson concludes that NDEs are clearly not toxic psychoses.[103]

The most thoroughgoing study of the physical conditions of the patients was that conducted by Osis and Haraldsson, who specifically looked for factors that might have led their subjects to hallucinate. They found that the vast majority of their subjects were dying from diseases or operations unrelated to the brain and that they typically had no history of mental problems. The majority had body temperatures of less than 100°F, so their visions could not be ascribed to delirium or fever. The large majority of subjects had little or no medication of a sort known to influence their minds, and most were rated as being "clearheaded" at the time of the vision. Furthermore, most subjects were not diagnosed as having any other hallucinogenic conditions by their physicians. They concluded:

> Hallucinogenic medical factors could not explain the phenomena in a majority of cases. . . . Drugs that might have caused hallucinations neither significantly affected the main phenomena nor the clarity of consciousness. . . . We analyzed the interactions of medication and the seven main characteristics of the visions. There was no relationship whatsoever between medication and experiential characteristics suggestive of an afterlife.[104]

From these studies and responses it should be clear that, in many cases, neither anoxia, anaesthesia, nor hallucinogenic drug effects were causally involved in producing NDEs.

Yet another important point can be noticed from Osis's results: a number of his subjects who seemed to "see into another world" were not yet in coma. Although they were to die in a matter of minutes (sometimes despite contrary predictions by their physicians), they were generally calm, clearheaded, and interacting normally with those attending them, with the exception that they also had visions of relatives, saints, or heaven at that time.[105] On the other hand, there are also cases in which these same sorts of visions are reported after revival by people who had been temporarily pronounced dead or who were clearly unconscious of their surroundings.

The conclusions are fairly clear. If NDEs share the same sorts of contents regardless of whether the patient is asleep or awake, nonanoxic or even anoxic, already dead or still on the brink of death, then oxygen supply and hallucinogenic drugs alone are inadequate to explain them all fully. Rather, it would be more logical to seek a cause for these visions which is present in all cases and not merely in an isolated few. The single outstanding factor present in all cases is simply the proximity of death. It is more appropriate to attribute NDEs to the nearness of death itself than to force them into physicochemical categories that demonstrably fail to account for a large portion of the samples studied.

NDEs are not like hallucinations. Investigation shows that NDEs are not essentially *like* the experiences of anoxia, hypoxia, anaesthesia, or drug hallucinations. Here we must make some careful distinctions. Reductionists would want to claim that, even if anoxia, drugs, etc., are not themselves present, at least the visions are due to some analogous chemical process (perhaps toxins or endorphins secreted by the brain itself) so that the underlying mechanism is still physicochemical. There is no evidence for this claim, but if it were shown that the content of visions experienced under these other known conditions (anoxia, ether, drugs) were very similar to the content of NDEs, then there would be at least an ad hoc credibility to this idea.[106] But there is no such similarity between the content of the cases suggested by critics and the NDE visions we are studying. Let us first look at the effects which each of the critics we have cited would expect his mechanistic model to produce.

In the first such model, anoxia should be expected to produce anxiety, disorientation, and perceptual distortions.[107] But there is no anxiety, disorientation nor perceptual distortion in the majority of the NDE visions studied. On the contrary, there is a feeling of peace, a feeling of knowing exactly how one is oriented, but also a feeling of knowing some things which are not obvious to humans in normal states.

Hypoxia, by contrast, leads to feelings of well-being and the projection of one's own hopes, fears, or preoccupations. But it has been demonstrated that deathbed visions did not correlate with the hopes and fears of their experiencers. Many visions were distinctly contrary to the religious or areligious expectations of their percipients.[108] Moreover, Ring found that there was an inverse relationship between knowing about NDEs and having them; those who had studied NDE material seemed less likely to experience them themselves, and those who had never heard of NDEs more likely to have such visionary experiences![109] This might be due in part to a difference in critical or intellectual levels. But the important point is that NDEs are not merely the projections of the hopes or preoccupations of their experiencers.

Last, ether anaesthesia and the death flash of bioelectric radiation are expected to produce OBEs and lights. If it is admitted that ether produces genuine OBEs, this is not a denial but a confirmation of some form of mind-body dualism. While OBEs coupled with apparitions have evidential values discussed in the previous chapter, the mere fact of OBEs during the NDE is not our concern here. Here again, we are not considering the mere vision of light to be significant or indicative of the nature of the next realm.

In sum, none of the causes mentioned above produces anything like the visions of departed relatives, saints, or heavenly realms that are central to NDEs' relation to conscious survival of death.

Siegel's Similarities

The critic closest to our concerns is Ronald K. Siegel, who cites numerous similarities between NDEs and drug hallucinations in parallel quotations from NDE subjects and hallucinators. Therefore, his analysis deserves more careful scrutiny. In essence, he compares four objects of visions: tunnels, cities, lights, and memories.[110] From the outset, we have recognized that tunnels and life-review memories may be triggered by brain mechanisms, and we have not even considered them seriously as evidence of survival.

Siegel argues that "similarities between tunnels and memories in drug experiences and tunnels and memories in NDEs shows that neither is survival-oriented." Of course, the opposite might be true: it might be the case that *both* NDE subjects and drug-trippers are dangerously close to death, and that *both* are catching glimpses of the afterlife. But even if Siegel's syllogism proves correct, he is simply refuting a straw man, for no one has seriously claimed that tunnels or memories prove survival.

This leaves the questions of cities and lights. Siegel's assertion is that these too are similar in drug and NDE cases. But here the comparisons he cites are stretched and rather tenuous. The NDE subject whom he cites actually describes a "city of light," whereas the drug-hallucinators simply see geometric forms. Even if it were granted that "geometric architecture" appears in both NDEs and hallucinations, or that "nets of great luminosity and brilliance" appear in both cases, our argument is still unaffected, for these cases too are not considered as good evidence for survival. By showing that geometric visions are not good evidence for survival, Siegel has not shown that visions of relatives, saints, or heavenly nature-imagery are not good evidence for survival.

When it comes to the question of visions of saints, relatives, or heavenly fields, Siegel can do nothing more than assert that these are all "retrieved memory images." Here he is simply uninformed, because some of the figures seen at deathbeds and recognized as dead relatives or saints are seen in different clothing or appearance than the percipient had ever remembered seeing them. Siegel's silence on visions of saints and heavens in NDEs implies that he was unable to draw such comparisons at all.

When we deal with the important issues of relatives and holy figures (as opposed to the red herrings of which Siegel is fond), we immediately find striking discrepancies. While more than 80 percent of dying subjects with NDEs had visions of dead friends or relatives, only about 20 percent of drug hallucinators saw dead people in their "trips." Only a tiny fraction of these, in turn, had any sort of "purpose" at all, in striking contrast to the well-documented "take-away purpose" expressed by 80 percent of the departed friends or relatives perceived at deathbeds. While terminal patients saw religious figures frequently—as much as 50 percent of the time— living hallucinators saw religious figures almost never (2–4 percent);[111]

NDE subjects who anticipated grim reapers or a judgment seat often witnessed scenery of flowery fields surpassing any they had seen in life. This not only violated their expectations and religious teaching, but is unlike the geometric imagery common to drugged hallucinations.[112] In summary, then, it is not the case that these NDEs are produced by hallucinogenic drugs. Nor is it the case that the important contents of NDEs (friends, saints, heavens) are similar to the sorts of things perceived by drug hallucinators. The analogies just fail to hold.

To recapitulate a previous argument, even if there were analogies between NDEs and drug hallucinations, it need not follow that neither is nonreferential. Even critics must ultimately admit that a paranormal basis for the content of deathbed visions is not invalidated by a medical reason for their mere occurrence. In other words, it is conceivable that even chemically induced "trips" could occasionally give veridical insights into another world. Further study is needed on both NDEs and hallucinations. But the verdict at this point still stands: NDEs of the sorts we consider significant are neither analogous to nor reducible to physicochemically induced malfunctions of the brain.

NDEs are Defense Mechanisms or Mental Disease

Another attempt to reduce NDEs to nonreferential hallucinations is the claim that they are merely psychological mechanisms or temporary schizophrenia. As in the previous section, we shall (a) present the arguments, (b) see whether NDEs actually are psychological problems, and (c) see how closely they are like defense mechanisms or mental disease. First, however, we must be aware of some curious ambiguities in this behaviorist line.

In the beginning, we must distinguish psychological conditions from physicochemical states, or else this whole argument collapses into the arguments of the previous section. If in this section we are to present genuinely new and interesting arguments, then we should expect evidence about mental states that is not reduced to chemical processes. Behaviorists wishing to reduce NDEs to psychological phenomena will have to claim either that psychological problems are ultimately nonreducible to physicochemical states or that psychological problems will someday be reducible to physicochemical states. The first argument is distasteful to the behaviorist because it tends to concede that there are nonphysical aspects of reality. The second argument, on the other hand, is a highly speculative assumption at this time. Although the clinician may act pragmatically without having a well-reasoned understanding of mind or survival behind his practice, these questions are real and important to the philosophical psychologist.

For the purposes of this section, we shall assume that there are some mental states or diseases whose physical correlates are incompletely known and unimportant for the purposes of argument. Of course, to the extent that such mechanisms are not known, so-called "explanations" of NDEs on the basis of other inadequately understood phenomena are a very shaky business. It might even be argued that a survivalist interpretation of NDEs gives us a better model for certain mental diseases than a reductionist interpretation of mental diseases gives us of NDEs. In short, we do not gain much explanatory power or value by reducing NDEs to instances of mental disease. But as long as such classifications are comforting to those who brook no violations of their already finalized worldviews, we shall continue to face the charges that NDEs are either reducible or analogous to defense mechanisms or mental diseases.

The argument. Jan Ehrenwald and Russell Noyes have been the major proponents of the defense-mechanisms view. Ehrenwald propounds that NDEs "exhibit an assorted set of defenses and rationalizations aimed at warding off anxiety originating from the breakdown of the body image, . . . in the last analysis, from the fear of death as a universal experience."[113] Noyes reiterates the theme of "depersonalization" as an escape from "life-threatening danger" in a dozen articles with the same interpretations of the same body of data in different periodicals.[114] Others have suggested that diseases of the temporal lobe may lead to hallucinations of bright lights or to cases where schizophrenics have occasionally hallucinated relatives, ghosts, priests, stars, mountains, and even God.[115] If NDEs are simply another case of such mental disease, they tell us nothing about the nature or possibility of survival.

NDEs are not mental diseases. It is simply not true that most NDE subjects are exhibiting mental diseases or defense mechanisms. Some of the patients, as indicated above, were clearheaded and in apparently good mental health. Some of them neither expected to die nor feared death before their NDEs. There is neither motive nor precedent for "psychological escapism" or defense mechanisms in the majority of these cases. Moreover, in studying the nature of hallucinations due to psychological causes, it has been established that "patients who hallucinate are generally those with a history of hallucinations."[116]

However, very few of the NDE subjects had such histories of hallucinating. Thus, the probability that they were hallucinating on their deathbeds is rather low. Nor have many of the patients in these studies been psychiatrically or medically diagnosed as having either brain diseases or schizophrenia.[117] Thus it is inappropriate to reduce all NDE cases into charges of mental disease. But there is admittedly a small minority of crisis cases, to which Noyes untiringly refers, in which a sort of depersonalization occurs. This leads us to the more important question of the content of NDEs, and their similarities to and differences from other defense mechanisms and mental diseases.

NDEs are not like defense mechanisms or mental disease. Most NDEs are not only not caused by depersonalization or mental diseases; they are not even like them. First let us look at Noyes's claims of depersonalization. Noyes has surveyed a number of accident victims, finding that 40–60 percent of them felt detached from their bodies, felt joy and "great understanding," and had subjective impressions that time was drastically slowed down (or in some cases, sped up). But Noyes does not carefully classify experiences of saints, dead relatives, or heavenly realms, relegating them all to the category of "visions, images, or revelations."[118]

There is no conflict, then, between Noyes's findings and those of other researchers, insofar as they are talking about two separate sorts of phenomena. Noyes is talking about depersonalization and time distortion, while survivalists are more interested in the visionary content, especially when providing intersubjective material. It is interesting that people experience OBEs and time distortion during accidents, but this fact by no means contradicts the fact that they may also have visions of people or heavens.

Even if it were found that none of Noyes's accident victims had NDEs of the sort we are studying, this finding would have no negative bearing on the issue of survival. Noyes's feeling that people do not survive bodily death and that OBEs are temporary psychological phenomena which help them avoid "facing the facts" of the emergency is clearly a bias that predates his research, and it is not a finding based on his data. On the contrary, the finding of large numbers of OBEs among his subjects might even lend support to the survival thesis. The points to be noted here are that Noyes's evidence does not refute other NDE evidence, that his label of *depersonalization* does not help us understand OBEs, and that his findings tell us nothing about whether people survive.

The Freudian critic of survival may allege that "matrices in the unconscious could result in experiences of life-review, divine judgment, hell, purgatory, etc."[119] But we should reiterate that the existence and structure of these matrices remains a questionable hypothesis and not an established fact. If the critic is correct that hellish images are as ubiquitous as heavenly ones in our unconsciousnesses, then there is a rather poor match between those unidentified structures and the NDEs themselves, which lean heavily to the side of heavenly imagery and only rarely to the unpleasant.[120]

As far as mental diseases are concerned, there is a striking contrast between the contents and behaviors produced by mental diseases and the contents and behaviors produced by NDEs. Whereas schizophrenic patients tend to have long drawn-out periods of hallucination, often in monochrome, NDE patients tend to see their visions in full color, but only for a few brief moments.[121] The mentally ill tend to see an irrational assortment of images, ranging from people with turkeys' heads to clouds, shadows, or dirt specks where there is nothing.[122] Temporal lobe seizures also lead to "bright flashes," but not to clear images of religious figures clad in light.[123] It is also common that seizure victims completely lose awareness of what they were doing, and either continue to do what they had planned to do without consciousness of it, or else commit utterly irrational acts.[124] None of these problems are characteristic of the NDEs we are considering.

Of course, there remains a small minority of mentally disturbed and schizophrenics whose mental imagery superficially resembles that of our NDE subjects.[125] What may be deduced from this? Their visions of religious figures or God are atypical of mental disease and typical of NDEs. Therefore, we cannot conclude that all NDEs are like mental diseases.

On the contrary, the opposite suggestion might be in order. It is quite possible that, in certain cases of mental disease, patients experience NDE-like images precisely because they are in fact psychologically close to death, with or without their doctor's realization. While it is possible that a few NDEs are pathological and a few schizophrenics have NDEs, for the most part they are two distinct phenomena. In any case, it is inappropriate to reduce all NDEs to psychological and mental diseases, or even to try to explain them on those inadequate models. Visions of survival may be calumniated for occasionally resembling pathology, but they cannot be logically dismissed on such grounds.

Attacks on the Veridicality of NDEs

The earliest of the attacks on the veridicality of NDEs was the allegation that NDEs simply reflect the religious beliefs of the people who experience them. Empirical studies have refuted this claim from several standpoints. Agnostics and atheists have had visions of "heaven" or religious figures, while devout churchgoers expecting judgment or purgatory found none. The cultural expectations that there is no life after death and that pain is as likely as pleasure in the next world (especially for sinners or nonbelievers) were simply not reflected in NDEs either.[126] So NDEs cannot be written off as mere projections of one's beliefs, desires, or cultural training. The cross-cultural uniformity among Christians, Jews, and Hindus also seems to indicate that more than a cultural image is being seen here. There are elements of broad similarity, if not universality, among many NDE experiencers.[127] Moreover, there is sufficient difference between NDEs and pathological or psychological mechanisms that they cannot be reduced or explained away on such models.

NDEs are a "replay" of the birth experience. Astronomer Carl Sagan, famous for his studies of Venus, believes he has the solution to this universality of NDEs. He asserts that the death experience is likely to produce common images of light and tunnels because we have all traveled through tunnels into light before: at birth. This leaves an indelible imprint on our brains that is replayed during the traumatic moments when we face death. In Sagan's own words:

> The only alternative, so far as I can see, is that every human being, without exception, has already shared an experience like that of those travellers who return from the land of death: the sensation of flight; the emergence from darkness into light; an experience in which, at least sometimes, a heroic figure can be dimly perceived, bathed in radiance and glory. There is only one common experience that matches this description. It is called birth.[128]

Sagan goes on to reduce all religion and speculative science to an analogue of the birth experience. He sees the satori or nirvana of Eastern religions as no more than a desire for a return to the warm, selfless nondistinction of the womb state. He calls Western fascination with punishment and redemption a poignant attempt to make sense of uterine contractions around the foetus.

> If religions are fundamentally silly, why is it that so many people believe in them? . . . The common thread is birth. Religion is fundamentally mystical, the gods inscrutable, the tenets appealing but unsound because, I suggest, blurred perceptions and vague premonitions are the best that the newborn infant can manage. It is rather a courageous if flawed attempt to make contact with the earliest and most profound experience of our lives.[129]

Finally, Sagan goes on to analogize scientific theories about the universe to the birth experience: steady state theories are analogous to the womb state; oscillating universe theories are analogous to the uterine contraction state; and Big Bang theories are analogous to birth into an ever-widening world. He concludes that our perinatal experiences may determine not only our NDEs but our psychiatric predispositions to scientific cosmologies![130] A number of things need to be said about Sagan's theory, since it appears superficially seductive and is couched in striking language in a best-selling book.

Sagan knows a lot about the surface of Venus, but precious little about philosophy or psychiatry. His dilettantism in these fields has been repeatedly castigated by other scientists.[131] It is trivially true that everything is either in a steady state, shrinking, or growing. So anything at all can be analogized to uterine states, contractions, and birth. But this does not mean that there is any *real* connection between uterine states and whatever is analogized to them. Sagan shows gross naïveté in equating cosmological and psychological models, and then attempting to reduce them both to analogues of the birth experience.

Apparently the only source for Sagan's flights of analogistic imagination is the work of Stanislav Grof, who found some analogies between mystic, drug, and NDE consciousnesses, particularly in their "visions of light."[132] Grof, however, while seeking causal explanations for NDEs within brain functions, is careful not to reduce NDEs to nonreferential hallucinations. On the contrary, he leaves open the possibility that changes in brain chemistry set up altered states of consciousness that give access to alternate realities not recognized in our ordinary waking states of mind.[133] Grof allows that NDEs and other altered states of consciousness may show us something about other realities, but Sagan crudely reduces all such visions to muddleheaded attempts to remember our own births.

There is a further consequence of Sagan's theory, however, which even he would reject if he had the objectivity to recognize it amid his rapture with the uterus. Sagan wants to say that, because NDEs are analogous to the birth experience, they can be reduced to memories of birth and, therefore, refer to nothing real outside of the birth experience. He also says that the universe studied by astronomers is analogous to the birth experience, and the Big Bang theory he accepts may be a superimposition of our birth memories on our views of the universe.

But if such analogies make NDEs nonreferential, they should also render his pet Big Bang theories equally nonreferential. If they make NDEs into meaningless delusions, then they should also make the Big Bang theory a meaningless delusion. By Sagan's own line of reasoning, science is not the finding of the truth about the universe, nor do laws of science refer to anything but the projections of the birth experiences of the leading scientists. Sagan almost admits this himself when he says, "I suppose it is too much to hope that the originators of the Steady State hypothesis were all born by Caesarean section, but the analogies are very close."[134]

Sagan tries to find delusory psychological origins for all of his opponents' theories, without realizing that the same line of criticism must apply to his own. If his theory is true, all the highly touted objectivity of science and scientists is a myth, reducible to the manner of their births and their predilections derived from it. The "scientific knowledge" which Sagan pompously opposes to the "foolishness of religion" becomes reduced to neurophysiology, and scientific theories have no better status than the survival theory he hopes to destroy with them. But Sagan is blind to these consequences in his zeal to attack the religious.

The inadequacy of the infant-perception model. If we study infant perception more scientifically, we find that most newborns simply cannot perceive anything well enough for Sagan's thesis to hold true. The key point in Sagan's analogy between birth and NDEs is that both include the vision of "some godlike figure surrounded by a halo of light—the Midwife or the Obstetrician or the Father."[135] But if newborn infants do not perceive such figures of light, then it is impossible to ascribe NDEs to such infantile perceptions. To examine this claim, we need to turn to the results of extensive studies of infant perception and memory, of which Sagan is obviously ignorant.

A generation ago, it was believed that infants could perceive almost nothing. Recent research on infant perception has made clear that infants perceive far more than was previously imagined. At the same time it has confirmed that, although infant perception develops rapidly in the first few months of life, there are severe limitations on newborn perception, especially at birth and within the few weeks thereafter.[136]

Some limitations on infant perception are neuro-optical, for at birth, many neurons are not in their proper layers. There are no Nissl bodies or neurofibrils, there is little chromophil or myelin, and macula are still underdeveloped.[137] Infant vision at birth is approximately 1/60, compared to 20/20 for normal adults.[138]

Recent European studies have demonstrated the limitations of infants' binocular or stereo vision, which is critical to perceiving and recognizing distant objects. Stereo vision and distance focusing are very poor in newborns. Binocular vision and depth perception do not even begin until several months have passed.[139]

Binocular acuity more than doubles from four months to one year, and doubles again between one year and four years.[140] Other experiments show that even at the age of eighteen months, infants' stereo vision is four times worse than five-year-olds'.[141] So half of all newborns cannot coordinate at all their visual perceptions of objects an arm's length away; and no infants under a month old have been found to fully coordinate their visual perceptions of things five feet away.[142]

Moreover, there is no stability to the images which newborns perceive. Eye movements of newborns are jerky and inaccurate. Newborns cannot make sense of images which do not hold perfectly still with respect to their eyes for at least two or three seconds.[143] As it is almost impossible for a trained adult to hold a camera still for even a half second, the difficulty of holding an object still in relation to the infant's eyeballs for several seconds becomes apparent. The problem is intensified because infants' eye movements are "rapid and disorganized, especially when crying."[144] In fact, newborns have their eyes open and are fully awake and alert only about 11 percent of the time.[145] Thus infant visual perception is not only blurry but it is fragmentary.

Another problem with newborn perception is that of alertness. The newborn's eyes are generally blurred by tears. They are often closed, either from relaxation, napping, blinking, or from diseases, such as rubella or Down's syndrome. Even if their eyes are open and free of tears, they are often completely devoid of attention, like adults who may be momentarily oblivious to their physical surroundings even when their eyes are open.[146] Due to these low alertness levels and neurological immaturity, even infants with the physical capabilities of perceiving blurry patches of light and dark for several seconds at a stretch often completely fail to do so.[147]

Newborn perception is limited as much by their brains as by their eyes.[148] Even the newborns who appear to exhibit pursuit and fixation may be utterly without recognition of what their eyes pursue or fixate upon.[149] The retina, optic nerve system, and central nervous system are not yet developed to the extent that the blurry picture which the newborn sees can be interpreted.[150]

Newborns have no conceptual framework into which to fit their scattered visual images. In medical terms, the newborn has little capacity for encoding and can only learn perceptually through laborious investigation, primarily by feeling and tasting objects.[151] An adult's reliance on sight over taste and touch is a skill developed only after time and discipline. Adults may conceptually piece together a unified vision of a room, despite blind spots and distractions, but newborns have no idea at all of what they are "looking at," nor of how it fits together, even in the rare moments when they have managed to fixate and focus on a nearby, stable, contrasting object. So if newborn infants in fact remember the moments of their births, it is not due to their normal physiological processes of sight, as Sagan would imply, but to some supernormal psychic memory transcending the limitations of their blurry newborn eyes and unpracticed neural-cortical pathways.

Even if there were some sort of hidden memory ability in newborn infants (which experiments deny), we should expect that such memories would be almost inconceivably varied and not uniform as Sagan suggests.[152] Some babies would have their eyes open, others their eyes closed. Some would fixate momentarily on contrasting stationary objects at close range, like a nipple or forceps; others might never have a stable attentive moment, and all would be a chaotic blur. Some are born in even light, some under spotlights, and some in virtual darkness. Some might begin to sense light-dark contrasts, while others would fail to recognize even this distinction. Some might have some feeling for color or motion, others would be relatively color-blind and unable to track moving objects at all.

The possible combinations are so endless that even if infants all stored their birth experiences in memory, their "playbacks" should hardly be expected to resemble each other except in rare coincidences. Since Sagan's thesis assumes that infants can discern whole figures, with relative integrity and stability, in a certain part of their visual field, the evidence above is alone adequate to show that his theory is unfounded.

Other dissimilarities. Even if newborn infants were able to perceive their surroundings with any kind of completeness or uniformity at birth, the birth experience and death experiences with which we are concerned are not analogous enough to reduce NDEs to memories of birth. Let us review just a few of the more striking dissimilarities between NDEs and what newborns would perceive, even if it were possible for them to register images stably and consistently.

First, Sagan suggests that the birth canal would look like a long dark tunnel with a light at the end. This takes the word "canal" too literally. If he had ever witnessed a delivery, Sagan would know that the baby's head presses tightly against the walls of the uterus, allowing no light into the womb. The birth is more analogous to breaking through a membrane from a dark room into a lighter room, or to surfacing from a muddy swimming hole, than to peering down a long tunnel with a glowing light at the other end. Moreover, even if the opening did let light in, the baby would be unable to tilt either its head or its eyes upwards to see it.[153] If the light registered at all on the untrained brains of the infants, it would be remembered as light streaming in from cracks at the top of their visual fields, and not as light at the end of a long tunnel.

Second, Sagan suggests that the figure of the midwife or doctor may be taken for the "figure of light," heroic, loving, and surrounded by a halo of light. We have already seen that the baby could not focus on such a figure as its doctor or midwife—but if it could, would the figure seem heroic and haloed? The figure would more likely seem a clinical torturer, holding it upside down by the feet, spanking it, cutting its connection with its womb and food supply, putting silver nitrate in its eyes, and strapping bands around its ankles! There is also no reason to expect that the doctor or midwife would appear substantially brighter (glowing) or darker (haloed) than the surrounding room or background. On the contrary, many babies are born either in dim light or into environments lacking in sharp black-and-white contrasts.

Despite all the problems here identified, the greatest anomalies have yet to be exposed. Even if Sagan's reconstruction of the birth experience were to explain visions of tunnels, lights, flying, and a "fuzzy-figured light," it manifestly would fail to explain the sharp and detailed visions with which we are concerned. In survival-related NDEs, we expect visions of either deceased friends and relatives, or religious figures, or heavenly imagery of flowers, fields, a path and/or a boundary. Sagan's analogies are predominantly concerned with three figures: the tunnel with light at the end, a sensation of flight, and a dimly perceived "figure of light." The features Sagan has chosen to explain are not explicable on the simple model he chooses—but even if they were, they would not be features which confirm or refute survival in any case. Clear and distinct deathbed visions of dead relatives, of St. Gerard in friar's hood, or of Jesus with a bloodied chest, are neither explained nor refuted by Sagan's imagination.[154]

Lest it seem that we have devoted undue attention to such an indefensible theory, it should be noted that this "amniotic universe" theory of Sagan's has wide popular appeal, both for its superficial understandability, its purported explanatory power, and for the charismatic character of its concocter in the media.

Super-ESP Accounts for True Information in NDEs

In addition to showing that the people who have had NDEs have neither been dead nor truly seeing into a "next world," the antisurvivalist must fall back on the super-ESP hypothesis to account for the information gained during NDEs, information to which the patients had no normal access. But the super-ESP hypothesis has already been shown not only to lack explanatory power, but also to encounter difficulties in explaining reincarnation and OBE phenomena discussed above. The antisurvivalist arguments of this section are analogous to those of preceding sections, and can be summarized somewhat more briefly here.

To account for visions of deceased people not known to be dead by anyone attending the deathbed, some sort of superclairvoyance must be attributed to the dying persons having NDEs. While rare, verifiable memories of former lives and true predictions of future occurrences still have to be explained by psychic retrocognition and precognition. The anti-survivalist skeptic argues that NDEs are nonreferential hallucinations that occasionally provide true information when dying people unwittingly exercise super-ESP psychic faculties.

Inadequacy of this hypothesis. The first problem with this hypothesis has been noted above: it is peculiar that almost all of the information gained through super-ESP at deathbeds concerns deceased relatives. The ESP theorist must assert that dying people, instead of glimpsing a realm of the dead, are suddenly possessed of clairvoyant powers to obtain true information about certain of their deceased friends or relatives, but about nothing else. This is the only super-ESP theory that fits the data, but there is no reason such a theory should be plausible or desirable. Even if it were conceded that the brain states of people on their deathbeds had some unknown common factor that enabled their true envisioning of only deceased people, another problem may arise.

If we admit that dying people often clairvoyantly gain true information about those who have died, may there not be clairvoyant truth in their visions of angels, saints, or golden gates? The materialist, of course, draws a sharp distinction between those cases where new information is revealed clairvoyantly, embroidered in religious imagery (e.g., "I see Aunt Jennie in heaven!") and those where no new information is revealed clairvoyantly (e.g., "I see Jesus in heaven"). Those visions that later happen to be confirmed are called *clairvoyant*, and those that do not happen to be confirmed are called *fantasy*. But there is no materialistic medical or clinical basis for making such distinctions.

Although we have treated visions of relatives, saints, and heavens as three separate subject-headings, they often occur in the same vision or in identical contexts in different people's visions. They share the characteristics of light, peace, and sometimes soft music. The person or voice in the NDE seems to show a single purpose: to guide the dying person to another place. This purposefulness was an unexpected and striking aspect of apparitions studied above. It corresponds sometimes to the purpose of persons having OBEs, and sometimes to the purpose that might be expected of the deceased persons if they were still alive. The figures in NDE visions, whether they be friends, saints, or dead relatives, tend to show this same element of purposefulness.

This leaves the skeptic with an even harder proposition to defend: that dying people hallucinate images of dead relatives, saints, or heavens of certain types, but that some people gain true information regarding deceased loved ones while others gain no information about anything, although their mental conditions are otherwise analogous. The cynic must also claim that this power of obtaining true information during hallucination is possible to most people only in the moments before death, and only when a relative seems to "guide them away." If nonrelatives appear in visions to guide them away, it is not veridical clairvoyance but delusion.

Of course such a theory is possible. It is the only one open to the skeptic. But it begins to strain credulity. Its ad hoc contortions to fit the data deprive it of all simplicity and elegance. Lacking reasons and mechanisms for such phenomena, it has no explanatory merit. Its only value is in allowing a die-hard antisurvivalist to preserve that worldview. Such a dogma has no place in philosophy, when other theories explain the same data more straightforwardly and consistently.

Intersubjectivity. The death-blow to the super-ESP theory comes in the area of intersubjectivity. We have already noted that observers at deathbeds have occasionally witnessed the presence of deceased friends, relatives, or religious figures ("angels") in places and attitudes corresponding to those described by the dying persons. Such figures are seen in the same unlikely locations in each case, standing beside or hovering over the deathbed. They are seen with the same aura of light or benevolence, and with the same take-away purpose just noted. They cause sudden and otherwise inexplicable changes in the moods of those who witness them. In some cases, they are even seen to "reach out their hands" to the patient at the same time that the patient "puts her hands in theirs."

The super-ESP theorist must claim that nothing more objective or external than an intersubjective illusion is happening (presumably projected by the dying person). This involves attributing yet another unknown and previously unavailable power to the dying person: the ability to project his own hallucination into the minds of the people and animals who are watching him. But we have already seen that apparitions are detectable by instruments or animals even when other *people* cannot see them. It has been shown that the projector model (that apparitions are projected by the person they resemble) is a better model than the percipient model (that apparitions are generated by their perceivers).

These deathbed visions of relatives, friends, saints, or other worlds seem similar to apparitions in many respects: apparent purpose, provision of information paranormally, sudden appearance and disappearance, mental health of the percipients, etc. By analogy, then, it makes sense to theorize that these visions too may be produced at least in part by their projectors (the perceived) rather than by their percipients (the perceiver). If so, they have a kind of reality or objectivity of their own, although it is not material in the way that we now understand matter. This is ultimately a far simpler and more unified theory than the array of ad hoc super-ESP variations necessary to account for apparitions, OBEs, and NDEs independently.

The survivalist theory makes sense of all these phenomena: claimed memories of past lives, apparitions and OBEs, and NDEs with paranormal visions. It says that each of these phenomena is an indication that consciousness or mind can persist after the death of the physical body and can manifest itself temporarily to communicate to the living or dying. It also accounts for the apparent persistence of individual memory over time and space between human death and rebirth. The nature of the ethereal body of consciousness is not yet adequately understood, but it sometimes affects laboratory thermocouples and TV monitors.

With such good evidence for survival, why does the scientific community still reject the idea of survival so often? Our next chapter will try to answer this question.

4.

Philosophy of Science

In the previous chapters, we considered a wide range of evidence indicative of the possibility of human survival of physical death. We found that antisurvivalist interpretations are less adequate in interpreting the data than is the theory that at least some persons survive bodily death. Still, some scientists and scholars refuse to treat such evidence, arguments, and conclusions seriously, because they seem to conflict with what is already accepted as "modern science." This is a serious charge, and not to be dismissed casually.

For centuries now, great minds of Western philosophy and science have devoted themselves to understanding the world through experimentation and observation. The worldview at which they have arrived is a detailed account with significant predictive abilities. Their methodologies too have become widely standardized. If the methods or conclusions of modern science genuinely conflict with our conclusions, we should be well advised to seek another interpretation of our information.

Accordingly, this section will review the status of current scientific worldviews. Taking physics as the vanguard of scientific cosmology, let us see whether the physicists' understanding of our universe conflicts with our conclusions. Then let us examine both the rationality and social foundations of scientific and emotional reactions against survival research. Finally, we shall examine the gradual transition of the field of parapsychology toward the status of a science in order to find what factors are important in its acceptance or rejection.

The Ontology of Modern Physics

The worldview of physics is undergoing constant metamorphosis. As Nicholas Maxwell has proposed, its history can be loosely characterized in several stages, each with a distinct theory as to the nature of all phenomena:

> The *Aristotelian* model of physics was the earliest, governing physics for nearly 2,000 years. It asserts that all things move teleologically, in order to fulfill their natural potentials and affinities. For example, stones thrown into the air fall to earth because they "desire" to join their fellows, and plants turn towards the sun because they "desire" its warmth. Even today, we can still find people asserting that plant genes mutate "in order to survive more successfully," as if the plants in question had conscious desires for the success of their progeny, and as if those desires could in some sense affect the mutation of their genes. Since the eighteenth century, scientists have almost completely discarded this model. Most physical things are unconscious, and do not operate from "desires."
>
> The *Cartesian* model mechanistically described a world of solid corpuscles which interacted through physical contact. This is the so-called "ping-pong" or "billiard ball" model of the universe, often taught to schoolchildren to explain ideas like the law of cause and effect. It easily leads to the misconception that interactions are between objects which somehow "touch" each other. We now know that material objects are in fact primarily energy and empty space; the few particles that really exist, like protons and electrons, never touch each other at all.
>
> The *Newton-Helmholtz* model suggested that interaction was rather between mass points in motion, interacting across distances by attractions and repulsions. This model was partly successful in explaining certain phenomena like gravity, magnetism, and simple electrical phenomena, but still carried with it the illusion that investigable "things" were responsible for everything.
>
> The *Einsteinian* model of relativity explained all phenomena in terms of fields (rather than particles) which are ultimately conceivable in terms of

a unified single field. While sometimes misinterpreted to mean that nothing can be taken as absolute, Einstein himself affirmed the reality of the physical universe, and even believed in its ultimate knowability. His theory of relativity simply suggested that knowability was related to the location and speed of the observer related to those of the fields observed.

The *Quantum* model of the post–World War II era asserts the existence of dozens of subatomic particles which cannot be objectively investigated, and the ultimate nondeterminism (and unknowability!) of the universe.[1]

There is little need to debate Maxwell's description of scientific change. It serves adequately to illustrate the fundamental sorts of changes in philosophical assumptions that each succeeding age has undergone. The more important point to notice is that common persons employed in fields other than the vanguard of physics often treat and think of the world in terms of either a Cartesian or a Newtonian model. We imagine atoms in terms of basketballs bouncing off each other in a rigidly rectilinear Cartesian space, following laws of motion we would expect of visible-sized objects. In fact, however, this picture has been abandoned by serious physicists for nearly a century. To understand whether our conceptions of survival are compatible with those of science, then, we must first get a clearer conception of the world of science in the 1990s.

Views of Physical Entities

To begin with, the entities discussed in modern physics are so inconceivably tiny that they cannot be "observed" or "experienced" at all. The tools of the modern physicist are mile-long particle accelerators which exert invisible forces on invisible particles. "Observations" are made in terms of submicroscopic fluctuations, magnified and computer-analyzed before they are ever presented on a screen or printout to the human eye. Even the "presence" of many subatomic particles is not observable in any sense at all; they are merely postulated to "explain" some of the otherwise even more mysterious anomalies in the data now being analyzed. Some have become widely accepted for their "explanatory value"; others are still hotly debated. In any case, we have abandoned the old idea that we can ultimately observe or even "convert into observable terms" all the entities and processes in the world.

Since the objects of inquiry themselves differ so far from the traditional objects of physics, it is not too surprising to find that the rules held to govern them are also drastically different from those which we might intuitively expect. As Burt says: "The fundamental concepts of modern science are so remote from actual observation and from ordinary sense perception that it becomes ludicrous to insist, or even to suggest, that they should be 'limited' by the 'basic principles' which were derived from the observable behavior of what I have called man-sized operations and processes."[2]

Just as the physical objects and the principles supposed to govern them have become increasingly elusive, our fundamental assumptions about the nature of things have also begun to crumble in the eyes of many physicists. Werner Heisenberg demonstrated that it is impossible to investigate small particles without influencing them by the process of investigation, and that it is theoretically impossible to determine both the location and mass of small particles with precision. The more precision is demanded for determination of a particle's position, the less it will be possible to determine the particle's mass, and vice versa. This "uncertainty principle" shook physics to its roots. Heisenberg himself came to believe that the advances of theoretical physics refuted the "impossibility of invisible vital forces."[3]

Henry Margenau concludes:

> To put it bluntly, science no longer contains absolute truths. We have begun to doubt such fundamental propositions as the principle of the conservation of energy, the principle of causality, and many other commitments which were held to be unshakable in the past. . . . The old distinction between the natural and the supernatural has become spurious.[4]

Views of the "Nature of Things"

Let us recall some of the problems and discoveries in physics that have rendered the scientific worldview of the physicist so open-ended. Even as long ago as Newton, the problem of action at a distance—that gravity and magnetism work on other objects across empty space without medium of wave or particle—was recognized as a problem. More recently, a range of post-Einsteinian experiments have blown open the notion of the "nature of things" even further. Koestler's survey is readable and informative:

> Half a century ago, Einstein, De Broglie, and Schrödinger between them had dematerialized matter. . . . Dirac populated the universe with holes; out of these holes pop, occasionally, particles of anti-matter, ghosts with negative mass and negative energy. Then there is Thompson's famous experiment in which an electron is apparently made to go through two slits at the same time. There is time reversal—Feynman's positrons traveling back into the past. There are Black Holes in astronomy into which matter is sucked. There, according to the equations of relativity, the laws of physics are suspended and matter disappears into the blue yonder. . . . Quantum physics can perfectly well visualize a square that is a circle or two parallels that meet, because of the curvature of space.[5]

If there are so many anomalies in our conceptions of the universe, if laws like causality and principles of objective observation no longer work, if even the objects of research are unobservable, where does all this leave modern physics? It is humbler, at least, than its nineteenth-century predecessors and its modern neighbors in behaviorist biology. Modern physicists are less certain of the nature of "truth" and more aware of the limitations of human knowledge. The new physics is far less dogmatic and more open to new theories than its predecessors have ever been.

Physicists now speak neither in terms of facts and figures alone nor in terms of the "laws" of matter, but rather in terms of probabilities and of the consistency of certain experimental results with certain other theories. There is in fact a close analogy between the statistical methods and probabilities used to document subatomic physics and those used in so-called ESP experiments.[6] Lawrence LeShan, in a now-famous paper, has shown that the statements of modern physicists about the nature of things are frequently indistinguishable from the statements of classical mystics.[7]

Compatibility of Physics and Parapsychology

It is not surprising that physicists and philosophers of science have become increasingly open to parapsychological theories about aspects of reality.

Notions of invisible bodies or fifth dimensions are no longer ridiculed by those scientists most in touch with the study of the universe. As George Kneller says: "We probably do have faculties which science has yet to employ, such as the capacity for travel with the 'astral body'."[8]

An even more widely accepted proposition is that there may exist other spatiotemporal dimensions we have hardly begun to detect, or which may be in principle impervious to detection, but which nevertheless exist and contain "universes" of their own. Physicist Ernst Mach debated the fourth dimension of space as a construct, holding that the sudden appearance or disappearance of objects would constitute good evidence of such a spatial dimension.[9] This is precisely what appears to happen in the cases of apparitions discussed above, as well as in experiments using Esaki and Zener tunnel diodes.[10]

Such phenomena have led some physicists to suggest that there exists a "hyperspace," which has explanatory value in both physics and parapsychology.[11] Parapsychologists also have taken up the suggestion, either as a literal or allegorical construct, to further demonstrate their compatibility with the worldviews of leading physicists.[12] The appropriateness of such explanatory models is debatable,[13] but this is ultimately a question for resolution by further empirical experimentation rather than by philosophical debate.

The important point here is that physical scientists of the highest caliber are open to the possibility of other forms of matter and other dimensions. They believe that such hypotheses would have explanatory value in their own fields as well as in parapsychology. While the subject matter of parapsychology and physics is significantly different, their fundamental insights curiously coincide.

The "laws" and insights of physics have long been thought to provide the best model of the nature of the universe. They are the rules according to which scientists in other fields as well are supposedly trained to view the world. Physics has become the paradigm of a "hard," mathematically modeled, empirically investigable field, which many other sciences would like to attain or emulate. This is precisely the field in which many of the mechanistic materialist laws of Descartes and Newton have been most radically overthrown and rejected.

Unresolved Philosophical Questions

The above accounts show cases in which parapsychologists try to assimilate their own survival theories with the openness and indeterminacy of modern physics. On the other side, there is another school of parapsychologists whom we might label *metaphysical dualists* or *superphysicalists.*

Metaphysical dualists claim that the materials studied in parapsychology, including OBEs and NDEs, are in principle not the sorts of things that may be studied by physicists and physical methods. Such phenomena are held to be "mind dependent," and mind is not on the same continuum as the things which physicists study, nor is it open to the same kinds of explanations. Thus, within parapsychology itself, there is some philosophical debate as to whether paranormal psychic phenomena will ultimately be explicable according to physics-like models, or whether they shall always be impenetrable to interpretation by behaviorist and empirical models.[14]

The issue in this case is not about the nature of the phenomena themselves; it is the old philosophical debate between monism and dualism, as Charles Tart claims: "The monistic view of mind and matter, the psychoneural identity hypothesis, so widely accepted in science, is one result of the worldview that totally denies the existence of psi phenomena as we experimentally know them. The existence of psi phenomena is clearcut scientific demonstration, however, that our knowledge of the physical world is quite inadequate . . ."[15] Tart concludes that only a thoroughgoing dualist interactionism can resolve the problem.

Gardner Murphy sees, on the other hand, a functional dualism that does not attempt to contrast realms of matter and ideas of mind as a possible alternative. He believes that physicists themselves are approaching a more Berkeleyan, idealistic view of reality.[16] John Beloff agrees that a Berkeleyan approach would make many psychic phenomena far more intelligible on a theoretical level, but he rejects the suggestion that physicists are no longer materialistic or monistic in their ideology.[17]

Philosophically, there are several options, each believed by serious philosophers of science. First, there are out-and-out dualists, like Tart and J. B. Rhine, who believe in the irreconcilable dissimilarity of mind and matter. There also are would-be monistic idealists, as Murphy was at times, who believe that ultimately everything will be explainable on the same continuum and that that continuum must contain idealistic elements. And finally, there are materialistic monists who believe that all will be ultimately explicable on physical terms, but that physics has yet to uncover many features of reality.

Clearly, there is no readily available resolution to this classical problem. But the adherents of each of these views have recognized that (1) present science is unable to explain fully all of the phenomena it encounters, including experiences surrounding death, and (2) since the generalizations or laws of physics are about different domains than those of parapsychology, there need be no inherent conflict between the two, despite their differences.

Whether the solution is ultimately dualistic or monistic, any generalization describing OBEs and NDEs will have to be of a different sort than those generalizations now applied to objects falling in a vacuum. There will have to be some sort of revision in any theory that "prohibits" OBEs and NDEs from happening, because they violate an obsolescent worldview. The facts must be the basis for the theory, and not the theory the basis for the rejection of data. We may hope that continued experiments will bring about a better understanding of the phenomena involved, with no loss in our understanding of present concerns. As Remy Chauvin has put it, we are not yet able to reconcile physics with psychic phenomena, but we cannot say that they contradict each other, and their reconciliation may demand an entirely new reconceptualization of the world.[18]

In summary, then, physics has advanced beyond Newton into indeterminacy, and physicists have come to expect anomalies in the universe. Some parapsychologists have hastened to draw analogies between the new physics and psychic phenomena; others emphasize the important and irreducible differences between the two fields. In their view modern physics, however mind-opening, sheds no new light on OBEs, NDEs, etc., and the central problem remains a philosophical question of monism versus dualism. But it is widely agreed that charges of "nonobservability" or "acausality" do not impugn the scientific status of parapsychology, and that there is no inherent conflict between physics and survival evidence.

Rational Objections to Paranormal Evidence

Despite the disclaimers of physicists that there need be no conflict between science and parapsychology, biologists and behaviorist psychologists still level a number of philosophical and methodological objections against the sorts of survival research we have described.[19] In addition to the specific criticisms already addressed in our previous chapters, there are three logical objections to the use of so-called paranormal evidence in scientific contexts. For convenience, we may label them the arguments from (1) repeatability, (2) theory-requirement, and (3) inherent probabilities. Let us examine each of these in turn, and see how they are answered by scientists. Since these constitute important questions in the philosophy and methodology of science, it is appropriate that they be carefully addressed before any further conclusions are drawn.

Repeatablllty

The argument from repeatability very simply holds that "repeatability is essential to the idea of a natural science; the notions of repeatability and of a law of nature are inseparably linked, while the latter is essential to the idea of a natural science."[20] We shall return to the question of "laws of nature" in the next argument about theory-requirement. For the moment, the challenge is to the repeatability of parapsychological survival data. It is first claimed that, if an experiment is repeated under the same conditions, it should produce uniform results, regardless of who conducts it or where. Then it is further claimed that phcnomcna indicative of possible afterlife do not correspond to this model, and that such investigations produce conflicting results. Critics conclude that such research need not be taken seriously as scientific evidence for anything at all, much less for personal survival. Are these charges justified?

Repeatability not theoretically required. In the first place, it is not the case that identical repeatability is required for an experiment to be accepted as scientific or legitimate. LeShan declaims that such requirements of repeatability are "drawn from billiard-ball physics, which was abandoned a century ago in the physical sciences which originated the model." There are many reasons why the most scientific of experiments may be non-repeatable. Some, such as those of nuclear physics, deal only in probabilities, where values are never likely to be precisely identical to those in previous experiments. Other experiments, like those in pharmacology with which LeShan has worked, already recognize the intrinsic importance of mood, value, and belief as variables.[21] For example, medicine is considered to be a science, but there are many experiments in medicine that are unrepeatable, and in which the influence of the beliefs and moods of the patients and practitioners are known to strongly affect the outcome of a given test.

Repeatability lacking in many sciences. Even today, there are a number of so-called "historical" sciences in which repeatability is not held to be a necessary or central issue. In "historical" sciences, the events under study happen only once, by their very nature. Michael Scriven explains: "It is important to stress that concern with repeatability is *not* the crucial matter. The Lisbon earthquake is not repeatable but its occurrence is extremely well established. *If* we can get repeatability, so much the better; and eventually, it is highly desirable. But it is not a requirement of all scientific claims that they be subject to test by repetition" [italics in original].[22]

Astronomy is concerned, among other things, with cosmic events which happen only once, as are archaeology, geology, and psychiatry.[23] We may improve our instruments to be better prepared to investigate cosmic, volcanic, or psychiatric disturbances when they arise, but we have only one chance to observe them when they do happen. Surely the nonrepeatability of our observations does not render either the event itself less real nor the scientific approach less valuable. Apparitions, possession cases, memories of past lives, OBEs and NDEs are equally unrepeatable in this sense. Just as all human history is unique, these experiences occur only once, unpredictably if at all. Yet the claim that they are not repeatable does not detract from the value of studying them any more than it would from the study of earthquakes.

Repeatability possible in some survival research. There is a continuing debate in the hard sciences about the merits of studying concrete cases in detail versus broad sampling with statistical techniques,[24] but neither holds a monopoly on the sciences. In either case, it is not true that there have been no confirmations of studies indicating past or future lives. These can occur in two ways: (1) when groups of scientists independently test the claims of a given subject, as in the Bridey Murphy or Shanti Devi cases, or (2) when scientists performing similar studies on different subjects arrive at similar results.

In each of the three fields of our concern (former lives, OBE/apparitions, and NDEs), repeatability of these sorts has been shown. Independent researchers have confirmed the results of hypnotic regressions and claimed memories of former lives, the experiments on the nature of apparitions, and the observations on deathbeds. In fact, it is precisely this similarity of many deathbed visions that seems so remarkable despite the wide range of individual differences of the percipients. In short, the arguments from repeatability "that survival research cannot be scientific" simply do not stand.

Theory-Requirement

The argument from theory-requirement is the claim that, in order for any facts to be "scientifically" meaningful, there must be some explanatory network into which the data are integrated and by which they are explained. Conversely, this requirement justifies the rejection of data that fall outside the bounds of known theories.[25] This argument contends that the scientific method is a continuous process of hypothesis-confirmation (or as Sir Karl Popper would have it, falsification); therefore facts must be set within a hypothesis before they acquire any real meaning. It then holds that the facts of psychic phenomena or NDEs lack such explanatory frameworks, and therefore are meaningless. Is this requirement justified? Does it apply here?

Facts must precede theories. It is not true that the collection of facts is of no value before a unified hypothesis has been worked out to account for their existence. An important part of the natural sciences, including biology, geology and, again, astronomy has consisted of collecting isolated and curious examples of data, photos, or radio wave patterns. At first these may be completely tangential or anomalous to any previous hypothesis.

Only after the collection of such data can scientists step back and hypothesize that, for example, coelocanths, or tectonic plates, or pulsars really exist. After that, they try to confirm their data collection by other methods, and they begin to construct hypotheses that would reconcile these new bits of knowledge with previous hypotheses. As Murphy has stressed, "Collection of isolated facts *is* necessary before full-fledged theory building."[26] What makes the enterprise scientific is not that the theory precedes the data collection, but that the data are collected with all possible precision, and that care is taken to observe as many variables as possible which might affect the outcome or analysis of the data.[27]

On explanations and theories. "Scientific explanations" are often really no more than a well-accepted description of a given process. When we label something a *quasar* or a *quark*, or call a process *evolutionary* or *gravitational*, we have not necessarily increased our understanding of it in any way. We have merely labeled it in a class with others and, in time, we may come to feel more comfortable with it since it is labeled. This is an important insight into the philosophy of science:

> Physics itself has come to accept the existence of inexplicable events. . . . There comes a point at which sufficiently elaborate *description,* documented and worked with for years, gives us the feeling that we have an understanding of the phenomenon thus described. We have not reduced it to another phenomenon, but this only offends our sense of aesthetics, not our scientific sense.[28]

To take a more specific example, how shall we explain why material *A* contracts when it is put through process *X*? We may respond that *A* is one of a class of *B*'s which always contract in process *X*. Or we may suggest that process *X* is a special case of process *Y*, which always causes *A*'s to contract. Such accounts often pass for "explanations" for some situations, but do they really explain why *A* contracts during *X*? Clearly not.

Another type of "explanation" would say that the molecules of *A* fit together in one way when they have not undergone *X*, but in condition *X* they come to fit together in another way, so that their total volume is smaller. This may be satisfying in some other contexts, but still, it is hardly a complete explanation. For we may yet again ask, how and why does X produce the refitting of molecules in A? Ultimately, the answer often comes down to "that's just the way the world is."

Even Newton's famous law of gravity, which says that "gravity is what made the apple fall," is no more than a disguised way of saying that the world works in such a way that smaller objects tend to move towards more massive objects. The case of the apple falling to earth is simply one instance of that regularity of nature. If we ask *why* or *how* gravity works, no further answer or mechanism is now available.

It is certainly premature to say that we have an adequate explanation of possession, or crisis apparitions, or visions of relatives at deathbeds. As Scriven says, we need to "document and work with for years" the details of these phenomena. We must better define the variables involved and try to understand them in terms of other known mechanisms or analogies, if possible. However, when we know much more about them, we may well come to ask, "Why did that happen?" and accept as an explanation an answer like "Oh, that was a crisis apparition," or "That was another fully conscious intersubjective religious NDE." It need not be assumed that any more elaborate "explanations" will be possible.[29]

Explanatory theories available. It is not that no explanatory theories have been offered for the data discussed above. These theories may not coincide with other traditional theories about the way the world works, but then there is no need for all new theories always to mesh harmoniously with all older theories. On the contrary, we have already observed how Ian Stevenson has staked his professional reputation on defending the novel hypothesis that reincarnation best explains the particular phenomena he has researched.

Similarly, theories that OBEs produce apparitions, or that the similarities in the content of NDEs is in fact due to an accurate intersubjective view of a real postmortem experience, are precisely the kinds of explanatory hypotheses the "theory-requirement" advocates demand. It is inappropriate, however, for them to demand additionally that these new data and hypotheses coincide with what is already thought to be known about the world. Nor need there be any conflict here. In Scriven's words:

> There is no clash between psi phenomena and other scientific discoveries—only between laws which are extrapolated too far from those prior discoveries. Evidence for present scientific laws cannot be appealed to refute ESP [OBEs, NDEs, etc.]. All it does is say, "Do not believe in ESP unless you have direct evidence for it," and of course, we *do* have direct evidence for it.[30]

So theory-requirement cannot be a valid objection to the scientific meaningfulness of data from carefully investigated paranormal sources.

Inherent Probabilities

The argument from inherent probabilities looks innocuous enough. It takes as its model the case where the physics student reports a different value for a wavelength of light or a coefficient of friction than the professor has expected. In such cases, it asserts, it will always be preferable to attribute the discrepancy to some error of method or observation on the part of the student than to admit that there could be variation in nature. In more general terms, it says that "antecedent probability" is always on the side of the previously established rule, against the occasional anomalous facts which seem to throw it into question.

In any instance where a few isolated and freaky facts appear to contradict a well-established "law," it is always more probable that the law will be correct than the putative facts. In terms of research on survival, this says that it is always preferable to reject survivalist interpretations of data in favor of psychological or physiological ones. When such psychological or physiological explanations seem lacking and survivalist interpretations are the only ones possible, the "inherent probabilities" are that the experimenter is either deluded or committing a fraud.

Analogy not appropriate. The first glaring flaw in this argument is that the analogy of the student in the physics class is not at all appropriate to the case of independent investigators finding new properties of yet-unstudied phenomena like OBEs or NDEs. In the case of the physics class, we have at least three conditions which are not paralleled in the survival research-ers' case: (1) The laws and variables governing the phenomenon are already well-established, (2) the crucial variables are already well defined, and effects of other conditions minimized, and (3) the experiment in question is *known* to fall within the purview of the law or hypothesis being demonstrated.

In such cases, it would indeed be more reasonable to reject the student's data than to question the laws under which he or she is working. In survival research, it is clear that *not* all the laws and variables governing survival have been established, that the determination of which variables are important and which conditions are incidental to survival research is *not* yet complete, and the experiments concerning survival are *not* known to fall under any of the traditional laws of science.

A better analogy would be the case in which the laws stated that "live birth is a defining characteristic of mammals." If scientists studying biol-ogy come up with evidence that platypi lay eggs and sharks bear live young, we have several options. We might choose to restrict the domain of our generalization (say, to mammals defined by some further criteria) so that its truth is not affected. Or we might revise the definition of mammals to include platypi as exceptions, or even create new classifica-tions for platypi and sharks. But we certainly need not reject the data because they are "inherently improbable," after independent researchers have confirmed the behaviors of platypi and sharks.

Paranormal phenomena also seem to constitute exceptions to what many people assume to be universal generalizations. But a generalization can in no way deny that the phenomena occur. What is needed is either careful restriction of the domain of the former generalizations, or revision of them to include new facts.

Mechanistic assumptions. The "inherent improbability" of survival is based on a materialistic, monistic, billiard-ball-interaction view of the universe. In his criticisms of survival, George Price emphasized this point: "The essence of science is mechanism. . . . Suppose that some extraordinary new phenomena is [*sic*] reported: should we be narrow-minded or receptive? The test is to attempt to imagine a detailed mechanistic explanation."[31] If a mechanistic theory is unavailable, Price contends, we should choose to be narrow-minded! But we should recall that physicists, who were responsible for providing the world with mechanism, have largely abandoned mechanism as an explanation for most phenomena.

The obsolescence of mechanism and its inadequacy as a criterion of "inherent probability" is almost too glaring to repeat. Perhaps the best response to this sort of assertion was that of J. B. Rhine:

> As a universal law, [mechanism] has never had any truly experimental confirmation whatsoever. How in the nature of things could it have? Actually, this whole mechanistic business means only that in those areas of nature in which most of the scientists of the world have been working—the various physical sciences—physical theory *has been* adequate. Naturally. Consequently, mechanism grew just like Topsy and became a habit of mind, a way of looking at the universe. . . . But to establish that this physicalistic interpretation applies to the whole of nature, and that there are no other kinds of principles in the universe, would call for a complete understanding of nature. Of course, we have nothing like that, as everyone well knows.[32]

In short, if the claim of "inherent improbability" is based on the assumption that everything is explicable in terms of mechanism, it is itself a metaphysical (and not empirically knowable) claim about the nature of things, and lacks scientific justification.

Hume's argument on miracles. The phrase "inherent improbability" sometimes appears in a different guise. In the words of Scottish skeptic David Hume, "A miracle is a violation of the laws of nature." Since the laws of nature are more consistent and absolute than the perceptions of any human being, in the case where there appears to be a miracle, it is always more probable that there is delusion or deception on the part of the observer than that the laws of nature had been temporarily abrogated.[33]

There are two ways to resolve this apparent rejection of new or "miraculous" evidence. If we accept Hume's dictum that miracles never happen because laws of nature are never violated, then we shall also have to say that faith-healing, OBEs, NDEs, etc., are not miracles, but by definition also accord with the laws of nature. In this case, we must take exception to Hume's implied premise that the laws of nature are already known or even in principle knowable. It may in fact be the case that there are laws governing everything. We do not know that they will in any way resemble the laws we presently believe. Nor can such laws be used to "rule out" OBEs or NDEs; those laws will necessarily include them. In this case, the problem is only a pseudoproblem, based on the false eighteenth-century assumption that we already know all the laws of nature.

The other possibility is to assert that Hume was wrong about the "fact" that laws of nature can never be violated. According to the great majority of contemporary philosophers of science, laws are no more than descriptive generalizations of what is already known. They are not only "violable" but are in fact violated every time an interesting new discovery is made, whether it be of quarks or sharks. Such discoveries indeed appear miraculous to people who believe them impossible. But their violation of known generalizations by no means demotes them to fraud or nonexistence.

The inappropriateness of this Humean view of miracles and laws of nature is well discussed in Paul Feyerabend's "Inherent Unreasonability of the Consistency Condition," and "The Self-Deception Involved in All Uniformity."[34] Ducasse states succinctly, "Assertions of impossibility are based on the metaphysical creeds of the scientists of the day. . . . Incapacity to admit nonphysical action is an occupational disease [of material scientists]."[35] And Rhine hits close to the heart of the matter when he asserts: "When anyone gives to such belief the almost dogmatic finality that Price apparently does, it suggests that the doctrine has taken the place of a security-giving theology, and is playing much more than a scientific role in his life."[36]

We shall examine the theological implications and problems of survival research shortly. For the moment, however, we should note that arguments from "inherent probability" are all based on assumptions that we know more about the world than we do.

Survival Research as Empirical Science

The above arguments refute the claims that there are methodological or theoretical reasons that survival research is inherently unscientific. On a more positive note, let us look briefly at the important ways in which survival research *is* scientific. LeShan and Margenau emphasize that the following principles are central to science:

1. A domain of experience is selected for study.
2. Observable variables are chosen [may be observed or inferred].
3. Some terms are procedurally defined in terms of others.
4. We ask not, "What is *X?*" but "How does *X* function or relate to *Y?*"
5. We expect regularity of interaction [with sufficient control of variables].
6. We find no contradictions internally, nor with other systems *in the same domain.*[37]

These features can demonstrably be applied to many fields of psychical and survival research. The point most open to question might seem to be number 2, the requirement of observable variables. But it is not required that the variables be public, macroscopic, and/or previously understood. Thus, deathbed visions can serve as the objects of such a science, just as much as subatomic particles or dream analysis can, without questioning their ontological status.

Nonrational Objections to Paranormal Evidence

Despite the evidence of paranormal phenomena indicative of survival, and despite the empirical and scientific methods of collecting such data, many scientists still insist that such data is illusory or nonexistent. The dogmatism of empirical scientists on this point seems to contradict the image of scientists as impartial objective observers of experience.[38] Marcello Truzzi[39] and R. A. McConnell[40] have made long catalogues of the objections often leveled by scientists against evidence of paranormal phenomena. (Most of these objections have already been answered, either immediately following the analysis of data in the previous chapters or in our preceding discussion of "rational objections" to paranormal sciences.)

We already noted that J. B. Rhine detected a tinge of religious fanaticism in George Price's rejection of paranormal occurrences. Considering the sorts of phenomena we have discussed, even scientists of the status of Hermann von Helmholtz have asserted that "neither the testimony of all the Fellows of the Royal Society nor the evidence of my own senses . . . would lead [him] to believe in the transmission of thought from one person to another independently of the recognized channels of sense."[41]

Surely such a statement is as unscientific as it is philosophically untenable. What could lead such a competent scholar to such a blind and headstrong assertion? Here we need to examine the motivations behind scientists' nonrational objections to survival evidence. We may classify the types of resistance broadly as psychological, intellectual, religious, and sociological. In each instance, let us examine the origins of these beliefs and their validity, if any. In so doing, we shall see whether survival evidence is vulnerable to such attacks and, at the same time, develop a case study towards the current literature in the history and philosophy of science.

Psychological Resistance to Cognitive Dissonance

In the early 1950s, Jerome Bruner and Leo Postman conducted a number of experiments in which subjects were asked to identify playing cards they saw flashed for a small fraction of a second in a tachistoscope. Among the cards were "impossible" anomalies, such as red sixes of spades and black queens of hearts. Some subjects became very disturbed emotionally by the difference between these cards and their expectations. (This difference is known as cognitive dissonance.) The vast majority of subjects, however, identified all the cards as normal; for example, they would call a red spade either a heart or a spade, and not even recognize that these cards combined features of two incompatible suits.

These remarkable experiments led their authors to conclude that we humans instinctively dislike anomaly to the extent that we will unconsciously misperceive reality—forcing our perceptions to conform with our ordered expectations—rather than accept incongruities within the system.[42] Thomas Kuhn cites these same tests in arguing that "data will be beaten into line" to conform with previous theories about the nature of things.[43] In Trotter's words, "The mind likes a new idea as little as the body likes a strange protein."[44] In other words, we subconsciously do everything possible to reject such new ideas.

The mind intuitively shuns and seeks to eliminate cognitive dissonance from our perceptions. This same phenomenon can be found in the mind's treatment of memory and interpretation of experience. As one example, we may read William James's own account of a spiritualist session, conducted in bright light and good test conditions. After his description, he quite self-consciously adds:

> Now, after four days' interval, my mind seems strongly inclined not to "count" the observation, as if it were too exceptional to have been probable. . . . I should be as one watching an incipient overflow of the Mississippi of the supernatural into the fields of orthodox culture. I find, however, that I look on nature with unaltered eyes today, and that my orthodox habits tend to exclude the would-be levee-breaker.[45]

James was at least intellectually honest enough to recognize the psychological repression that had taken place within himself. But he was not strong enough to resuscitate the memory and force it to take a place in his view of the universe!

A more recent instance is given in the account of Ernst Rodin, a Detroit physician who had an NDE with a euphoric vision of heaven in 1953. At the time, he was convinced that he was going to heaven and begged to be allowed to die. A quarter of a century later, however, he has reinterpreted his experience in terms of his medical beliefs, and he no longer believes that his experience had any inherent reality or meaning.[46] Here again, we find a scientist suppressing cognitive dissonance (the disagreement between his experience and his conceptualizations) by denying his experience rather than by changing his mind. This is indeed a vivid documentation of the strength of conceptual systems. Our preconceptions are stronger than our sensory experiences, for they actually dictate the way we will perceive objects.

Eminent psychologists and doctors can totally discount the importance of their own personal experiences, reinterpreting them in accord with their more comfortable and traditional worldviews. How much more then, would people be inclined to discount such phenomena as OBEs or NDEs as delusion, nonsense, or fraud—anything to preserve their systems of thought? Scientists who are educated to be concerned with consistency find the survival data to be incompatible with their worldviews. By vigorously denying the existence and even the possibility of such data, they eliminate the data from their worldviews rather than modify their worldviews to fit the data.[47] We might call this the psychological reaction to dissonance. It does not really change the truth of the situation, but it provides a psychological mechanism whereby the organism can avoid becoming too upset.

Intellectual Resistance to Reeducation and Paradigm Shift

In the course of their educations, philosophers are expected to learn a wide range of unpopular as well as popular theories, and to discern the important truths or fatal mistakes in each system. By contrast, scientists seldom study the history of their discipline. When they study it at all, they tend to study those particular branches of science that directly contributed to their own particular traditions.[48] The contributions of alchemy and astrology to science, for example, are only mentioned in their rejections, but are not taken seriously as alternative worldviews. Thus, scientific education tends to be monolithic, monovalent, and to emphasize the superiority and correctness of its own peculiar metaphysics. In the words of philosopher of science Thomas Kuhn:

> Scientific education inculcates what the scientific community had previously with difficulty gained—a deep commitment to a particular way of viewing the world and of practicing science in it. . . . Preconception and resistance seem to be the rule rather than the exception in mature scientific development. . . . They are community characteristics with deep roots in the procedures through which scientists are trained for work in their profession.[49]

The scientist learns not just facts and experiments, but a whole worldview and approach to the world, which Kuhn calls a "paradigm." Through textbooks and repetition, one paradigm is learned to the exclusion of all others. It becomes invested with strong emotional value as the best, if not the only, way of looking at the world.[50] Thus, the chosen paradigm becomes an extremely emotional rather than a rational affair. It has never been viewed with philosophical objectivity, and the idea that it might be inferior to some other paradigm is rejected by the entire scientific community of believers.[51] Changing paradigms does not simply involve "changing one's mind"; it rather entails a conversion experience—a new way of looking at the world.[52]

It is little wonder that scientists would rather ignore conflicting evidence than modify their long-reinforced pet worldviews. The responses of scientists themselves to such a breakdown of their worldviews further documents this theory. One mathematician said of psychic or paranormal evidence, "If that were true . . . it would mean that I would have to scrap everything and start again from the beginning."[53] Of course, there is no inherent conflict between mathematics and paranormal evidence, but this shows how much he connected his personal worldview with his understanding of his profession. As LeShan has observed: "Ours is a culture that has made a tremendous investment in the mechanistic concept of the cosmos, in Descartes' 'clockwork universe'—we are terribly threatened in our very being [if it is challenged]."[54] Whately Carington and others have found a connection between the rejection of paranormal phenomena and the belief that parapsychology would break down our traditional notions of causality, thought to be the framework within which the sciences have grown up.[55]

These attitudes are not rational. There is nothing in paranormal research that demands either the sacrifice of mathematics, causality, or even of Descartes (except where he was pretty clearly mistaken, as about animals, billiard balls, or the pineal gland). The fear expressed here is born of ignorance and reluctance to revise old ideas.

Many physicists have already abandoned or substantially revised both their commitments to Cartesian geometry and to traditional notions of causality in exploring the atom and the cosmos. Thus people like Werner Heisenberg are no more threatened by survival research than by the inherent uncertainties of scientific empiricism. Survival could also prove to be compatible with special cases of dimension theory or energy fields.

Most of the resistance to survival studies comes from the biological, psychological, and even social sciences, which are on weaker theoretical grounds than physics.[56] The violence with which they reject survival "may prove to be an index of its importance."[57] For example, it is natural that neurophysiologists studying the human brain would not want to admit a huge range of yet ill-defined and perhaps uncontrollable variables. The mind-brain identity theory is a comfortable way for them to reassure each other that nothing is being ignored, that all will ultimately be known by the tools at their disposal. Survival evidence gives the death-knell to that theory. But rather than admitting that other variables might affect their discipline than the ones they have already defined, most neurophysiologists prefer to ignore the evidence itself.

Religious Resistance to Heretical or Occult Forces

Paranormal phenomena ranging from spirit possession and astral travel to resuscitation of the dead have been known for thousands of years in Europe as well as Asia. They have been consistently banned and suppressed by the church, not because their reality was doubted but because they were dangerous, opening the gates to heterodoxy and perhaps to the work of the devil himself. Scientists, too, have very human religious commitments and presuppositions. In some cases these involve rejecting survival as impossible or unimportant, in others, of limiting it to articles of faith, consciously segregated from the sorts of issues held to be open to scientific inquiry. The evidence that persons are more than material or that life might survive the grave is a mind-boggling proposition to many dogmatic people, who quickly anathematize it.[58]

William McDougall suggested that men of science fear that the admission of paranormal phenomena might open floodgates of public credulity, "for they know that it is only through the faithful work of men of science through recent centuries that these distressing beliefs have been in large measure banished from a small part of the world."[59]

In his masterful survey of scientific attitudes towards the paranormal, Prince concludes that there is an "enchanted boundary" that deprives scientists of their objectivity and reason in dealing with such phenomena. He documents in painstaking detail how great scientists such as Faraday, Tyndall, Thomas Huxley, and dozens of others simply refused to believe such evidence. Some stooped to name-calling and ad hominem attacks, others to deliberate distortion of the material they disliked. In another scientific study, a questionnaire was sent to a large number of scientists asking them how they would interpret a hypothetical example of a psychic phenomenon if it had occurred in such-and-such a manner. The majority of respondents were unable to answer the questions or even to entertain the hypothesis in their imagination.[60]

Scientists in survival research now find themselves in good company with orthodox churchmen who have other reasons for not wanting people to believe that afterlife could be proved. The orthodox fear that people may think church membership and sacraments are not necessary to attaining heaven; others argue that proof of heaven might justify a rash of suicides or atrocities like Jim Jones's Guiana massacre.[61] The men making these statements are committed to objectivity and inquiry in other departments of their lives, but this does not seem to affect their religious fears. Nor is this resistance new:

> Consider the violent antagonism encountered by the theories of Copernicus and Galileo in astronomy, Buffon and Hutton in geology, Darwin and Huxley in biology—most of them theories which are now almost unanimously accepted. In these cases, the resistance, as has so often been remarked, arose largely out of the time-honored metaphysical preconceptions or prejudices associated with religious beliefs.[62]

We cannot prophesy the future enough to suggest that the field of survival research will at some point become an independent science like biology or geology. But the symptoms of metaphysical resistance are visible in full strength. Religious objections are neither logical nor scientific reasons for rejecting evidence of survival. However, they play an important role in shaping what is believed acceptable to the scientific community, and thereafter by the public.

Social Resistance and Fear of Ridicule

We have just seen that the real motives for rejecting the evidence of survival may be psychological and metaphysical rather than scientific. Thus the neglect of survival research may be more attributable to sociological reasons than to any inherent flaws in its methods.[63]

Practically all scientifically educated persons found that fear of ridicule, plus their own very reasonable recoil from the seemingly irrational, was more powerful than alleged facts which did not fit into the scheme of things; so, humanly enough, like the man who refused to look through Galileo's telescope for fear that what he saw would not suit his views, they safeguard themselves by ignoring the evidence.[64]

Darwin postponed the publication of his *Origin of Species* for twenty years because he feared challenging the biblical account, and even more because he "hesitated to defy public opinion."[65] William James privately expressed the fear that his name might be discredited because of his interests in psychical research.[66]

Nor is such fear of ridicule totally groundless. Sir John Eccles, the Nobel laureate whose trialistic worldview has won much popular acclaim, has been blasted for his unorthodox attempts to reinstate mind-brain interactionism.[67] Wilhelm Reich was incarcerated and his books were destroyed when his theories became too radical.[68] In survival research, Drs. Kübler-Ross and Moody have come under repeated attack for being popularizers or even loonies. We have already noted the courage required of Stevenson to publish articles on reincarnation in the face of attacks in the *Journal of Nervous and Mental Disease*.[69] In short, fear of ridicule may not be a logically legitimate reason for avoiding survival research, any more than for refusing to sail west across the Atlantic for the first time. But it may be very effective in suppressing scientific interest in survival until the tide of public opinion slowly turns to accept the legitimacy of such investigations.

In summary, there are a number of nonrational origins for scientists' objections to research on survival and paranormal phenomena. Taken together, they amass a strong, sometimes almost impenetrable, barrier between the world of real experience and the world recognized by science. Such attitudes of scientists in fields outside of their own in no way refute our evidence or conclusions. At most, they demonstrate the dogmatic conservatism and mechanism of many scientists. At the same time, we need to understand the methods and channels through which scientists manage to denigrate the importance and deny the legitimacy of survival research.

5.

A Model of Resistance and Change in the Sciences

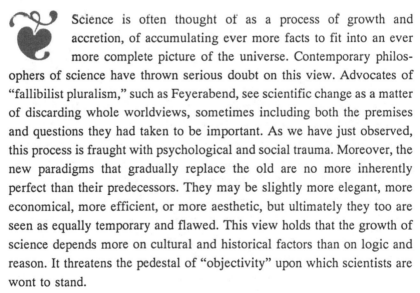 Science is often thought of as a process of growth and accretion, of accumulating ever more facts to fit into an ever more complete picture of the universe. Contemporary philosophers of science have thrown serious doubt on this view. Advocates of "fallibilist pluralism," such as Feyerabend, see scientific change as a matter of discarding whole worldviews, sometimes including both the premises and questions they had taken to be important. As we have just observed, this process is fraught with psychological and social trauma. Moreover, the new paradigms that gradually replace the old are no more inherently perfect than their predecessors. They may be slightly more elegant, more economical, more efficient, or more aesthetic, but ultimately they too are seen as equally temporary and flawed. This view holds that the growth of science depends more on cultural and historical factors than on logic and reason. It threatens the pedestal of "objectivity" upon which scientists are wont to stand.

We must be careful to distinguish between replacement of paradigms and mere replacement of facts. Viewing the world as a sphere instead of as a plane was largely a correction of a matter of fact. It did not require discarding a whole set of old questions as unanswerable, but simply gave a different answer to an old set of questions. By contrast, the theories of gravity and heliocentricity replaced old teleological theories and led to a new set of questions and answers, a new way of looking at everything—in short, a shift to a new paradigm.

Our study of survival research contributes some important documentation and insights to this historic debate about the nature of scientific change. We can note several phases in its development: rejection, suppression, independent growth, and assimilation/acceptance. In this chapter, let us see just how far (or how little) survival research has come towards being recognized as a science or as a legitimate empirical study.

Rejection of the Evidence

When anomalous facts or phenomena emerge which do not comfortably coincide with a prevailing worldview, the first tendency of people already educated within that worldview is to deny the existence or possibility of such anomalies. Some people simply refuse to look at the evidence, while others attempt to discredit it circumstantially, without examining the evidence on its own merits.

Refusal to Consider

Rejection of the evidence of survival may take several forms. It may be the blunt and obstinate sort of rejection published in *Science* magazine that "not a thousand experiments with ten million trials and by a hundred separate investigators" could lead the individual to accept survival.[1] This particular scientist clearly prefers to put blind faith in his materialistic metaphysics over the objective empiricism which his scientific training should have imparted to him. Some prefer to couch their objections in the more sophisticated-sounding language of analytic philosophy, such as Flew's discussion of the "insurmountable initial obstacles" in believing in survival.[2] But this too is no more than a thinly-veiled way of saying, "I just can't bring myself to believe that a man's mind survives his body."

Others choose the tack of screaming, "Fraud!" This was the charge leveled against the early table-rapping spiritualists and modern channelers, with whom scientific survival researchers would part company. George Price used the Humean argument that "it is more probable that a few people out of the world's billions would lie than that nature would change" to accuse some of the greater names in modern psychology of conspiracy and fraud.[3] Price withdrew his criticisms after honestly studying the subject himself, but they appear again in Hansel (1966) and Gibson (1979).[4]

Whether the language is nasty or nice, the message is clear. But these accusations of fraud are not based on any knowledge, or even any legitimate suspicion, that such a conspiracy really exists. They are simply using ". . . the fraud hypothesis as a soothing addendum to some version of the a priori [impossibility] argument. Though ESP is seen as a priori impossible, the phenomena explained by the parapsychologists must still be explained away. The fraud hypothesis fills this lacuna."[5]

We recall how Ruth Reyna repudiated the reincarnation hypothesis by casting aspersions on the researchers of claimed memories of former lives. The independent collection and confirmation of hundreds of cases does not change her view. It emerges later in her work that she had already decided that reincarnation cannot happen, so any apparent evidence for it had to be fraud or folly on the part of the investigators.[6] The fraud hypothesis became a cover for irrational justification of her own presuppositions in the face of evidence which throws them open to doubt.

Discrediting by Association

Another tactic for impugning survival research is to associate it with the more incredible sides of the occult fringe, casting doubt by implication on the integrity and sanity of its researchers. This may be a more or less conscious ploy. R. A. McConnell argues that "much of the reluctance of orthodox scientists to endorse extended support for ESP research arises from their failure to make a clear distinction between popular and scientific belief."[7]

Both believers and nonbelievers in survival tended to agree with a survey statement that increasing popular interest in parapsychology will damage its scientific reputation.[8] Scientists unreceptive to survival research are equally aware of this phenomenon, and deliberately use it to their advantage where possible.[9] By associating survival research with the occult fringe, which lacks respectability in the eyes of most Americans, Christians, and scientists, critics insinuate that the evidence found by OBE or NDE research does not deserve further serious study.[10]

Criticism by Authority

Another manner of rejecting the evidence for survival has been alluded to in our discussion of claimed memories of past lives. Adults often criticize their children's statements which do not neatly coincide with the adults' worldview. This tends to suppress vocalization of such memories and eventually to stifle them altogether as being of no value in this world. Garrett describes a time in her childhood when she clairvoyantly "saw" the death of a relative and described it to her guardian. Her guardian's response was, "Don't ever speak of things that you see like that, for they might *again* come true!"—as if the child were somehow causally responsible for the tragedy because she had foreseen it.[11] The irrationality of this response is obvious, and hardly helpful to the child being criticized. As the child has neither the capacity nor the authority to reason with its elders, the effect is simply to suppress discussion of death-related and paranormal experiences altogether.

Similar criticism takes place on a broader scale from intellectual authority figures. Many people may hesitate to speak of parapsychology when an authority figure like the ex-director of the U.S. Bureau of Standards can use the *Bulletin of the Atomic Scientists* to pontificate in this way:

> There used to be spiritualism, there continues to be ESP. . . . Where corruption of children's minds is at stake, I do not believe in the freedom of the press or freedom of speech. In my view, publishers who publish or teachers who teach any of the pseudo-sciences as established truth should, on being found guilty, be publicly horsewhipped, and forever banned from further activity in these usually honorable professions.[12]

The Bureau of Standards did not like deviations from visible norms. It avails little to protest that this "authority" knows almost nothing about the field he is condemning, much less of democratic political and penal theory. The net effect of such statements in respectable publications is to suppress free expression of experiences, ideas, and dialogue. It is just such dialogue which might lead, if unrestricted, to a better understanding of what really does and does not happen.

Suppression

Blatant rejection of survival evidence by authority figures constitutes an irrational but head-on repression of nontraditional information. Other methods of suppression may be more indirect, such as limiting publications and funding.

Limiting Opportunities for Publication

An even more effective method for suppressing "undesirable" discussion of survival evidence consists in strict controls over the channels of legitimization. Most obvious is the policy of leading journals of science and medicine to avoid material that might question the paradigms under which the majority of their authors conduct research. Until recent inquiry on the social controls and sanctions of knowledge became of interest to philosophers, there had been no empirical studies of when and why scientific journals published what sorts of articles. So their opposition to nontraditional sciences remained very covert, and other alibis could always be found for rejecting articles of "inappropriate subject matter."

H. M. Collins and T. J. Pinch researched cases in which papers submitted to leading publications like *Science* were rejected despite recommendations by a majority of readers and referees.[13] Paul Allison suggests that the low number of articles in traditional journals "was not due to lack of submissions."[14] There can be little doubt that "the refereeing system frequently operates to suppress the publication of new and important material that happens to be personally distasteful to the referee to whom it is referred."[15]

Of course, this may well be the case in other fields such as philosophy. But unlike philosophy, where journals may specialize in positivism, monism, humanism, idealism, and other conflicting views about the nature of things, scientific journals seldom represent opposing viewpoints or methodologies. Rather, the sciences are dominated by a few journals whose presuppositions uniformly preclude contrary or paradigm-shaking material—and there are few alternative publications open to investigators of survival.[16]

The other alternative of the journals is to grant publication to an occasional article on survival, and then to dilute it by playing up the critical reactions to it.[17] This sometimes takes the form of collusion among several journals, so that several critical articles appear simultaneously with one favorable article. Or it may be the tacit policy of some editors to publish only those articles that demonstrate the limitations and inconclusiveness of paranormal research.[18]

By these unwritten and normally invisible policies, established scientists can avoid the increasing evidence of the nonmechanistic aspects of human being. Many who are interested in survival and psychic research get the impression either that nothing is being done or that it lacks scientific respectability. Professionals in the sciences might be stimulated to think about other approaches to their research, or upset to find their monolithic conceptions threatened. But they are spared the challenges and the distractions by editors who screen out such material from their reading fare.

Moreover, when material on survival fails to appear in leading scientific journals, it cannot be excerpted for a broader public audience by potential popularizers such as *Scientific American, Psychology Today,* or even *Reader's Digest.* It does not find its way into the printed and computerized indices of scientific and periodical literature; this makes literature reviews and bibliographic searches immensely more difficult. The implication that survival research is somehow unscientific or illegitimate is conveyed quietly without the need for offering reasons or risking strong counterarguments.

At least through the mid 1970s, this means of rejecting survival evidence was widely practiced and apparently highly effective. It has only been since the late 1970s that the *Journal of Psychiatry,* the *Journal of the American Medical Association,* and the *Journal of Nervous and Mental Disease* have begun to give space to the interpretations of survival research, with only the most circumspect and tentative of articles. This suppression of publishing channels is easy to quantify and document; other means of suppression may be even more subtle.

Suppression of Academic Fraternity, Opportunities, and Funds

As much or more than other disciplines, science depends on a close-knit social structure, which Kneller calls "an invisible college." There are networks and groups of collegial scholars working on particular problems, trading their views and interacting with the larger scientific community through conferences, letters, summer sessions, and even camps.[19] Therefore, "getting ahead" in science is due not only to good ideas and careful experimentation, but on personal connections with the right people and groups. Survival researchers have generally been excluded from this scientific community. When admitted as somewhat offbeat members (like J. B. Rhine or Charles Tart), they may be restricted in the topics they are allowed to present at conferences of "straight" scientists.

Harder to document, but even more critical, is outright discrimination against parapsychologists. In his thesis at Wisconsin, Allison found 183 instances of claimed discrimination among members of the Parapsychology Association because of their interests in parapsychology.[20] Over half of these cases concerned hiring, promotions, or use of facilities. They tended to come from those already within academic environments.

This may also be an unintentional by-product of the conservatism of funding sources. It is relatively difficult to win funds, grants, or positions to research or teach subjects outside of traditional departmental lines of demarcation. The problem becomes even more complex in parapsychology, because it potentially bridges (or falls into the chasms between) disciplines as disparate as neurophysiology, physics, electronics, psychology, and philosophy of religion. In this era of recession and cutbacks in academic funding, such radical departures from traditional structures are not likely to find sanction. This in turn can result in the loss of funding for proposals researching the borders of present knowledge.

Reinterpretation

Reinterpretation to "explain away" the data is yet another approach of scientists to rejecting survival research. It is hardly necessary to reiterate all the many tacks that have been taken by critics in the previous chapters, but a summary of some of their methods may be illustrative. The most traditional approach is to say that the phenomena in question are no more than manifestations of an already well-known condition; thus Kenneth Dewhurst attempts to explain OBEs as heautoscopy, and Ronald Siegel tries to reduce near-death visions to hallucination. Such tactics are only made possible by ignoring some of the unique and crucial features of the

OBEs or NDEs, but the impression given to the uncritical or uninformed reader is that "nothing significant is happening here." The situation becomes almost humorous when opponents of a particular survivalist interpretation attempt to replace it with something apparently more scientifically reputable. We recall, for example, Leonid Vasiliev's attempts to define a new condition between life and death called "parabiosis" to account for the fact that some people have revived after all of their bodily functions have terminated. Then there are the attempts to define NDEs as projections of Jungian archetypes. And the super-ESP hypothesis is widely used by A. J. Ayer and Antony Flew.

There is a double irony here. First, as we have mentioned earlier, parabiosis, archetypes, and even ESP are themselves very vague hypotheses, whose functions and even existence are more in doubt than the phenomena being studied. Second, the ascription of an authoritative or scientific-sounding name is felt somehow adequate to explain away the phenomena and keep them from further serious consideration. The existence of the data is not denied, and the "explanations" proffered are more uncertain and mysterious than that which they are to explain. Yet such subsuming of new evidence under traditional rubrics somehow absolves people from the need to study the issues further and brushes them under the rug.

Independent Growth

As the evidence for anomalous phenomena gains an increasing following on the fringes of respectable academia, the more daring and progressive of investigators have begun to bypass previous publications and organizations, and form their own new organs which will enable their communication and recognition of new ideas.

Publications

When a community comes to believes that its existing scientific paradigm is inadequate, among its first and most important countermeasures is the promulgation of its own nontraditional viewpoints in print. The survival topic represents an excellent example of this trend within the history of science. A generation ago, there was only one serious scientist publishing material on reincarnation evidence. Only a few pioneers like Stanislav Grof and E. Kübler-Ross were working on NDEs. Their work was so disguised in traditional forms that the revolutionary impact of their writings was not then felt, and they were relatively unknown to others working in similar fields.[21]

However, with the publication of Raymond Moody's *Life After Life* in 1976 and Karlis Osis's cross-cultural comparisons in *At the Hour of Death* the following year, the floodgates were opened. It is not that the scientific community recognized the legitimacy of their research and conclusions. Rather, individuals who had been previously interested in and working in related fields were at last emboldened to attempt publication of their own results. In the past decade alone, at least thirty books centering on the near death experience have emerged.[22] Extracts and interviews with their authors in popular magazines such as *Time, Life, Newsweek,* and *McCall's* soon followed these early publications.

Equally or more important is the creation of periodicals specifically designed to deal with the survival problem. Of course, it was this which first inspired the creation of branches of the Society for Psychical Research in London, Boston, and California. More recently, journals on death and dying such as *Death Education, Theta, Omega,* and the *Journal of Near-Death Studies* have rapidly populated thanatologists' bookshelves, and a significant portion of each journal is concerned with issues of survival.

Professional Organizations

Behind many of these new publications are new associations of people interested in the evidence of survival, outside of the old framework of mechanistic materialism. These organizations are of several types. Some, like the International Association for Near-Death Studies (IANDS), have affiliation with and support from recognized university departments, and they stress the scientific nature of the research being conducted, although accepting contributions from other sources.[23] Others, like Lumena and ERICLAL (European Research and Information Center About Life After

Life) encourage participation from those who have had near-death experiences, and may be more or less committed to survivalist interpretations of the evidence.

Survivalist scientists may also join forces with existing antiparadigm organizations, such as the Parapsychology Foundation. This foundation holds annual conferences, usually in Europe, of the leaders in parapsychology and a number of related fields, from physics and statistics to neurophysiology and psychokinesis. In recent years, an increasing participation and interest is observed by scientists studying NDEs and OBEs as well.

We can discern two stages in the development of counterparadigm societies. First there are those which are simply devoted to the objective study of phenomena that have not yet been adequately studied under the old paradigm. And then there are those that advocate new and relatively well-defined platforms to replace the old paradigms. This approach says to the traditional scientific community, "If you don't think our work is valuable or worthy of consideration, we shall congregate and organize with those who do." Thus, in addition to publishing books as individuals, these counterparadigm scientists can publish conference papers and reports, and set up their own research groups, which over time can take on the forms of legitimate science.

Grants and Funding

In order to establish journals and hold conferences, substantial funding becomes necessary. Some of this comes from the pockets of the participants, particularly if they are strongly devoted to their own research organizations. Even more important, however, is the legitimate funding that can be gained from government and private foundation grants. These not only enable research of a particular nature to be carried out, but also confer the appearance of respectability on the investigators. Collins and Pinch observe the trends towards legitimate funding in parapsychology:

> The strategy of the parapsychologists has been that of metamorphosis —of becoming scientists. Thus they have acquired university posts (at many American universities [also Freiburg, Utrecht, Andhra, Jaipur]), Ph.D. studentships (in three British universities), chairs (Surrey, Edinburgh), and government funding for research.[24]

Similarly, in the area of survival research, a chair has been established at the University of Virginia Medical School specifically for such investigation. Faculty of many universities are spending part of their time studying and teaching about death and dying. Dissertations on survival are becoming acceptable today, when a decade ago they would have been unthinkable.[25]

One of the problems with funding in this area is that some of the sources have less than academic connections: old ladies who wish to have their faith confirmed by science, or the Arizona prospector James Kidd, who left $300,000 to anyone who could prove the survival of the human soul with photographs![26] Would-be scientists are concerned with "laundering the funds," with appearing to receive them from already respectable sources.[27] Thus, the sociological process of scientific recognition takes into consideration both the funds and their sources in according prestige to new entrants.

Assimilation and Acceptance

In the course of becoming more "scientific," groups favoring new paradigms slowly win acceptance from organs and individuals within the traditional establishment. The process of becoming scientific, as we have seen, is not complete when the methods and thinking of the investigators have become scrupulous and objective. Rather, it is a matter of taking on the forms and trappings of an accepted science, of gaining social recognition within the limited community of these persons already considered scientists. Such acceptance of the members and findings of an out-group by in-group scientists may take any of several forms, including recognition without conversion, paradigm conversion by personal persuasion, and supersession of an old paradigm by a new one. Let us examine each of these cases, with specific reference to the growth of survival research as a scientific discipline. First, however, let us briefly review the nature of paradigms.

Kuhnian philosophers use the term paradigm to describe (1) a way of looking at and investigating the world, including both basic assumptions of how that world will fit together and of the kinds of questions that need to be answered, and (2) the particular experiments that vindicate one worldview rather than another. We shall use the term here in the former sense exclusively. The term *antiparadigmatic* thus refers to an opposition to the prevailing traditional paradigm, and not to all paradigms whatsoever. By the same token, a paradigm shift is not from error into truth, nor can we depict the battle between paradigms in such black-and-white terms. Rather, a paradigm switch is more analogous to a religious conversion, or to changing jobs. The new way of looking at the world redefines the terms and reorients problems of the "converted" scientist. The new paradigm may answer some questions better than had the old one. But it may leave other questions unanswerable which were purportedly understood under the old paradigm.

We have seen that each traditional paradigm is established and reinforced by a narrow and repetitive process of science education, which does not encourage the historical reappraisal of rival paradigms. It is thus a major first step for some scientists to admit that there might be important fields of knowledge whose investigation requires tools or methods utterly different from those now employed by modern science. It is even a more difficult step for a scientist to try to change his worldview in midstream, and be "converted" to an utterly new methodology for investigating the world. As we have seen, many scientists adamantly resist such paradigm shift throughout their lives. These individual reactions can also be seen replicated in the reactions of the scientific community as a whole. Let us now return to those reactions common from the community of established scientists towards the infant field of survival research in its stages of growth.

Recognition without Paradigm Conversion

For a generation, parapsychologists have tried without success to gain recognition from the scientific community. Douglas Dean documents some of the problems involved in this process. The first step was to form the professional Parapsychological Association (1957). Over the following decade, this association repeatedly tried to win recognition from the American Association for the Advancement of Science. It was finally admitted in 1969, following an enthusiastic endorsement speech by Margaret Mead at a meeting of the AAAS membership. Dean reports on this approach:

> The [AAAS] came to the conclusion that it [the PA] is an association investigating controversial or non-existent phenomena; however it is open in membership to critics and agnostics; and they were satisfied that it uses scientific methods of inquiry; thus that investigation can be counted as scientific. Further information has come to us that the number of AAAS fellows who are also members of the PA is not four as on the agenda, but nine.[28]

We may note several interesting factors in the legitimization process. The role of Mead's appeal cannot be overestimated. Her personal stature and persuasion had a strong effect on the membership, which had voted to keep out the PA for so long. Mead's comparison of members of the PA to anthropologists, who also claim to be scientists while not claiming to believe the myths of the people they study, was another point in the PA's favor. Furthermore, we can notice the appeal to loyalty to one's own membership. If "not four, but nine" members of the AAAS program were already PA members, this too could be taken to bespeak an acceptability and legitimacy not previously admitted. Needless to say, the PA had worked hard to get nine of its members on the program.

It is all too clear that the AAAS admission did not indicate acceptance of the conclusions of the PA's research, but simply accepted the parapsychologists' use of scientific methods. This admission to the AAAS, however, has made it substantially easier for later survivalist researchers to gain admission to other professional organizations and conferences. In particular, sections of recent national conferences on religion, psychology, and psychiatry are often devoted to discussions of survival. The fact that such national organizations admit the existence of interesting issues in the research of survival by no means implies that they agree with the ultimate importance of such problems, the survivalist answer, or the necessity of revising their own paradigms.

Thomas Kuhn analogizes the interactions between traditional scientists and paradigm-challenging scientists to a breakdown in communication. He proposes that gradual participation in the same community demands translation of problems that exist for both communities from one language game to another:

> Taking the differences between their own intra- and inter-group discourse itself as a subject for study, they can first attempt to discover the terms and locutions that, used unproblematically within each community, are nevertheless foci of trouble for inter-group discussion. . . . The availability of techniques like these does not, of course, guarantee persuasion. For most people, translation is a threatening process, and it is entirely foreign to normal science.[29]

In survival research, as well as elsewhere, the increasing use of compatible terminology, or at least learning to see the world through alternative terminologies, is part of paradigm change. We can see examples in the use of terms coined by Moody, such as *life-review* and *figure of light,* and Osis's *mood elevation,* as well as in the acronyms *OBE* and *NDE.* These terms are now widely used by the scientific community, even by those critical of the survivalist interpretations of such phenomena.

An example of an individual's gradual conversion process may be seen in the case of Marcello Truzzi. Truzzi started the *Zetetic* magazine in order to scientifically criticize paranormal literature. However, after several years of studying the material, his own position softened considerably. Truzzi then abandoned the *Zetetic* to a hard-core group which (like himself five years earlier) was committed to debunking all paranormal phenomena as unreal. He then started a new publication, the *Zetetic Scholar,* to take a "critical but objective look" at survival and other central issues in parapsychology. Truzzi says (from experience) that we cannot change science by convincing the skeptics, who are not open to such conversion in the first place, but only by slowly persuading the more liberal and open-minded members of the scientific community.[30]

Paradigm Conversion by Personal Persuasion

As not many trained scientists have actually switched their allegiance from an old paradigm to a new one, they are all the more striking for their rarity. One famous early example of a drastic switch in worldview occasioned by persistent study and persuasion is the Conan Doyle/Harry Price case. Doyle himself had been a critic of spiritualism until he began studying it, after which he became increasingly convinced of its importance and of the truth of personal survival. In his later years he wrote less fiction, and instead devoted himself almost full time to this subject. Harry Price, the scientist who spent most of his time debunking mediums, was agnostic if not hostile to the whole idea of survival. But after "Doyle himself" appeared to Price in a seance, and when other information inaccessible to the medium through normal means was revealed about the ill-fated crash of the R-101 dirigible in 1930, Price himself at last became a believer in survival.[31]

A softening in antisurvivalist posture may be noted by chronological surveys of the writings of philosophers such as C. D. Broad, Gardner Murphy, and even Antony Flew. After decades of studying survival research in order to criticize it, they became less able to declare categorically that "it just can't happen," and in Broad's words, came to feel they would be "more disappointed than surprised" if survival turned out to be the truth.

The most striking conversion is undoubtedly that of George Price, whose diatribe against ESP in 1955 we cited above. Over a period of more than ten years, Price corresponded with J. B. Rhine and his associates at Duke. In the end, Price at last became convinced of their integrity and, concomitantly, of the actual existence of forces that apparently contradict mechanistic paradigms and make sense of survival.[32]

Nonconversion and Supersession of the New Paradigm

The other side of the conversion coin is that many scientists are simply never able to re-view their world through new paradigms. Kuhn's books on scientific revolutions are littered with examples of scientists, famous in their day, who died in staunch opposition to theories that were becoming increasingly acceptable and would ultimately replace their own completely. Prince's *Enchanted Boundary* also lists a number of great scientists who would not change their minds on the survival issue even in the face of strong evidence.

Facing such intransigence, how can science ever hope to change?

Physicist Max Planck summed it up in his autobiography: "[Boltzmann's triumph over Ostwald] gave me also an opportunity to learn a fact—a remarkable one in my opinion: A new scientific truth does not triumph by convincing its opponents and making them see the light, but rather because its opponents eventually die off, and a new generation grows up that is familiar with it."[33]

Coming from a scientist who rubbed shoulders with the leaders of twentieth-century physics and philosophy, this statement is a scathing denial of the widely touted "objectivity" of scientists. Planck confirms that the reasons for theory rejection are more psychological and educational than theoretical or scientific.

To put the case a little strongly, many of the logical positivists and Skinnerian behaviorists of the 1950s and 1960s neither converted to nor consented to the new waves of psychology. But they are now becoming supplanted by a new breed of scientists who have themselves experimented with meditation and mind-altering drugs, and who can no longer accept the mechanistic philosophy of the nineteenth century and are hence much more open to the possibilities of survival research.[34] The next century may see an increasing liberalism in this area, coinciding with an increasing interest of "legitimate" young scientists in alternative paradigms which allow for the survival or reincarnation hypotheses.

Public Opinion and Scientific Change

One further factor is the effect of public opinion on scientific investigations and determination of the boundaries of "legitimate science." Of course, this is more important in free than in totalitarian countries. We have already noted that the scientific community may use charges of occultism or "playing to the vulgar crowd" to discredit survival researchers. But a growing number of philosophers of science in the West are beginning to recognize public interest as an important element in the decision of scientific legitimacy.

Paul Feyerabend, for example, is outspoken against the tyranny of traditional scientists. He upholds the public interest in UFOs, astrology, and survival as probably having important glimpses of truth; and he repeats that the public should be the ultimate arbiter of what science studies.[35]

According to Feyerabend, this is partly because a great deal of the money of science comes out of the pockets of the taxpayers. Even more importantly, the common man is smart enough to see through the "monumental ignorance behind the most dazzling display of omniscience."[36]

Scientists disagree as to whether such issues should be left completely in the hands of laymen. The mood of a country towards its sciences, whether of apathy or of worship, has tremendous impact on the support they receive.[37] The growing literature and public awareness of NDEs and OBEs have substantially influenced the legitimation of survival research as a field of study—regardless of the final outcome and conclusions to which these scholars of survival will ultimately arrive.

We have seen that objections based on repeatability, theory requirement, and inherent probabilities are ill-founded and inadequate to impugn the value of survival research. We then turned to psychological, educational, religious, and social resistance to survival research. These types of objections do not stand as real reasons for rejecting or revising survivalist conclusions. However, they do help to explain the origins of dissent among those who have not studied carefully the issues and evidence. We demarcated four separate phases in the growth of survival studies, showing a transition from rejection or suppression to independent growth and finally to assimilation and acceptance from traditional science.

Survival research is, in principle, just as scientific as any other empirical study. On the basis of this chapter, we can understand the psychological motivations and sociological methods for the rejection of survival research by some authorities. We have seen the slow process by which the fields of parapsychology and survival research are working their way towards academic respectability. At the same time, there is always the danger of becoming associated too deeply with occult or religious movements, which would bias the direction of the research and cast doubt on the objectivity of the researchers.

In our concluding section, we shall venture some tentative conclusions to the research we have reviewed above. Of course, additional data may help to support or deny these conclusions. But the reasoning we have laid forth in the preceding sections should enable us to review any future data and objections with understanding as well as detachment.

6.

What Will the Next World Be Like?

The empirical studies we have reviewed in this book tend to show that there is an extremely wide range of experiences surrounding death. Even among civilized, literate, modern peoples, there is a tremendous variety in the nature of our personalities, consciousnesses, and experiences while alive. Similarly, there seem to be tremendous variations in the nature of the causes and situations of death as well. Therefore, it should not be too surprising to find that people report having very different experiences on different deathbeds, or in their apparition/OBE type experiences.

The Wide Range of Experiences at Death

On the whole, it is remarkable that people of such different backgrounds and body types experience such similar NDEs. Of these experiences, some may be caused by chemical changes in the dying brain, indicating nothing of the nature of a future existence. Some may have physical correlates but not necessarily physical causes. Others have no neurophysiological correlates whatsoever, but appear to be simply a different level of experience.

The question, "What is the next world like?" is too broad to answer in one breath, and the questions "What will it feel like to die?" or "Will my consciousness survive the death of my physical body?" are too specific

165

and personal to answer with assurance. Rather, we must begin by asking: What is the *range* of experiences which some humans may possibly undergo during and following their physical deaths?

This range of possible experiences has already been alluded to by scholars like Raymond Moody and Kenneth Ring, who itemize a number of "stages" through which dying people pass.[1] We have emphasized that these are not sequential steps through which everyone will pass. But each of these stages has been reported by someone, so it is quite possible that others will experience them again in the future.

When they die, many people experience a whooshing sound, or they find themselves passing through a black vortex, tunnel, or void. Some may see colorful nets, lights, and geometric imagery. Some may have veridical OBEs, seeing their bodies from outside them. Others may have dreamlike hallucinations of chemical origin and doubtful referentiality. Some may have visions of departed loved ones, holy figures, or heavenly scenery. Some of these events are at least partly neurophysiological; others are inexplicable except on the survival hypothesis.

Whether in peace or in pain, most people die without reporting any remarkable experiences or saving grace.[2] Based on the evidence alone, it seems that only a minority of dying people have OBEs or NDEs. The number reporting "memories of past lives" veridically is still far smaller. So we are not entitled to jump to the conclusion that everyone will survive death or be reborn. Rather, it seems more probable that there is a wide range in the ways different people will experience survival—if indeed they experience anything at all.[3]

It is a common theme in many books on survival that the persons' expectations determine whether and in what way their conscious experiences continue. This is the theory Price and Hick have advocated earlier.[4] It is reiterated by many mystics, religious writers, and scholars of survival.

[The afterlife] shall be a reflection of the ideas and desires held by them during their period of earth life—a dramatization of their desire-ideals of their past life. In short, the Indian really finds his "happy hunting grounds," and the other primitive peoples their particular paradises as pictured in their creeds and faiths. . . . The conception of the "golden gates" is but a little higher in the scale than that of the "happy hunting ground," for it is purely material, and reflects the ideals of a race whose desires are for glittering and costly things.[5]

This argument is also turned against the nonbeliever: "The Viking's Valhalla, the Indian's Happy Hunting Ground, could also have a real existence for a number of psyches. The convinced materialist could experience the total emptiness he anticipates after death; the only essential difference would be that he finds himself still psychically living and conscious."[6] This makes for a very "neat" theory indeed, with an ironic tinge of cosmic justice to it: if materialists want meaninglessness and emptiness at death, that is just what they shall find. This proposal is not clearly false, and it might be reworked to square with empirical studies, but as it stands, it is premature. For we have seen cases in which "convinced materialists" and atheists had "heavenly," mind-opening experiences on their deathbeds. And there are devout religious people who die in agony and report nothing, or who experience only unconsciousness while temporarily pronounced dead.[7]

It still might be true on some subtle level that at death "we experience what we believe." But it is clear that belief in a certain species of afterlife is not alone adequate to produce that experience immediately upon death. Yet it is reasonable to expect that the mental state of the dying person strongly influences subsequent conscious experience, if there is any.

We have seen that people may experience many things at death—and many people may experience nothing. Let us now think further about the nature of the postmortem state. The possibilities range from ethereal bodies to idealistic other worlds or transcendent nonpersonal (nirvanic) states.[8] In the popular religious mind, however, the most widely expected postmortem state is one of reincarnation—either in a physical body here on this earth, or in a paraphysical body in a heavenly or "resurrection" realm. Let us briefly reconsider the status of these concepts in relation to the evidence adduced above.

Reincarnation

Regardless of the trouble some Westerners may have with this concept, reincarnation has been shown to be the most reasonable hypothesis to explain verifiable memories of former lives. When children exhibit memories that could only be attributed to people now dead, and insist that they *were* those persons before they died; when they show linguistic, athletic, artistic skills and talents they could not have learned in their present life and which the deceased had had; when, at the same time, marks on their bodies correspond to marks on the bodies of the deceased—then no other hypothesis can fit the data as well as taking the children's claims at almost face value. There is a sense in which they were someone else in a former life on this earth, and now they are as they appear. Under carefully controlled conditions, cases of possession or hypnotic regression may provide similar evidence. On the basis of such combined evidence, it is most reasonable to accept that at least some people are reborn in new human bodies after their deaths in former human bodies. Theologian John Hick concludes:

> There are forms of reincarnation doctrine which may be broadly true pictures of what actually happens. It may be true, as Vedantist teaching claims, that an eternal "soul" or "higher self" lies behind a long series of incarnations. . . . Or it may be true, as Buddhist teaching claims, that "units" or "packages" of karma (as distinguished from higher selves) produce a series of persons, one of whom is me.[9]

Hick believes that persons do not evolve through a series of prehuman incarnations, but are created *ab initio ex nihilo* by God.[10] Either case is possible, but the evolutionary one is easier to square with scientific cosmology.

Christian believers in resurrection find themselves in exactly the same situation on this point. Because resurrection, like reincarnation, is not instantaneous upon death but occurs some time later, some carrier of personal identity is necessary. Consciousness alone is not enough because, if it rests, it is thereby extinguished forever. There is a gap, an interim between this life and the next embodiment, if there is one.

If we are to make any sense of personal identity at all, there must be both the process of consciousness and its ontological substrate present during this interim between incarnations. This locus of consciousness may be a vehicle or blueprint invisible to the human eye.[11] But it must exist, for if not, we would have the paradoxical situation of only paranormal memories and replica bodies with no genuinely real memories of past lives. Conversely, the existence of subtle bodies or ideal realms wherein consciousness might temporarily exist in a nonphysical state are the only ways that resurrection and/or reincarnation, as well as other forms of survival, can be meaningfully understood.

An Apparitional World

In our study of OBEs and apparitions, we found that apparitions were most often produced by the dreams or projections of the consciousness of the person who corresponded to the apparition. We saw that people having veridical OBEs perceived the physical world from perspectives and places distant from their physical bodies, and that devices or animals could sometimes detect a "presence" in that same place. If purposeful apparitions are produced and detectable in such ways and show no significant differences from apparitions of the dead, then it seems reasonable to impute the same causal process to apparitions of the dead, especially when they provide information and motives unknown to any but the deceased. We may then assert that the deceased person was in some sense dreaming or projecting consciousness to an area where his or her apparition was perceived.

The similarity between this theory and that of traditional ghosts or spirits may lead to its immediate rejection by hasty critics. In fact, this discarnate body theory is the easiest way to make sense of individual identity and personality after death. This theory would suggest that humans have two "bodies": a physical, material body, and an invisible, ethereal or "astral" body. At death, the ethereal or astral body leaves the corpse, as it may do temporarily during OBEs. Sometimes its leaving the corpse may be perceived by people attending the deathbed. In other cases, it may appear to loved ones in other locations, as if to inform them of the death or counsel them on some matter of importance to the deceased.

Far from invalidating the theory, this problem of spirits is the problem of human destiny after death.[12] And such a theory of invisible bodies need not conflict with modern science. Such bodies might well evolve through processes paralleling the evolution of our physical bodies from lower animals.[13] They may be the sorts of entities so commonly encountered in Indian literature as the *linga sharīra* or the Buddhist *ālaya-vijñāna*—a subtle body of consciousness.[14]

Such a theory of normally invisible bodies might be made completely compatible with modern non-Newtonian physics, for "even the grossest materialism would have to allow that it is conceivable that the seat of consciousness and personality is not the physical brain after all but an 'astral' brain that can survive the death of the physical body."[15] Some materialists might wish to disagree with this statement, but their disagreement, as we have seen above, would be based upon the faulty assumption that modern science has identified and understood everything in the universe. In fact, it is only one system in a long history of systems that have needed continual revision. "We are never entitled to declare that a certain effect must be nonphysical just because it happens to be incompatible with any certain system of physics."[16]

Ethereal Bodies Reconcilable with Materialism

There are at least three ways in which invisible bodies might be reconciled with modern materialism: they might be some form of yet-unstudied particle or wave-like energy substance; they might be analogized to force fields; or they might exist in other dimensions which sometimes interact with or interpenetrate our own.

Particle wave theory. It may be that discarnate bodies are made of as yet inadequately studied particle or wave-like stuff. This theory was first formulated by F. W. H. Myers eighty years ago. Myers speaks of a meta-ethereal universe "which appears to lie after or beyond the ether; the spiritual world in which the soul exists."[17] This theory was developed by Gardner Murphy into what he called the "Myers-Newbold theory," a system he feels is midway between traditional Spinozistic monism and Cartesian dualism.[18] The existence of an unstudied ethereal order is somewhat demonstrated by psychic phenomena and supported by such researchers as G. N. M. Tyrrell.[19]

Other investigators have proposed various names for the wave/particles which might account for psychic phenomena and make sense of survival of invisible consciousness after death. Adrian Dobbs calls such particles *psi-trons,* and attributes to them an imaginary mass with the status of other yet-unidentified imaginary subatomic particles.[20] Whately Carington coins the term *psychons* to refer to such particles which interact primarily with consciousness and might survive death;[21] C. D. Broad uses the term *psi factor* in similar ways.[22] William Roll, emphasizing the survival aspect over the psychic aspect of this material, calls them *theta agents,*[23] while R. H. Thouless and others call them *shin* after the Hebrew character.[24]

There are three points of note here: (1) there may exist types of matter/particles/waves which we have not yet adequately studied, (2) the fact that they have not yet been studied by science does not make their existence any the less probable, (3) they may help to explain psychic phenomena and apparitions before death and to make sense of what survives after death. This ethereal stuff may be analogous to other wavelengths of color or radioactive rays that had not been discovered until the beginning of this century. The more we come to understand our universe as a continuum of waves, rather than as discrete, billiard ball-like entities, the more plausible it appears that there are parts of this energy continuum which have escaped scientific study heretofore. The notion of such subtle matter would not only make sense of survival, but would tally well with the Asian worldview that there are sorts of matter other than those which we normally perceive with unaided eyes.[25]

Force fields. Alternatively, the "body" which survives might be analogous to a force field—an invisible organizing principle—which assists in the interaction of consciousness and body during life and structures some kind of body-consciousness after death. J. L. Randall is among the major proponents of this view, holding that psi-factors are like magnetic fields selectively bounded by material fields.[26] J. B. Rhine also prefers to think in terms of energy over matter: "Back of the phenomena of psi must exist an energy that interoperates with and interconverts to those other energetic states already familiar to physics. Psi energy is imperceptible by the sense organs and does not in any way yet discovered function within the frameworks of time and space and mass, and yet does lawfully operate."[27]

Yet another, more recent, version of the force field theory is the so-called holon or holographic theory. It was first proposed by Karl Pribram as an explanation of memory systems in the brain, and picked up rather uncritically to account for phenomena ranging from apparitions to survival.[28] In brief, a hologram is an image formed when in-phase laser light is shined through a film on which the interference patterns from similar sources have already been refracted and recorded. Holograms resemble the brain in only one respect: when a portion of either is destroyed, the images stored therein are sometimes retained in toto, unaffected by local damage.[29]

Aside from this curious similarity, Pribram has not shown in what sense the brain could resemble a hologram, for there are no films and no laser beams scanning within the brain. Ferguson and Ring, however, expound that this brain theory somehow gives us access to a whole new "realm of meaningful, primary pattern reality that transcends time and space."[30] It is unclear how the brain relates to this reality, nor are we justified in calling either such realms "holographic reality."[31] If such a theory were developed into a workable system, it would fall closer to fields than waves or particles, and yet it is still sensorially connected to our construction of the physical realm.[32]

The energy-field theory is somewhat more problematic than the "straight" wave-particle theory for several reasons. At present, we do not really understand how fields like magnetic, gravitational, or subatomic force fields work. We simply know that there appear to be regularities on those levels, and we name the domains in which they work *fields*. To adopt field theory at this time would be just another case of "explaining" one unknown with reference to another but feeling more comfortable because of the analogy.

Ultimately, of course, there may be some sense in which matter and energy fields are interconvertible. If so, then both theories may be correct. At present, the contrast between waves-and-particles and energy fields is a useful distinction. The majority of survival theorists speak in terms of wave-particle models. But we should bear in mind that these are not the only possible contenders, and that field theory might also make sense of survival without contradicting science.

Fourth-dimension theory. Yet another way of explaining the survival of invisible bodies by a minor revision of present physical theory is the admission of a fourth spatial dimension. Such theories are sometimes called fifth-dimension theories by those who count time as a fourth. But time is clearly not the same sort of dimension as the first three physical dimensions, nor is it clear that any other dimension has temporal aspects to it. We shall speak of a fourth dimension as referring to a physical realm or dimension (*not* time) in addition to the three dimensions in which we consciously live. Such dimension theories are not lacking in proponents either.

In the early part of this century, physicist Ernst Mach considered the fourth spatial dimension as a purely mathematical concept that would also explain the sudden disappearance or appearance of objects in this world, if it occurred.[33] Peter Ouspensky made some rather wild speculations along this line[34] before Hornell Hart first applied dimension theory to psychic phenomena in 1953.[35] Hart's work failed to distinguish between purely mathematical constructs and the metaphorical conceptions of other dimensions that are not unequivocally identifiable with mathematical versions.[36] More recently, Herbert Benson worked out a version of the fourth dimension which would make sense of both psychic phenomena and physical systems like tunnel diodes.[37] A growing number of physicists are inclined to accept the possibility of other dimensions, or "hyperspace," analogous to the dimensional system in which we live, but either inaccessible to or invisibly interpenetrating our own.[38]

Such theories would also lead to the suggestion that the other realms seen by people temporarily dead may be located in other dimensions, into which we can enter only by penetrating a dimensional tunnel between this and the next. Another dimension may operate on different time frequencies than our own and enable objects to freely enter and leave our own three dimensions, which can be perceived from that dimension as we would perceive a "flatland," but perhaps lacking some physical aspects.[39] If there is one other spatial dimension, then there may be any number of "planes," each perpendicular to the plane in which we live, each providing a realm of existence for its inhabitants which need not contradict the geography of any other such realm. To use Hart's crude analogy, it is rather like the fact that the dreams of people all sleeping in the same room need not invalidate or conflict with anyone else's.[40]

If they can be adequately formulated, dimension theories will have tremendous explanatory power and implications. At present, however, we know so little about other dimensions or how we might access them—and about whether mathematical dimensions are in fact similar to psychic fourth dimensions—that we must let the matter rest until physics, electronics, and other branches of science come up with further evidence. In the meantime, we may admit that a fourth dimension might be possible. We may be unconsciously living in it right now, or able to move to it at death, given the proper circumstances. In any case, the worldviews just mentioned do not destroy but rather expand physicists' conceptions of the world.

If there are other forms of matter, waves, energy, fields, or dimensions, why is it that we are so unconscious of them? This question may be leveled as a rhetorical attempt to discount the probabilities of there existing such entities. More serious examination, however, opens up a deeper understanding of the ways we view humans and the universe.

Humans cannot exhaustively understand their universe with their senses alone. Not only can we not see ultraviolet or infrared, hear dog whistles or bat calls, but we are just beginning to expand our understanding of the electromagnetic spectrum in this twentieth century. We have used our intellects and intuitions gradually to understand a small part of our universe, but in terms of detecting the range of possible waves and dimensions, we are but terribly primitive physical organisms.

Many philosophers believe that our brains might be inherently capable of receiving more information than they do—but that the opacity of our senses to other phenomena has practical value. Immanuel Kant reasoned that the body was not the cause of our thinking, but rather a condition restrictive of it.[41] In his essay "Human Immortality," William James developed the idea that the brain was a restrictive filter of reality.[42] Building on Henri Bergson's ideas, Malcolm Moncrieff put the theory of sense-limitation in an evolutionary context: "The function of the sense organs is to restrict or canalize the clairvoyant powers which every sentient organism has, and to limit them . . . by shutting out what is biologically irrelevant."[43]

This may be one reason we cannot normally see the subtle material forms primitives and schizophrenics claim to see, or sense the myriad psychic impulses that may be whirling around us—because they are not conducive to our effective functioning in this material world.

Forty years ago, Ryle argued that the mind was nothing more than a computer-like set of actions and tendencies. He called the concept of mind a "category mistake," and he attempted to exorcise from common language the concept of the "ghost in the machine" controlling our brains.[44] Only a few years had passed before Sir John Eccles could answer, from his studies of brain physiology, that the brain is "precisely the sort of thing that a ghost might operate."[45] Charles Tart has more boldly propounded that our brains and decision-making functions are governed not by sensual and chemical inputs, but by psychic and telepathic forces, especially by the nonphysical mind exercising telekinesis on the brain.[46] Lawrence LeShan theorizes that the brain acts as a transducer between levels of reality (e.g., physical reality, dream reality, clairvoyant reality) and that field theory enables us to understand the brain, mind-body interaction, and survival as well.[47] The evidence surveyed on OBEs and apparitions in particular enables us to propose that subtle bodies might exist and play a part in survival. Harrison proposes that

> Apparition bodies . . . have the advantage of not being visible to everybody, which could explain why we cannot see people in heaven or hell. Since apparitions do not exclude material objects from the space which they appear to occupy, there would be no difficulty about finding room for them. . . . This suggests the possibility of a community of people with apparition bodies communicating by auditory apparition words or apparition gestures. . . . The difference between a real body and an apparition body becomes something like one of degree.[48]

These statements are not to be taken as authority that such realms of apparitions do in fact exist. Rather, they are mentioned to show that some scientists are comfortable with these concepts. The evidence has already been supplied in our previous sections, and it is not refuted by modern physics. The existence of such realms is similarly asserted by Hindus and Mahayana Buddhists. An apparitional survival world (or worlds) might contain body-like structures, images, memory, and continuity. Thus it might make sense of survival in a way that even the positivists would not object to.

Astral Bodies are Not Enough

A couple of cautionary observations are in order here. First, the existence of subtle matter or fields does not in itself simplify the mind-body problem. Even if there is an "astral body," it is not itself equal to consciousness. We are still faced with the unanswerable question of their interaction, as C. D. Broad realized:

> There are plenty of fairly well-attested facts which afford prima facie empirical evidence of the ghost in the machine theory, if ghost is used in its proper sense . . . astral traveling, out-of-the-body experiences, haunting, bilocation, materialization, etc. . . . We shall then have to consider, in the case of each living person, *two* relationships, viz., (1) the relation of his mind to his ghostly or astral body, and (2) the relation of the latter to his ordinary, physical body.[49]

Thus, astral-type bodies are a significant contribution to the survival question, but they in no way solve the traditional mind-body problem. This humbling point should not be forgotten.

Second, the existence of an astral body is still inadequate as a description of survival. As H. D. Lewis has put it, the assurance that his astral body would continue to exist is as of little comfort as the assurance that his bones would not deteriorate. As long as astral bodies are not themselves equal to consciousness, but merely a carrier of it, they do not guarantee the sort of survival we seek. It is equally possible that some astral bodies continue for some time like corpses without continuing consciousness.

It is the conscious aspects of the astral body that are important to us, not the astral body by itself. But we are still far from knowing much about the association of consciousness and the body. Although material and astral bodies may be used by humans to identify one another, and they provide convenient domains in which we can interact, it would be just as wrong to *reduce* humanhood to an astral body as to a physical body.[50]

Thus, we are not really concerned with ethereal survival unless it is somehow fundamentally mental. Our studies of OBEs and apparitions provide some indication that their structures are fundamentally mental in a deeper sense than our bodies. People reporting their OBEs, for example, say that their mere volition could bring about the performance of the desired action. Apparitions may appear fully clad within locked rooms. What provides this clothing is surely not the existence of ethereal hatmakers and boot factories, but the power of the mind of the projector (as in the case where a mother sees her son dying before her in his bloody fatigues).

Thus there is a sense in which the subtle or apparitional realm is more psychically malleable, more open to direct volitional influence than our present physical universe appears to be. To carry the argument to its ultimate conclusion, we might assert that the psychic waves, fields, or ether in which apparitions appear to exist and function may be in some way intermediary between mental activity and physical observability. While this intriguing hypothesis accords with the evidence we have presented, we cannot say much more about which theory (waves/fields/dimensions) best accounts for apparitions at this point.

An Idealist Next World

A Nonmaterialist Hypothesis?

To be meaningful, any sense of survival in a next world must include consciousness, and perhaps memory and volition as primary characteristics. The physical body will not live after death, and we have seen that even an astral body living after death will be quite meaningless unless it is intimately associated with consciousness. Since it is the mind or consciousness whose survival we are considering, it need not surprise us if the "realms" of which it is conscious after the decease of the physical body are also mind-dependent, or idealistic. (The term *idealism* here refers not to the "starry-eyed" sort of idealism found in people with ideals, but rather to the philosophical idealism that holds that the underlying essence of all things is not material, but idea or ideational.) Many thinkers have supported this suggestion.

G. N. M. Tyrrell and Ellis, among others, have argued that idealism makes the best sense of "other worlds" in their relation to this world.[51] Mundle and Beloff cogently argue that if ESP evidence counts in favor of dualism, then it counts even more strongly for Berkeley's forms of idealism.[52] In a Berkeleyan idealism, there is no problem of how minds interact with matter at all, since experience of "matter" is merely certain kinds of ideas in mind, and mind-to-mind interaction is taken as fundamental. Gardner Murphy has found that even physicists are coming closer to the acceptance of a Berkeleyan idealism,[53] and this claim is at least superficially substantiated by Lawrence LeShan's surveys.[54] In accounting for the objects of NDE visions, Kenneth Ring reaches similar conclusions:

> Just where do the landscapes, the flowers, the physical structures, and so forth come from? In what sense are they "real"? . . . This is a realm that is created by interacting thought structures. . . . Since individual minds "create" this world (out of thoughts and images), this reality reflects, to a degree, the "thought-structures" of individuals used to the world of physical reality. . . . "The world of light" is indeed a mind-created world fashioned of interacting (or interfering) thought patterns. Nevertheless, that world is fully as real-seeming as is our physical world.[55]

Let us push Ring's suggestions one step further. Why is it that people in cultures around the world have "religious figure" experiences, but those religious figures vary from culture to culture? Americans tend to see Jesus, while the Indians see Yamaraj, and the Japanese see a Bodhisattva. We saw above that these experiences cannot be reduced to, or interpreted merely in terms of, personal or cultural expectations. Yet the cultural "coloring" given to the image is clear.

Or again, why do people in cultures around the world have different "barrier" experiences? Japanese see a river they cannot cross; some Englishmen a wide moor or stone wall; some Arabs a burning desert; others, a cliff or deep chasm. The meaning of all these symbols is the same: you may not cross this place and return again whence you came. But the images are those each person can easily understand from within his or her own cultural background.

One possibility is this: there are no physical figures, no bodies, and no physical barriers in the next realm of experience. But there are noumenal beings, guides of compassion, and places from which one may not return after crossing into. We, who have learned to experience everything with our visual senses, add visual imagery to these ultimately nonphysical people, places, and experiences. So naturally, the visible imagery is that which we can envision, just like the imagery we project in our dreams. Yet there is a common underlying noumenal basis for these experiences of divine guidance or a barrier to irreversible crossing, unlike purely personal dreams.

We noted earlier that at least one possible afterlife scenario is idealistic. Idealism could also be true of ethereal realms, and even of this material world, as Bishop George Berkeley has cogently argued. John Hick concluded that Berkeleyan idealism made the best sense of resurrection in future worlds. The major differences between this world (if it is idealistic) and an idealistic next world are in the degree of apparent objectivity—of the environment's imperviousness to human volition—rather than in the nature or kind of "stuffs" composing this universe and the next. Hick himself wrestles with this problem without really resolving it: "Given a Berkeleyan account of a postmortem world (or worlds), we must go on to ask why this should not also apply to our present world. . . . Why should this world differ from any other worlds in fundamental character?"[56]

Hick concedes that an idealist view of this world would make equal sense, and says that the only reason for not adopting an idealist view is "the assumption that Berkeley's theory is not true of this world." It would be more philosophically consistent and aesthetically pleasing to apply the idealistic model to this world as well, if we really believe that other worlds will prove to be so. This is precisely what numerous Buddhist and Indian philosophical schools would contend is the case. In the nineteenth century, Arthur Schopenhauer, F. H. Bradley, and Mary Baker Eddy also showed how idealistic interpretations of the universe make good sense, each in their own way.

The idea that the "next world" has idea-based images and perceptions receives some support from psychologists as well as philosophers and NDE researchers. All agree that such an idealism makes consistent sense, both of the mechanisms of various psychic phenomena and of the "scenery" of the next world in NDEs. Such an idealism is also in keeping with the suggestions of meditators and mystics in both Western and Eastern traditions. It would appear that such predictions of an idealistic next world need not conflict with the physicists' conceptions of this world, since this world and the next are fundamentally distinct realms. But how could we ever know that the next world is in fact idealistic? Are such claims subject in any way to the sorts of verificationist/falsificationist principles we want to apply to statements about this world?

The confirmation of the idealist nature of the next world need not seem so impossible as the question might presuppose. Further investigations of just the sort we have considered in this study (OBEs NDEs, etc.) may yield additional facts that tend to confirm or deny the idealist hypothesis. Moreover, if the Buddhists are correct that mysticism gives previews of the same realms that are visible at death, then we need not wait until death but can conduct other sorts of research with living meditating subjects.[57] Of course, we might have to devise new methodologies of science to investigate a realm that is in essence capable of being experienced but mind-dependent and nonmaterial.

One scientist to take this proposal seriously is Charles Tart. He has suggested that we should recognize ASCs (altered states of consciousness) as giving insights into other idealistic realities. Tart advocates research using teams of people who would volunteer to explore the realms of the mind much as we now explore the sea or the stratosphere. They would be trained in methods of reporting and objectivity, and learn to verbally report experiences as they were having them, or to remember them in such ways that they could be recorded immediately on return to waking consciousness and "this world." They could be given carefully controlled doses of drugs known to produce ASCs or rely solely on their natural meditative abilities to achieve altered states, if they showed talents in that direction. Tart knows that the public is not receptive to such proposals at the moment, and he is also aware of the dangerous side effects of some hallucinogens.

However, the important philosophical point is that we can make a cogent case for the scientific study of ideational realms through altered states of mind, and whether his program is adopted or not, its canons and principles harmonize with those of modern science.[58]

That we should be able to construct a "geography" of idealistic landscapes, while mind-boggling to many Westerners, is nothing new to India. There Patanjali's Yoga system, the *Visuddhimagga* of the Abhidharmists, the *Meditation Sutras* of the Pure Land sects, and the *Tibetan Book of the Dead*—to name but a few—are step-by-step guides to achieving other states and experiencing other realms. They presuppose that the practitioners will be able to verify the teachings for themselves through discipline and practice.

If a program like Tart's were ever adopted, we might gradually learn what psychological, religious, and physical variables contribute importantly to enabling or producing visions of what nature, and how we can better compare the visions of different subjects. It might even become possible to take intersubjective trips, where two or more people experience themselves going together to another realm, just as it is possible to have shared dreams. In addition to more extensive studies of NDEs, studies of meditative or altered-state access to idealistic realms might give verification to statements about the status and contents of such realms. Thus, the statement that the next world is an idea-based realm is in principle verifiable, and not subject to the materialists and positivists charges of "meaninglessness."

Personhood and Personal Identification

Several major objections are leveled against any theory of survival that no longer seems to require physical bodies, and against talks about mind-dependent realms. Let us lay these skeptical objections to rest.

Solipsism. One common argument against survival in an idealist next world is that such experiences would be inescapably solipsistic or subjective, lacking any physical basis. Numerous responses are available to this challenge. In the first place, the nature of the next world is the way it is, and it cannot be changed or argued against simply because we would rather have it another way. If the idealistic life after death were indeed solipsistic, it might take a while to discover the fact, but our desire that it be otherwise would not necessarily make it so. It is possible that the phase of solipsism after death is only a temporary stage, prior to encountering other beings, or that the combined thoughts of minds on roughly the same "level" might produce environments common to an entire set of such minds.[59] There still might be an aspect of subjectivity in the sense that elements of private experience remain, that the other-minds problem remains a real one, and perhaps that some of the experiences one projects in the presence of other minds are not fully experienced by the others.

On the other hand, there might be considerable intersubjectivity. The fact that this intersubjectivity is influenced by the experiencers themselves is analogous to Werner Heisenberg's discovery that the very act of investigating changes the object investigated.[60] The difference is one of degree, not of kind. The demand that the external world be somehow "objective" is increasingly giving way, even in the "hard" sciences; objectivity, in short, is now conceived of as intersubjectivity. Intersubjective norms are not agreed to by the members of a society because they are objective; they are objective because they are jointly accepted.[61]

Thus, the naïve materialistic sort of "objectivity" presupposed by the objection concerning solipsism is not even thought to be attainable in this world. So its absence in the next world need prove no obstacle to the reality of that realm. On the contrary, if the realm entered at death is indeed an image projection of numerous minds in concert, there might be a distinct feeling of material reality and intersubjectivity. So the argument from solipsism (1) does not keep idealist worlds from existing, (2) need not apply to an idealistic next world any more than to an idealist view of this world, and (3) presupposes desiderata which are not attainable even in this world.

Identification. Another commonly raised pseudoproblem is that people in an idealistic next world might be unidentifiable, since it would lack "real" bodies. On the other hand, there is nothing inherent in the notion of an idealistic world that need make it any less public, less identifiable, or less real-seeming than the world we presently inhabit. Berkeley's dialogues well illustrate that an idealistic world may include perceived bodies, persons, and sensations of all sorts. The only significant difference is that their underlying essence would be not material but spiritual or ideational. It is possible that all the apparently "real" bodies in this world are just so many impressions in our minds kept harmoniously coordinated by God or by a law of psychic nature. Similarly, it is quite possible that an idealistic "next world" might have real-seeming bodies and perceptions. These might be the projections of the minds in those next worlds, individual or collective, and they might behave according to different principles, lacking material or wave-form substrates.[62] Once we realize that perceivable bodies are possible in an idealistic universe, the problem of identification is no more.

Another pseudoproblem we should lay to rest is A. J. Ayer's old claim that disembodied minds are logically possible after death, but that they would not constitute persons.[63] In other words, it is admitted that survival of my mind is possible, but not that this mind would equal me. We may respond with two related observations.

In part, the question may be a purely semantic one. Let us imagine a situation in which Ayer finds himself continuing to have experiences: he feels his perceptual locus drifting out of his head, looks down on his body and hears a doctor pronouncing him dead, feels himself pass through a dark tunnel, and upon arrival in "heavenly fields" is greeted by his grandmother. A bit of mental experimenting—moving and stopping, telepathizing and getting telepathic messages—might serve to demonstrate that his new existence is decidedly mental and idealistic in a way his former existence has never been. Ayer could now choose for himself either of two lines of reasoning:

1. I know that this body I perceive is not physical in the way that my former body was. And I know that the former kind of physical body is essential to the definition of a person. Therefore, I am no longer a person—but a mind, spirit, fantasy, or what-have-you!

Or

2. I no longer have a physical body of the sort I had previously. But I still continue to remember my previous self and my experiences. I am

continuing to have experiences, desires, and even quirks of personality. I guess that I was wrong that physical bodies are essential to selfhood. For I still exist, and I should like to call myself a person still, even though I now lack a gross physical body.

One line of reasoning leads to the conclusion that persons cannot survive bodily death; the other, that they can. But nothing important in the situation has changed except the definition of the term *person,* and our ability to apply that word to the new sort of existence in which survival is experienced. Then the argument that persons do not continue to exist after death is really quite hollow, for it says nothing about what really happens, but only makes a stipulation about how we use certain words. Murphy puts it this way: "The question for science should be not, 'Is this Myers or not?' but 'What are the similarities between this evidence [or state] and Myers?' The question is not, does a physical person exist after death, but what are the similarities between what exists after death and what exists now."[64]

The characteristics of memory, continuity, and consciousness can certainly be maintained in an idealist next world. Ayer tries to define *persons* so that what survives would not be "persons," because they lack physical bodies. But this simply skirts the main issue and does not deny significant survival except in the obvious and trivial sense that the body does not survive.

There is another type of survival however, to which such criticisms might apply with greater force. That is, if there is some sort of depersonalized, transcendental, nirvana-like state in which memory and volition as well as bodies are eradicated, there might be more serious reason to ask whether such survival is truly personal. It might be personal in the sense that a stream of consciousness might continue distinct from other streams of consciousness; yet without memory or volition, such minds might not merit the label of *person* in the way we are accustomed to using the term. Such arguments do not in any way diminish the likelihood of such states existing. Rather, they make such a prospect simply more or less appealing according to one's religious predilections, and they approach the boundaries of the indiscussable.

On the other hand, it is possible that death may represent the end of all personal limits and boundaries, without necessarily being the end of conscious experience altogether. A radical removal of the limitations of consciousness might lead either to a sense of union with a "collective unconscious," to an "explosion" or expansion of consciousness into trans-personal states, or into other states of disembodied consciousness difficult to depict or identify. This theory is central to the Buddhist theory of nirvana. But in the Buddhist view, this is not automatic; people with normal desires and cravings will soon be reborn into other bodies, and only those most transcendent and desireless of persons can achieve a personless nirvanic state at death.

Michael Grosso, Gardner Murphy, and C. D. Broad see the depersonalization of mind at death as an inevitable consequence of the loss of bodily restrictions. Harry Price and John Hick, by contrast, also recognize the possibility of transcendent nirvanic states after death, but they deny that they will be automatic. Instead, they hold, these states must be achieved after much further spiritual development. Hick concludes his massive study of survival with this prediction:

> In progressively "higher" worlds, . . . self-protective egoity withers away, so that the individual's series of lives culminates in a last life beyond which there is no further embodiment but instead entry into the common Vision of God, or nirvana, or the eternal consciousness of the *atman* in its relation to Ultimate Reality.[65]

The End, A New Beginning

In previous chapters, we have consistently advocated that the variety inherent both in the human condition and in the experience of death implies that not everyone should be expected to experience the same thing —if anything at all—at death. Speaking purely from the available evidence, and relying only on principles of induction, we may arrive at least at the following tentative conclusions.

Some people will be reborn into other human bodies. They will be most likely to remember their former lives if their deaths were violent and if their culture does not suppress such reports. Except for cases in which young children are reborn, there will normally be a period of years intervening between reincarnations. (No one reports being reborn immediately upon physically dying.) In rare instances, spirits may manifest themselves "incarnate" through the medium of channeling or spirit possession.

Some people will survive in ethereal bodies after the decay of their physical bodies. The fact that most apparitions of living people are produced by the people they resemble suggests that most apparitions of the dead are also produced by the people they resemble. This case is strengthened because apparitions sometimes convey information or motivations known only to the deceased. Apparitions are most intelligible on the assumption that there are other forms of matter, fields, or dimensions physics has not yet studied. To persons surviving in ethereal bodies, it will feel as if their locus of conscious thought and perception was released from their heads at death and they are now living in a permanent out-of-body experience.

Some people will find themselves passing away into realms that are ideational or idealistic in their ontology. While some of the scenery and images perceived in such states will be unique to each individual, other features may be intersubjectively perceived by many consciousnesses. Such idealistic realms need feel no less physical for their lack of material substrate or their violation of "laws of matter." An idealist model best accounts for the phenomena of meditative and deathbed visions.

It is possible that, at some point after death, some people may experience selfless transpersonal or transcendent (nirvanic) states. However, we lack the appropriate language and experience to characterize such states further, and since they are superpersonal, they go beyond the present discussion of personal survival.

Oversimplified, then, our conclusion is this: there is good evidence that some persons have survived death in the past and, by induction, that some people now living will continue to have conscious personal experiences after bodily death. In the measured phrasing of philosopher C. J. Ducasse: "The balance of the evidence so far obtained is on the side of the reality of survival, and in the best cases, of survival not merely of life on earth, but survival also of the most significant capacities of the human mind, and of the continuing exercise of these."[66] Ducasse arrived at these conclusions after careful studies of his own forty years ago. The best evidence for survival has just emerged from the research of the past ten years, and it fully supports his judgment. Our conclusions should be tempered by several important caveats on the limitations of this study.

If there is even a fair chance that consciousness may survive, we should cultivate our minds, which will be more lasting, rather than seeking first material goods, status, wealth, etc. Many near-death experiencers have gained new visions of morality through their life-review experiences. They emphasize the importance of thinking of others, or of the community of life on the planet. We need not wait for death to take their ideas seriously.

Survival is an issue of immense ethical importance. It may cause us to rethink the ways we look at abortion, euthanasia, suicide, or the "right to die." The implications are very important for future studies. Furthermore, many wise and spiritual men of many cultures have stressed that there is a moral nature to the universe and that this will be more clearly discerned in the next world. If so, this too has very important implications for how we live and think here and now.

There are other issues that are particularly important for future studies to confirm or falsify, and which may affect our conclusions here. More rigorous studies of the mechanisms of ESP are essential. Discovery of such mechanisms might lead to alternative (nonsurvivalist) explanations for some of the phenomena we have surveyed. Conversely, they might suggest that the phenomena indicative of survival do not use the same mechanisms, further invalidating so-called super-ESP theories.

We need more extensive and rigorous studies of NDEs, particularly with regard to physical causes and cultural influences. Further published proof of brain inactivity prior to resuscitation and reporting of NDEs is important to set straight the widespread belief that experience of any kind is impossible without cranial activity. Such studies would literally refute the already obsolescent mind-brain identity theory. Comparative studies of atheists, Buddhists, or unlettered jungle tribesmen may also give us important data on how universal deathbed visions really are, and to what extent they are a product of cultures that more or less consciously believe and expect them.

We also need a deeper understanding of altered states of consciousness. Whether altered states give perspectives into other realities or merely image the psychological state of the subject, there is much to be learned from such research. Someday, perhaps Tart's plan for universities or laboratories of people researching meditative states—pooling, comparing, and analyzing their findings—may become a reality. Then we shall learn much more about the nonphysical "geographies" of the minds in which we live. In the meantime, we still have the option to attempt to explore such realms individually, preferably under the careful supervision of trained masters.

The question of personal survival of physical death is actually the question of the nature of personhood, and the relations of consciousness to reality and to the body with which it normally seems affiliated. One in ten people may give us usable evidence about the nature of survival on their deathbeds—once in their lifetime. If mystics are correct that glimpses of other realities, including the afterlife, may be gained through disciplined meditations in this life, then this offers us another course worthy of investigation. This theory that meditation allows insights into other realms is certainly not nonreferential nonsense; it is a path which may be practiced and evaluated on its own merits.

Many sincere religious individuals may be disappointed in the limited scope of these conclusions. They may claim to know more than we have demonstrated here, without the need for such dry philosophical analyses. Conversely, many other people may reject these conclusions for sociological and psychological reasons, as we have seen. This study, however, has adduced the insights of field researchers and logicians, and of physicists and psychologists, to rigorously demonstrate that several sorts of personal survival of bodily death are probable.

The probability that persons shall survive bodily death does not make this world any less important, nor mean that we can escape present troubles through suicide. Death remains a painful and final parting from everything on this world. None of us can predict with certainty when our journey will end, or when we must change planes. It is up to us to make the most of each hour on the way, to live so that we can pass on with no regrets, regardless of what awaits us.

NOTES

The following is a list of abbreviations for the journals that have been cited in the notes:

IJPP *International Journal of Parapsychology*
IJPR *International Journal for the Philosophy of Religion*
JAMA *Journal of the American Medical Association*
JASPR *Journal of the American Society for Psychical Research*
JNMD *Journal of Nervous and Mental Disease*
JPP *Journal of Parapsychology*
JSPR *Journal of the Society for Psychical Research* (London)
PSPR *Proceedings of the Society for Psychical Research*

Chapter 1: Proof of Reincarnation?

1. Ian Stevenson, *Twenty Cases Suggestive of Reincarnation*, 2d ed. (Charlottesville: University Press of Virginia, 1974); cf. Martin Ebon, *Reincarnation in the Twentieth Century* (New York: New American Library, 1967), pp. 70–71.

2. H. N. Banerjee and Will Oursler, *Lives Unlimited: Reincarnation East and West* (New York: Doubleday, 1974), p. 160.

3. Nils O. Jacobson, *Life Without Death?* trans. Sheila La Farge (New York: Delacorte, 1974), pp. 199–200.

4. Cf. Rhea A. White, *Déjà Vu: A Bibliography.* (Dix Hills, N.Y.:

Parapsychology Sources of Information, 1989).

5. Arthur W. Osborn, *The Expansion of Awareness* (Wheaton, Ill.: Quest Books, 1967), pp. 98–99.

6. K. N. Jayatilleke, *Survival and Karma in Buddhist Perspective* (Kandy, Sri Lanka: Buddhist Publishing Society, 1969).

7. Erlendur Haraldsson and Ian Stevenson, "A Communicator of the Drop-In Type in Iceland," *JASPR* 64, no. 1 (1975): 33ff. On channeling, see Henry Gordon, *Channeling into the New Age: The "Teachings" of Shirley MacLaine and Other Such Gurus: An Unauthorized Edition,* (Buffalo, N.Y.: Prometheus, 1988); cf. also Robin Westen, *Channelers: A New Age Directory* (New York: Putnam, 1988).

8. T. K. Oesterreich, *Possession, Demoniacal and Other,* trans. D. Ibberson (New York: University Books, 1966), p. 207, citing Jacob Fromer, *Ghetto-Dämmerung* (Berlin: Schuster & Loeffler, 1911), pp. 64ff.

9. Dr. Weir Mitchell, "The Case of Mary Reynolds," in vol. 1 of *Transactions of the College of Physicians of Philadelphia,* 4 April 1888, cited in William James, *Principles of Psychology* (New York: Holt, 1890), p. 381.

10. E. W. Stevens, *The Watseka Wonder* (Chicago: Religio-Philosophical Publishing House, 1887), also in James, *Principles,* p. 397.

11. C. J. Ducasse, *A Critical Examination of the Belief in a Life After Death* (Springfield, Ill.: Charles C. Thomas, 1961), pp. 171–74.

12. A. Lemaître, "Fritz Algar," *Archives du Psychologie,* vol. 5 (n.p., 1906), pp. 85 ff.

13. Cornelius Tabori, "The Case of Iris Farczady," trans. Paul Tabori, *IJPP* 9, no. 3 (1967): 223–26.

14. C. T. K. Chari, "Paranormal Cognition, Survival, and Reincarnation," *JASPR* 56, no. 4 (1962): 160.

15. Morey Bernstein, *The Search for Bridey Murphy* (New York: Doubleday, 1956).

16. Ducasse, *Critical Examination,* pp. 276–99.

17. Arthur Guirdham, *The Cathars and Reincarnation* (London: Spearman, 1970).

18. Edward Ryall, *Born Twice: Total Recall of a Seventeenth-Century Life* (New York: Harper & Row, 1975), pp. 10–30, 165–75.

19. Joseph Head and S. L. Cranston, *Reincarnation: The Phoenix Fire Mystery* (New York: Julian Press, 1977), pp. 401–2.

20. Ian Stevenson, *Xenoglossy: A Review and Report of a Case* (Charlottesville: University Press of Virginia, 1974).

21. F. H. Wood, *This Egyptian Miracle* (London: John Watkins, 1955).

22. Ian Stevenson, "A New Case of Responsive Xenoglossy: The Case of Gretchen," *JASPR* 70, no. 1 (1976): 65–77.

23. Helen Wambach, "Life Before Life," *Psychic* 9 (Jan. 1972): 10–13; cf. also Thelma Moss, *The Probability of the Impossible* (Los Angeles: J. P. Tarcher, 1974), pp. 352–56.

24. Arthur Schopenhauer, *Parerga und Paralipomena,* vol. 2, trans. E. J. F. Payne (Oxford: Clarendon Press, 1974), chap. 16; cf. also Head, *Reincarnation,* p. 296.

25. Lafcadio Hearn, *Gleanings in Buddha Fields* (Boston: Houghton Mifflin, 1897), chap. 10.

26. Charles Lancelin, *La vie postume* (Paris: Henri Durville, 1920), pp. 309–63; cf. A. de Rochas, *Les vies successives* (Paris: Chacorna, 1911), pp. 338–45.

27. L. D. Gupta and N. R. Sharma, *Inquiry into the Reincarnation of Shanti Devi* (Delhi: Baluja Press, 1936).

28. J. Gaither Pratt, *The Psychic Realm: What Can You Believe?* (New York: Random House, 1975), pp. 240ff.

29. Stevenson, *Twenty Cases.*

30. Ian Stevenson, "Research into the Evidence of Man's Survival After Death," *JNMD* 165, no. 3 (1977): 153–63.

31. Cf. Banerjee and Oursler, *Lives Unlimited.*

32. Cf. Guy Lyon Playfair, *The Indefinite Boundary* (New York: St. Martin's, 1976), p. 163.

33. Karl Muller, *Reincarnation Based on Facts* (London: Psychic Press, 1971); cf. T. Locher, *Parapsychologie in der Schweiz* (Biel, Switzerland: Schweizerische Vereinigung für Parapsychologie, 1986).

34. Cf. Banerjee and Oursler, *Lives Unlimited,* pp. 180–81; cf. also the cases in Francis Story, *Rebirth as Doctrine and Experience* (Kandy, Sri Lanka: Buddhist Publication Society, 1975), two vols.

35. K. N. Jayatilleke, *The Message of the Buddha* (New York: Free Press, 1974).

36. Michael Scriven, "Personal Identity and Parapsychology," *JASPR* 69, no. 4 (1965): 312.

37. Gardner Murphy, "A Caringtonian Approach to Ian Stevenson's *Twenty Cases Suggestive of Reincarnation,"* *JASPR* 67, no. 2 (1973): 120.

38. Ruth Reyna, *Reincarnation and Science* (Delhi: Sterling Publishers, 1973), p. 29.

39. Ibid., p. 30.

40. Banerjee and Oursler, *Lives Unlimited,* p. 159.

41. Harold I. Lief, "Commentary on Dr. Ian Stevenson's 'The Evidence of Man's Survival After Death,'" *JNMD* 165, no. 3 (1977): 171.

42. Montague Ullman, in *JNMD* 165, no. 3 (1977): 174.

43. Moss, *Probability,* p. 356.

44. Jacobson, *Life Without Death,* pp. 194–98.

45. Playfair, *The Indefinite Boundary,* p. 166.

46. Stevenson, "Research," p. 165.

47. Renee Haynes, *The Seeing Eye, The Seeing I* (New York: St. Martin's, 1976), pp. 185–87.

48. Donald West, review of "Facts and Fallacies in the Name of Science" by Gardner Murphy, *JSPR* 39, no. 697 (Sept. 1958).

49. Ducasse, *Critical Examination,* pp. 275–99.

50. Stevenson, "Research," p. 165.

51. Jacobson, *Life Without Death,* pp. 28–32.

52. William Roll, "Pagenstecher's Contribution to Parapsychology," *JASPR* 61, no. 3 (1967): 219–40.

53. Louisa E. Rhine, review of *Twenty Cases Suggestive of Reincarnation* by Ian Stevenson, *JPP* 30, no. 4 (1966): 263–72.

54. Reyna, *Reincarnation,* p. 34.

55. C. T. K. Chari, "'Buried Memories' in Survivalist Research," *IJPP* 4, no. 3 (1962): 40; cf. Playfair, *Indefinite,* p. 171.

56. Reyna, *Reincarnation,* p. 34.

57. Berthold E. Schwarz, "Telepathic Events in a Child Between One and 3½ Years," *IJPP* 3, no. 4 (1961): 5–46.

58. Haynes, *Seeing I,* p. 183.

59. For the case that all memories are but special cases of ESP, see Robert L. Patterson, "The Case for Immortality," *IJPR* 6, no. 2 (Summer 1975): 91.

60. Stevenson, "Research," p. 165.

61. Michael Polanyi, "Tacit Knowing, Its Bearing on Some Problems of Philosophy," *Review of Modern Physics* 34 (1962): 601–16.

62. Michael Scriven, "Personal Identity and Parapsychology," *JASPR* 69, no. 4 (1965): 312.

63. Reyna, *Reincarnation,* pp. 32–34.

64. This seems true even of Europeans dying in Asia; cf. Ian Stevenson, "A Reply to Gardner Murphy," *JASPR* 67, no. 2 (1973): 132–34.

65. Stevenson, "A Reply," pp. 133, 135.

66. Adrian Parker, *States of Mind* (New York: Taplinger, 1975), p. 168.

67. Jacobson, *Life Without Death,* pp. 368–69.

68. Cf. Stevenson, "A Reply," pp. 130–36.

69. Ian Stevenson, review of *The Cathars and Reincarnation* by Arthur Guirdham, *JASPR* 66, no. 1 (1972): 117–19.

70. Ducasse, *Critical Examination,* pp. 248–56.

71. J. M. O. Wheatley, "The Question of Survival, Some Logical Reflections," *JASPR* 59, no. 1 (1965): 207–9.

Chapter 2: Invisible Bodies?

1. Sydney Maliz et al., "A Comparison of Drug-Induced Hallucinations with Those Seen in Spontaneously Occurring Psychoses," in Louis J. West, ed., *Hallucinations* (New York: Grune an& Stratton, 1962), pp. 50–61.

2. Wilder Penfield, *The Mystery of the Mind* (Princeton: Princeton University Press, 1975).

3. Irwin Feinberg, "Visual Hallucinations in Schizophrenia," in West, *Hallucinations,* p. 71; cf. also Walter Grey, "The 14th F. W. H. Myers Memorial Lectures," *PSPR,* 1960, p. 23.

4. Lawrence C. Kolb, "Phantom Sensations, Hallucinations, and the Body Image," in West, *Hallucinations,* pp. 239–43.

5. Ibid., pp. 244–46.

6. Ibid.

7. Cf. Louisa E. Rhine, "Auditory Psi Experience: Hallucination or Physical?" *JPP* 27, no. 3 (1963): 182–97.

8. William G. Roll, "Poltergeists and Hauntings," in *Papers from the 19th Annual Convention of the Parapsychology Association* (Metuchen, N.J.: Scarecrow, 1977), pp. 227–29.

9. William V. Rauscher and Allen Spraggett, *The Spiritual Frontier* (New York: Doubleday, 1975), p. 67.

10. A. T. Baird, ed., *One Hundred Cases for Survival After Death* (New York: Bernard Ackerman, 1944), pp. 47–49.

11. Hornell Hart, *The Enigma of Survival* (Springfield, Ill.: Charles C. Thomas, 1959), p. 186.

12. Ibid.; cf. p. 171.

13. Ludwig Lavater, *Of Ghostes and Spirites Walking by Nyght* (1573), ed. and trans. J. Dover Wilson (London: Oxford University Press [for the Shakespeare Association], 1929).

14. Jocelyn Pierson, "Old Books on Psychical Phenomena," *JASPR* 35, no. 3 (1941): 74–80, 98–104.

15. Edmund Gurney, F. W. H. Myers, and Frank Podmore, *Phantasms of the Living* (London: Trubner, 1894).

16. Henry Sidgwick, "Report on the Census of Hallucinations," *PSPR* 10 (1894): 36–44; cf. esp. table 5, p. 44.

17. Alexandra David-Neel, *Magic and Mystery in Tibet* (New York:

University Books, 1958).

18. "Cases," *JASPR* 15, no. 3 (1946): 163–85.

19. Hornell Hart, "Scientific Survival Research," *IJPP* 9, no. 1 (1967): 45.

20. D. J. West, *Psychical Research Today* (London: Duckworth, 1954).

21. G. N. M. Tyrrell, *Apparitions* (London: Duckworth, 1953).

22. Hart, "Scientific," p. 46.

23. Thelma Moss and Gertrude Schmeidler, "Quantitative Investigation of a Haunted House," *JASPR* 69 (1975): 341–51.

24. Louisa E. Rhine, "Case Study Review," *JPP* 33, no. 3 (1969): 260.

25. W. Dewi Rees, "The Hallucinations of Widows," *British Medical Journal* 4 (1971): 37–41.

26. Walter F. Prince, *The Enchanted Boundary* (Boston: Boston Society for Psychical Research, 1930), p. 173.

27. Abraham Cummings, *Immortality Proved by Testimony of the Sense* (Bath, Me.: J. C. Tobbley, 1826).

28. Hart, *Enigma,* p. 182.

29. Tyrrell, *Apparitions,* p. 69.

30. Hart, *Enigma,* p. 182.

31. C. E. M. Joad, *The Recovery of Belief* (London: Faber & Faber, 1952), p. 208.

32. Thelma Moss, *The Probability of the Impossible* (Los Angeles: J. P. Tarcher, 1974), pp. 325–26.

33. Gertrude R. Schmeidler, "Predicting Good and Bad Scores in a Clairvoyance Experiment," *JASPR* 37, no. 4 (1943): 210–21.

34. John Palmer, "ESP Scoring from Four Definitions of the Sheep-Goat Variable," in William Roll et al., eds., *Research in Parapsychology, 1971* (Metuchen, N.J.: Scarecrow, 1972), pp. 37–39.

35. Louisa E. Rhine, "Reply to Dr. Stevenson," *JPP* 34, no. 2 (1970): 161–62.

36. Prince, *Enchanted Boundary,* pp. 169–70.

37. Thomas R. Tietze, "The Mysterious Wax Gloves," *Psychic* 2, no. 5 (April 1971): 24–25.

38. Prince, *Enchanted Boundary,* p. 202.

39. Ibid., pp. 165–67.

40. Ibid., p. 181.

41. Ibid., pp. 175–76.

42. Gardner Murphy, "An Outline of Survival Evidence," *JASPR* 38, no. 1 (1945): 2–4.

43. Hart, *Enigma,* pp. 168–70; cf. also "Case of an Animal Apparition," *JASPR* 35, no. 4 (1941): 92–97.

44. Gardner Murphy, "Hornell Hart's Analysis of the Evidence for Survival," *JASPR* 65, no. 1 (1961): 9.

45. Indre Shira, "The Raynham Hall Ghost," *Country Life,* 16 December 1936, pp. 673–75; cf. also Moss, *Probability,* pp. 316–20.

46. Herbert Benson, "Physical Aspects of Psi," in Alan Angoff and Betty Shapin, eds., *A Century of Psychical Research* (New York: Parapsychology Foundation, 1971), p. 152.

47. Cf. Thelma Moss and Gertrude Schmeidler, "Quantitative Investigation," *JASPR* 62, no. 4 (1968): 399–409.

48. Gertrude Schmeidler, "Investigation of a Haunted House," *JASPR* 60, no. 2 (1966): 139–49.

49. E. P. Gibson, "An Examination of Motivation as Found in Selective Cases," *JASPR* 38, no. 2 (1944): 83–103.

50. Quoted in Hart, *Enigma,* p. 183.

51. W. H. Salter, *Ghosts and Apparitions* (London: G. Bell & Sons, 1938), p. 53.

52. F. W. H. Myers, "On Recognized Apparitions Occurring More Than a Year After Death," *PSPR* 6 (1890): 29.

53. F. W. H. Myers, "A Defence of Phantasms of the Dead," *PSPR* 6 (1890): app., 341.

54. M. P. Reeves, "A Review: Tyrrell's Study of Apparitions," *JPP* 8, no. 1 (1944): 64–83.

55. Jocelyn Pierson, "Externalized Images," *JASPR* 35, no. 2 (1941): 49.

56. Laura Dale et al., "Recent Survey of Spontaneous ESP Phenomena," *JASPR* 56, no. 1 (1962): 26–46.

57. Louisa E. Rhine, "Hallucinatory Psi Experiences," *JPP* 21, no. 1 (1957): 33–35.

58. Henry Sidgwick et al., "Phantasms of the Dead," *PSPR* 10 (1894): 394.

59. Prince, *Enchanted Boundary,* p. 172.

60. Laura Dale, "Spontaneous Experiences Reported by a Group of Experimental Subjects," *JASPR* 40, no. 2 (1946): 59–69.

61. Walter W. Prince, *Noted Witnesses for Psychic Occurrences* (Boston: Boston Society for Psychical Research, 1928), p. 150.

62. Nils O. Jacobson, *Life Without Death,* trans. Sheila La Farge (New York: Delacorte, 1974), pp. 120, 309; cf. Hart, *Enigma,* p. 158.

63. Hart, *Enigma,* pp. 184–86.

64. D. Scott Rogo, "Astral Projection in Tibetan Buddhist Literature,"

IJPP 10, no. 3 (1968): 278–83.

65. Michael Grosso, "Plato and Out-of-Body Experiences," *JASPR* 69, no. 1 (1975): 61–73.

66. Carlos Castaneda, *The Teachings of Don Juan* (New York: Ballantine, 1969), e.g., pp. 144–45.

67. Quoted by Curt J. Ducasse in "How Good is the Evidence for Survival After Death?" *JASPR* 53, no. 3 (1959): 97.

68. David C. Knight, ed., *The ESP Reader* (New York: Grosset & Dunlap, 1969), p. 279.

69. Robert Owen, *Footfalls on the Boundary of Another World* (London: Trubner, 1860).

70. Knight, *ESP Reader,* pp. 274–78.

71. F. W. H. Myers, *Human Personality and Its Survival of Bodily Death* (London: Longmans, 1903), pp. 209–11.

72. C. Leadbeater, *The Life After Death* (London: Theosophical Press, 1912).

73. Knight, *ESP Reader,* pp. 295–98.

74. Sylvan Muldoon and Hereward H. Carrington, *Projection of the Astral Body* (London: Rider, 1929) and *The Case for Astral Projection* (London: Aries, 1936).

75. Oliver Fox, *Astral Projection* (London: Rider, 1939).

76. Knight, *ESP Reader,* p. 286.

77. Robert Crookall, *The Study and Practice of Astral Projection* and *More Astral Projections* (London: Aquarian Press, 1960 and 1964, respectively).

78. Karlis Osis and Erlendur Haraldsson, "Out-of-Body Experiences in Indian Swamis Sai Baba and Dadaji," in *Research in Parapsychology, 1975,* ed. J. D. Morris and R. L. Morris (Metuchen, N.J.: Scarecrow, 1976), pp. 147–50.

79. Janet Mitchell, "A Psychic Probe of the Planet Mercury," *Psychic* 6, no. 4 (June 1975): pp. 17–21.

80. Karlis Osis, "Kinetic Effects at the Ostensible Location of an Out-of-Body Projection During Perceptual Testing," *JASPR* 74, no. 3 (1980): pp. 319–28.

81. Hart, "Scientific," p. 47.

82. Robert Crookall, *Events on the Threshold of the Afterlife* (Moradabad, India: Darshana International, 1967), pp. 6–10, 24, 87.

83. Benjamin Walker, *Beyond the Body* (London: Routledge & Kegan Paul, 1974), pp. 68–69.

84. Hart, "Scientific," p. 48.

85. Crookall, *Events,* p. 140; Walker, *Beyond,* p. 76.

86. Hornell Hart et al., "Six Theories About Apparitions," *PSPR* 50 (1956): 179.

87. Celia Green *Out-of-the-Body Experiences* (Oxford: Institute of Psychophysical Research, 1968), pp. 98–99.

88. Arnold Toynbee et al., *Man's Concern with Death* (London: Hodder & Stoughton, 1968), p. 197.

89. Crookall, *Events,* pp. 4–7, 83–85.

90. Dennis Bardens, *Mysterious Worlds* (London: W. H. Allen, 1970), p. 143.

91. Cf. Harvey Irwin, "Out of the Body Down Under," *JSPR* 50, no. 785 (1980): 453.

92. Rosaline Heywood, in Toynbee, ed., *Man's Concern,* p. 200; cf. also Adrian Parker, *States of Mind* (New York: Taplinger, 1975), p. 99.

93. "Cases," *JASPR* 18 (1924): 37; 31 (1937): 103; Helen Dallas, "Bilocation," *JASPR* 35 (1941): 71–73.

94. Crookall, *Events,* pp. 8–9.

95. Carl G. Jung, *Memories, Dreams, Reflections* (London: Collins and Routledge & Kegan Paul, 1963), p. 270.

96. Crookall, *Events,* p. 10.

97. Hippolyte Baraduc, quoted in J. Carrington, *Death, Its Causes and Phenomena* (London: Rider, 1911), p. 269.

98. Hereward Carrington, *Modern Psychical Phenomena* (London: Kegan Paul, Trench and Trubner, 1919).

99. Moss, *Probability,* pp. 316–20.

100. Karlis Osis, "Perspectives for Out-of-Body Research," in *Research in Parapsychology, 1972,* ed. J. D. Morris and R. L. Morris (Metuchen, N.J.: Scarecrow, 1973), pp. 113–16.

101. Cf. G. Henshaw, *The Proofs of the Truths of Spiritualism* (London: Kegan Paul, Trench, Trubner, 1919), pp. 117–26; cf. also Fred Gettings, *Ghosts in Photographs* (New York: Harmony, 1978).

102. William G. Roll, "OBE Experiments with a Cat as Detector," in *Research in Parapsychology, 1974,* ed. William G. Roll (Metuchen, N.J.: Scarecrow, 1975), pp. 55–56.

103. David C. Knight, ed., *The ESP Reader* (New York: Grosset and Dunlap, 1969), pp. 274–78.

104. W. F. Prince, *Noted Witnesses,* pp. 30–32.

105. Lucian Landau, "An Unusual OBE," *JSPR* 42, no. 717 (1963): 126–28.

106. Eileen J. Garrett, *My Life as a Search for the Meaning of Mediumship* (London: Rider, 1938).

107. Hornell Hart, "ESP Projection: Spontaneous Cases and the

Experimental Method," *JSPR* 48, no. 2 (1954): 121–46.

108. Ducasse, *Critical Examination,* pp. 160–63.

109. John Hartwell, "A Study of the Physiological Variables Associated with OOBEs," in *Research in Parapsychology, 1974,* ed. William G. Roll (Metuchen, N.J.: Scarecrow, 1975), pp. 127–29.

110. Karlis Osis, "Perceptual Experiments on OOBEs," in *Research in Parapsychology, 1974,* ed. William G. Roll (Metuchen, N.J.: Scarecrow, 1975), p. 53.

111. Charles T. Tart, "A Psychophysiological Study of Some OBEs," *JASPR* 62, no. 1 (1968): 3–23.

112. Moss, *Probability,* p. 303.

113. Montague Ullman, "Experimentally Induced Telepathic Dreams," *IJPP* 8, no. 4 (1968): 577–97.

114. Karlis Osis and Donna McCormick, "Kinetic Effects at the Ostensible Location of an OB Projection During Perceptual Testing," *Research in Parapsychology, 1979,* ed. William G. Roll (Metuchen, N.J.: Scarecrow, 1980), pp. 142–45.

115. Moss, *Probability,* p. 304.

116. Adrian Parker, *States of Mind* (New York: Taplinger, 1975), p. 104.

117. Karlis Osis, "Toward a Methodology for Experiments on OOBEs," *Research in Parapsychology, 1972,* ed. William G. Roll (Metuchen, N.J.: Scarecrow, 1973), p. 78.

118. Karlis Osis, "Kinetic Effects at the Ostensible Location of an Out-of-Body Projection During Perceptual Testing," *JASPR* 74, no. 3 (1974): 257–75.

119. John Palmer, "ESP and Out-of-Body Experiences: EEG Correlates," in *Research in Parapsychology, 1978,* ed. William G. Roll (Metuchen, N.J.: Scarecrow, 1979), pp. 135–38; also in *JASPR* 68, no. 3 (1974): 257–75.

120. Celia Green, *Lucid Dreams* (London: Hamish Hamilton, 1968), p. 18.; cf. also Celia Green, *Out-of-Body Experiences,* p. 41.

121. Bardens, *Mysterious Worlds,* p. 144.

122. Parker, *States of Mind,* pp. 110–11.

123. Michael Grosso, "Some Varieties of OBE," *JASPR* 70, no. 2 (1976): 176–92.

124. Walker, *Beyond the Body,* p. 66.

125. Charles T. Tart, "Reports to the Parapsychology Association Conventions," *JPP* 29, no. 4 (1965): 281, and *JPP* 30, no. 4 (1966): 278.

126. Janet L. Mitchell, "Out of the Body Experience," *Psychic,* March 1973, pp. 44–55.

127. Parker, *States of Mind,* pp. 103–6.

128. Charles T. Tart, *Psi* (New York: E. P. Dutton, 1977), pp. 177–97.

129. M. A. O'Roark, "Life After Death: The Growing Evidence," *McCall's,* March 1981, p. 28.

130. John Palmer, "Influence of Psychological Set on ESP and OBEs," *JASPR* 69, no. 3 (1975): 193–212.

131. Walter J. Kilner, *The Human Atmosphere* (New York: S. Weiser, 1973); cf. Benjamin Walker, *Beyond the Body* (London: Routledge and Kegan Paul, 1974), pp. 15, 52.

132. Robert Crookall, *The Mechanism of Astral Projection* (Moradabad, India: Darshana International, 1968), p. 52.

133. Cf. C. W. Leadbeater, *Man Visible and Invisible* (London: Theosophical Publishing House, 1907); Phoebe Payne, *Man's Latent Powers* (London: Faber & Faber, 1938); A. E. Powell, *The Etheric Double* (London: Quest, 1969).

134. Semyon and Valentina Kirlian, "Photography and Visual Observations by Means of High Frequency Currents," *Journal of Scientific and Applied Photography* 6 (1961): 397–403.

135. Moss, *Probability,* pp. 27–60.

136. J. Fraser Nicol, "Old Light on New Phenomena," *Psychic* 2, no. 6 (May 1971): 26–28; Carolyn Dobervich, "Kirlian Photography Revealed?" *Psychic* 6, no. 1 (November 1974): 34–39.

137. Sir Auckland Geddes, "A Voice from the Grandstand," *Edinburgh Medical Journal,* n.s. 44 (1937): 367.

138. Charlie Dunbar Broad, "Dreaming and Some of Its Implications," *PSPR,* 1958, 57–78.

139. Hart, "Scientific," p. 67.

140. West is quoted in Hart, *Enigma,* p. 163.

141. B. Abdy Collins, "Is Proof of Survival Possible?" *PSPR* 46 (1941): 361–76.

142. Prince, *Enchanted,* pp. 164, 170, 192.

143. Hart, "Scientific," pp. 48–50.

144. Hart, *Enigma,* p. 174.

145. Murphy, quoted in ibid., pp. 168–70.

146. Ralph Tymms, *Doubles in Literary Psychology* (Cambridge, England: Bowes and Bowes, 1949), p. 26.

147. Walker, *Beyond the Body,* p. 148.

148. Hart, *Enigma,* p. 185.

149. Louisa E. Rhine, "Hallucinatory Psi Experiences," *JPP* 21, no. 1 (1957): 33–35; cf. Hornell Hart, "Rejoinder," *JPP* 22 (1958): 59–62.

150. Seymour Fisher, "Body Image Boundaries and Hallucinations,"

in West, *Hallucinations,* p. 255.

151. Kenneth Dewhurst and John Todd, "The Double: Its Psychopathology and Psychophysiology," *JNMD* 122 (1955): 47.

152. Louis J. West, "A General Theory of Hallucinations and Dreams," in West, *Hallucinations,* pp. 282–88.

153. Kenneth Dewhurst, "Autoscopic Hallucinations," *Irish Journal of Medical Science* 342 (1954): 266–68.

154. Kenneth Dewhurst and John Pearson, "Visual Hallucinations of the Self in Organic Disease," *Journal of Neurological and Neurosurgical Psychiatry* 18 (1955): 53.

155. Claude Richet, *Thirty Years of Psychical Research,* trans. Stanley deBrath (New York: Macmillan, 1923); cf. E. R. Dodds, "Why I Do Not Believe in Survival," *PSPR* 42 (1934): 147–72.

156. Hereward Carrington, *Modern Psychical Phenomena* (London: Kegan Paul, Trench, Trubner, 1919).

157. Hart, *Enigma,* p. 140.

158. Gardner Murphy, "Difficulties Confronting the Survival Hypothesis," *JASPR* 39, no. 2 (1945): 67–94.

159. J. B. Rhine, quoted by Hart, *Enigma,* p. 143; cf. Murphy, *Challenge,* pp. 286–87.

160. Immanuel Kant, *Dreams of a Spirit-Seer* (1766), trans. E. F. Goerwitz (London: New-Church Press, 1915), II, 1, pp. 93–95.

161. Crookall, *Mechanism,* p. 48.

162. J. M. O. Wheatley, "Implications for Religious Studies," in Stanley Krippner, ed., *Advances in Parapsychological Research* (New York: Plenum, 1977).

Chapter 3: The Heart of Near-Death Experiences

1. Raymond Moody, Jr., *Life After Life* (Harrisburg, Pa.: Stackpole, 1976), p. ix.

2. Kenneth Ring, *Life at Death* (New York: Coward, McCann & Geoghegan, 1980), p. 40.

3. Moody, *Life,* pp. 33–51, passim, and p. 64.

4. Karlis Osis and Erlendur Haraldsson, *At the Hour of Death* (New York: Avon, 1977), pp. 217, 221.

5. Ring, *Life at Death,* p. 197.

6. Moody, *Life,* p. 64.

7. Ibid., pp. 67–68.

8. Quoted in David C. Knight, *The ESP Reader* (New York: Grosset and Dunlap, 1969), p. 398; cf. Ring, *Life at Death,* p. 67.

9. Jean-Baptiste Delacour, *Glimpses of the Beyond,* trans. E. B. Garside (New York: Delacorte Press, 1973), pp. 106, 160.

10. Maitland Baldwin, "Hallucinations in Neurologic Syndromes," in West, *Hallucinations* (New York: Grune and Stratton, 1962), p. 82.; cf. Wilder Penfield, *Mystery of the Mind* (Princeton: Princeton University Press, 1975).

11. Russell Noyes, Jr., "Near-Death Experiences: Their Interpretation and Significance," in Robert Kastenbaum, ed., *Between Life and Death* (New York: Springer, 1979), pp. 76–81.

12. Ring, *Life at Death,* pp. 212–13; cf. C. T. K. Chari, "Parapsychological Studies and Literature in India," *IJPP* 2, no. 1 (1960): 24–36.

13. 2 Kings 4:32.

14. Mark 5; Luke 8; John 11, esp. verses 47–48.

15. Acts 9; Acts 20.

16. Bede, *A History of the English Church and People* (Harmondsworth, U.K.: Penguin, 1955), pp. 290ff.

17. Carl Becker, "The Pure Land Revisited: Sino-Japanese Meditations and Near-Death Experiences of the Next World," *Journal of Near-Death Studies* 4, no. 1 (1984): 51–68.

18. Sir Edward B. Tylor, *Primitive Culture,* vol. 2 (New York: Harper, 1958), pp. 285–87.

19. Robert Kastenbaum and Ruth Aisenberg, *The Psychology of Death* (New York: Springer, 1972), chap. 2.

20. Fred R. Marvin, *Last Words of Distinguished Men and Women* (New York: F. H. Revell Co., 1901).

21. Thomas de Quincey, *Suspiria de Profundis* (London: MacDonald, 1956), pp. 511–12.

22. Delacour, *Glimpses,* pp. 108, 106, 5–10, 22, 18, 38, respectively.

23. Sir William F. Barrett, *Death-bed Visions: The Psychical Experiences of the Dying* (London: Methuen, 1926), pp. 10–11.

24. John Grant Fuller, *The Great Soul Trial* (New York: Macmillan, 1969).

25. Osis and Haraldsson, *At the Hour of Death,* p. 21.

26. Elisabeth Kubler-Ross, *Death: The Final Stage of Growth* (Englewood Cliffs, N.J.: Prentice-Hall, 1975).

27. Cf. Bruce Greyson, "Can Science Explain the Near-Death Experience?" *Journal of Near-Death Studies* 8, no. 2 (1989): 77–91; "Near-Death Encounters with and without Near-Death Experiences," *Journal of Near-Death Studies* 8, no. 3 (1989): 151–62; "Near-Death Experiences Precipitated by Suicide Attempt: Lack of Influence of Psychopathology, Religion, and Expectations," *Journal of Near-Death*

Studies 9, no. 3 (1991): 183–88; "The NDE Scale: Construction, Reliability, and Validity," *JNMD* 171 (1983): 369–75.

28. Robert Kastenbaum, *Between Life and Death* (New York: Springer, 1979): 16–19.

29. Raymond Moody, Jr., "Commentary on Rodin," in *JNMD* 168, no. 5 (May 1980): 264.

30. Michael Sabom and S. Kreutzinger, "The Experience of Near Death," *Death Education* 1 (1977): 195–203.

31. Charles A. Garfield, "The Dying Patient's Concern with Life After Death," in Kastenbaum, *Between,* p. 53.

32. W. Dewi Rees, "The Hallucinations of Widows," in *British Medical Journal* 4 (1972): 37–41.

33. Ring, *Life at Death,* p. 40.

34. Osis and Haraldsson, *At the Hour of Death,* p. 218.

35. Moody, *Life,* p. 53.

36. Osis and Haraldsson, *At the Hour of Death,* p. 149.

37. Ibid., p. 29; cf. Kubler-Ross cited in Ring, *Life at Death,* p. 208.

38. Barrett, *Deathbed Visions,* pp. 10–12.

39. A. T. Baird, *One Hundred Cases for Survival After Death* (New York: Bernard Ackerman, 1944), pp. 81, 87, 88, 83, respectively.

40. Ring, *Life at Death,* p. 207; cf. Delacour, *Glimpses,* p. 115.

41. Osis and Haraldsson, *At the Hour of Death,* p. 217.

42. Baird, *One Hundred Cases,* pp. 82–86.

43. Knight, *ESP Reader,* p. 392.

44. B. J. F. Laubscher, *Beyond Life's Curtain* (Capetown, South Africa: Howard Timmins, 1967), pp. 68–69.

45. Florence Marryat Lean, *There is No Death* (London: Kegan Paul, Trench, Trubner, 1891), p. 89.

46. Horace Traubel, in *JASPR* 15 (1921): 114.

47. Cf. Ring, *Life at Death,* p. 226, and Robert Crookall, *Events on the Threshold of the Afterlife* (Moradabad, India: Darshana International, 1967).

48. Osis and Haraldsson, *At the Hour of Death,* p. 150; Ring, *Life at Death,* pp. 59–60.

49. Moody, *Life,* pp. 56–57.

50. Knight, *ESP Reader,* p. 398.

51. Osis and Haraldsson, *At the Hour of Death,* p. 150; Ring, *Life at Death,* pp. 59–60.

52. Moody, *Life,* p. 134.

53. Ring, *Life at Death,* pp. 137, 210.

54. Moody, *Life,* p. 57.
55. Osis and Haraldsson, *At the Hour of Death,* p 152.
56. Ibid., pp. 44, 66–67, 108–17.
57. Ring, *Life at Death,* pp. 226–27.
58. Wellesley T. Pole, *Private Dowding* (London: J. M. Watkins, 1917), p. 101.
59. Ernest W. Oaten, *That Reminds Me* (Manchester, U.K.: Two Worlds, 1938).
60. Osis and Haraldsson, *At the Hour of Death,* pp. 41, 180.
61. Moody, *Life,* pp. 90–91.
62. Osis and Haraldsson, *At the Hour of Death,* pp. 162–63; 176–77; cf. Carl Becker, "Pure Land," pp. 51–66.
63. Archibald B. Campbell, *Bring Yourself to Anchor* (London: Rider, 1947).
64. Quoted in Knight, *ESP Reader,* pp. 394–96; Campbell also in Knight, *ESP Reader,* pp. 376–78.
65. Osis and Haraldsson, *At the Hour of Death,* pp. 163–68.
66. Becker, "Pure Land," p. 52.
67. Osis and Haraldsson, *At the Hour of Death,* p. 176.
68. "The Pseudodeath of Private Ritchie," in *Guideposts,* June 1963.
69. Ring, *Life at Death,* pp. 56–60; 137, 207.
70. Osis and Haraldsson, *At the Hour of Death,* pp. 173–82, 220.
71. Ibid., pp. 92–98; Knight, *ESP Reader,* pp. 385–89.
72. Delacour, *Glimpses,* p. 20.
73. Ibid., pp. 106–7.
74. Osis and Haraldsson, *At the Hour of Death,* pp. 43–44; Knight, *ESP Reader,* pp. 387–90.
75. Osis and Haraldsson, *At the Hour of Death,* p. 180.
76. Ring, *Life at Death,* pp. 68, 192–93.
77. Delacour, *Glimpses,* pp. 24, 144; cf. the many cases in Maurice Rawlings, *Beyond Death's Door* (Nashville, Tenn.: Thomas Nelson, 1979).
78. Delacour, *Glimpses,* pp. 34–36.
79. Ibid., p. 136.
80. Leonid V. Vasiliev, *Mysterious Phenomena of the Human Psyche,* trans. Sonia Volochova (New York: University Books, 1965), p. 200.
81. Ibid., p. 194.
82. Ibid., pp. 201–2.
83. Stanislav Grof and Joan Halifax, "Psychedelics and the Experience of Death," in Arnold Toynbee, ed., *Life After Death* (New York: McGraw-Hill, 1976), pp. 197–98.

84. Delacour, *Glimpses,* pp. 34, 44, 100, 59, 158.

85. Arthur Ford, *Unknown But Known* (New York: Signet, 1969), pp. 54–58.

86. Quoted in Head and Cranston, *Reincarnation,* p. 452.

87. Cf. Peter M. Black, "Brain Death," *New England Journal of Medicine* 299, no. 7 (1978): 342–44, nn. 25 and 26.

88. Moody, *Life,* p. 142.

89. Ring, *Life at Death,* p. 212.

90. Peter M. Black, "Criteria of Brain Death," *Postgraduate Medicine* 57, no. 2 (Feb. 1975): 69–73.

91. Karlis Osis, "Deathbed Visions and the Afterlife Hypothesis," *Journal of Indian Psychology* 2, no. 1 (1979): 15.

92. M. A. O'Roark, "Life After Death: The Growing Evidence," *McCall's,* March 1981, p. 28.

93. Ibid.; cf. Michael Grosso, "Toward an Explanation for Near-Death Phenomena," *JASPR* 75, no. 1 (1981): 48.

94. Tart has proposed that "state-specific sciences" could be established to explore the referents of altered states; cf. Charles T. Tart, "States of Consciousness and State-Specific Sciences," in Hoyt L. Edge and J. M. O. Wheatley, eds., *Philosophical Dimensions of Parapsychology* (Springfield, Ill.: Charles C. Thomas, 1976): 441–62.

95. J. F. McHarg, review of *At the Hour of Death* by Haraldsson and Osis, *JSPR* 49 (1978): 886.

96. Cf. Juan C. Saavedra-Aguilar, "A Neurobiological Model for Near-Death Experiences," *Journal of Near-Death Studies* 7 (1988): 205–22.

97. Ernst A. Rodin, "The Reality of Death Experiences," *JNMD* 158, no. 5 (May 1980): 262.

98. R. S. Blacker, "To Sleep, Perchance to Dream," *JAMA* 242, no. 21 (23 Nov. 1979): 2291.

99. Ronald K. Siegel, "The Psychology of Life After Life," *American Psychologist* 25, no. 10 (Oct. 1980): 923.

100. Janusz Slawinski, "Electromagnetic Radiation and the Afterlife," *Journal of Near-Death Studies* 6 (1987): 127–45.

101. M. A. O'Roark, "Life After Death," p. 28.

102. Kenneth Ring, "Commentary on 'The Reality of Death Experiences' by Rodin," *JNMD* 168, no. 5 (May 1980): 273–74, and *Life,* p. 211.

103. Ian Stevenson, "Comments on 'The Reality of Death Experiences' by Rodin," *JNMD* 168, no. 5 (May 1980): 271–72.

104. Osis and Haraldsson, *At the Hour of Death,* pp. 156, 172, 226, 230.

105. Raymond A. Moody, *Reflections on Life After Life* (Atlanta, Ga.:

Mockingbird, 1977), p. 109.

106. The value of phenomenological content comparisons is stressed in Gordon R. Lowe, "The Phenomenology of Hallucinations as an Aid to Differential Diagnosis," *British Journal of Psychiatry* 123 (1973): 630.

107. Karlis Osis and Erlendur Haraldsson, "Correspondence: Reply to Dr. McHarg," *JSPR* 50 (1979): 126–28.

108. Baldwin, "Hallucinations," p. 78; Osis and Haraldsson, *At the Hour of Death,* pp. 188–90.

109. Ring, *Life at Death,* p. 210.

110. All Siegel references are to "The Psychology of Life After Life," pp. 922–24.

111. Osis and Haraldsson, *At the Hour of Death,* pp. 63, 66; cf. 229.

112. G. B. Ermendrout, "A Mathematical Theory of Visual Hallucination Patterns," in *Biological Cybernetics* 34, no. 3 (Oct. 1979): 137. Context-independent geometric hallucinations are explicable on mathematical models; this works well for drug hallucinations, not at all for NDEs.

113. Jan Ehrenwald, *The ESP Experience* (New York: Basic Books, 1978), p. 161.

114. Russell Noyes, Jr., "Near-Death Experiences: Their Interpretation and Significance," in Robert Kastenbaum, ed., *Between Life and Death* (New York: Springer, 1979): 83–86.

115. Baldwin, "Hallucinations," p. 81, and Eugene L. Bliss and Lincoln D. Clark, "Visual Hallucinations," p. 104, both in West, *Hallucinations.*

116. Ihsan Al-Issa, "Socio-cultural Factors in Hallucinations," *International Journal of Social Psychiatry* 24, no. 3 (1978), pp. 167–76.

117. Osis and Haralddson, *At the Hour of Death,* pp. 73, 330.

118. Noyes, "Near-Death Experiences," pp. 76–77.

119. Grof and Halifax, "Psychedelics," p. 190.

120. Ring, *Life at Death,* pp. 192–97, 209.

121. Bliss and Clark, "Visual Hallucinations," p. 105.

122. Baldwin, "Hallucinations," p. 78.

123. F. A. Elliot, *Clinical Neurology* (London: Saunders, 1966), p. 143.

124. On the subject of automata, cf. Wilder Penfield, *The Mystery of the Mind* (Princeton: Princeton University Press, 1975), pp. 100ff.

125. Bliss and Clark, "Visual Hallucinations"; cf. Osis and Haraldsson, *At the Hour of Death,* pp. 63–66.

126. Ring, *Life at Death,* pp. 192–96, 132–37.

127. Richard A. Kalish, "Contacting the Dead: Does Group Identification Matter?" in Kastenbaum, *Between,* pp. 61ff.

128. Carl Sagan, *Broca's Brain* (New York: Random House, 1979), pp. 303–4.

129. Ibid., pp. 307–9.

130. Ibid., p. 312.

131. Vincent Fitzpatrick (review of *Broca's Brain* by Carl Sagan, *Best Sellers* 39 [Oct. 1979]: 234) calls Sagan "a smug illiterate" in philosophy and theology. Robert Jastrow, in the *New York Times Book Review,* 10 June 1979, p. 6, calls Sagan "fatuous and self-indulgent." Cf. Richard Restok, in *New York Times Book Review,* 29 May 1977, p. 8, who judges Sagan's work on brain research "embarrassingly naïve."

132. Stanislav Grof, *Realms of the Human Unconcious* (New York: Viking, 1975), pp. 139–41.

133. Quoted in Ring, *Life at Death,* p. 214.

134. Sagan, *Broca's Brain,* p. 313.

135. Ibid., p. 306.

136. D. A. Curnock, "The Senses of the Newborn," *British Medical Journal* 299, no. 6714 (16 Dec. 1989): 1478–79.

137. Daphne Maurer, "Infant Visual Perception: Methods of Study," in Leslie Cohen and Philip Salapatek, eds., *Infant Perception* (New York: Academic Press, 1975), I, pp. 8–9.

138. M. Warburg, "Synets udvikling [Development of sight]," *Ugeskrift for Laeger* 153, no. 22 (27 May 1991): 1571–75.

139. M. Reim, C. Teping, and J. Silny, "Vision stereoscopique: Etude objective et developpement pendant les premiers mois de la vie," *Journal Français d'Opthalmologie* 12, no. 10 (1989): 623–27.

140. F. Vital-Durand and A. Hullo, "La mésure de l'acuité visuelle du nourrison en six minutes," *Journal Français d'Opthalmologie* 12, no. 3 (1989): 221–25, and D. J. Heersema and J. vanHof vanDuin, "Gedragsmatige bepaling van de gezichtsscherpte bij kinderen van 1 tot 4 jaar [Behavioral determination of visual acuity in 1-to-4-year-old children]," *Tijdschrift voor Kindergeneeskunde* 57, no. 6 (Dec. 1989): 210–14.

141. E. B. Ciner, E. Schanel-Klitsch, and M. Schieman, "Stereoacuity Development in Young Children," *Optometry and Vision Science* 68, no. 7 (July 1991): 533–36.

142. Oliver Braddock and Janette Atkinson, "Accommodation and Acuity in the Human Infant," *Developmental Neurobiology of Vision,* ed. Ralph D. Freeman (New York: Plenum Press, 1979), p. 291.

143. Maurer, "Infant," pp. 31–32.

144. C. Schulman, "Eye Movements in Infants Using dc Recording," *Neuropediatrie* 4 (1973): 76–78, and cf. Warburg, pp. 1571–75.

145. D. A. Curnock, "Senses of the Newborn," pp. 1478–79.

146. R. L. Fantz and S. B. Miranda, "Newborn Infant Attention to Form of Contour," *Child Development* 44 (1975): 224–28.

147. B. Z. Karmel and E. B. Maisel, "A Neuronal Activity Model for Infant Visual Attention," in Cohen and Salapatek, *Infant Perception.*, p. 124.

148. D. A. Curnock, "Senses of the Newborn," pp. 1478–79.

149. R. D. Snyder, S. K. Hata, B. S. Brann, and R. M. Mills, "Subcortical Visual Function in the Newborn," *Pediatric Neurology* 6, no. 5 (Sept.–Oct. 1990): 333–36.

150. Warburg, "Synets udvikling" [Development of sight], pp. 1571–75.

151. Philip Salapatek, "Pattern Perception in Early Infancy," in Cohen and Salapatek, *Infant Perception*, pp. 172–75.

152. See M. L. Courage and R. J. Adams, "Visual Acuity Assessment from Birth to Three Years Using the Acuity Card Procedure," *Optometry and Vision Science* 67, no. 9 (September 1990): 713–18; and Leslie B. Cohen and Eric R. Gelber, "Infant Visual Memory," in Cohen and Salapatek, *Infant Perception*, pp. 378–81.

153. M. Jones, "The Development of Early Behavior Patterns in Young Children," *Pedagogical Seminary and Journal of Genetic Psychology* 33 (1962): 537–85.

154. Osis and Haraldsson, *At the Hour of Death*, p. 152.

Chapter 4: Philosophy of Science

1. Nicholas Maxwell, "The Rationality of Scientific Discovery, Part 2," *Philosophy of Science* 41 (Sept. 1974): 275–95.

2. Cyril Burt, "Psychology and Parapsychology," in *Science and ESP*, ed. J. R. Smythies (London: Routledge & Kegan Paul, 1967), p. 81. The notion of *Basic Limiting Principles* in modern Western science was first proposed by C. D. Broad in the 1940s as a description of rules man could not conceive of things or events violating—within our present worldview. Careful analysis shows Broad's BLPs to involve not only considerable disorder, but to be already disproven by quantum as well as Einsteinian physics.

3. Quoted by John C. Poynton, "Parapsychology and the Biological Sciences," in *Parapsychology and the Sciences*, ed. Alan Angoff and Betty Shapin (New York: Parapsychology Foundation, Inc., 1974), p. 117.

4. Henry Margenau, "ESP in the Framework of Modern Science," in Smythies, *Science and ESP*, p. 213.

5. Arthur Koestler, "The Perversity of Physics," in Alan Angoff and

Betty Shapin, A Century of Psychical Research: The Continuing Doubts and Affirmations (New York: Parapsychology Foundation, 1971), p. 165. On the demise of laws like causality, see also Max Planck, A Spiritual Autobiography (New York: Philosophical Library, 1949), p. 149.

6. Burt, "Psychology," pp. 107–8, 120–21.

7. Lawrence LeShan, "Physicists and Mystics, Similarities in World-View," Journal of Transpersonal Psychology 1, no. 2 (1969): 1–15.

8. George F. Kneller, Science as a Human Endeavor (New York: Columbia University Press, 1978), p. 41.

9. Cited by Nils O. Jacobson, Life Without Death? trans. Sheila La Farge (New York: Delacorte Press, 1974), p. 221.

10. Herbert Benson, "Physical Aspects of Psi," in Angoff and Shapin, A Century of Psychical Research, pp. 147, 152.

11. Cf. James Jeans, quoted in ibid., p. 148.

12. Hideo Seki, Five Dimensional World (Tokyo: Chūo-kōron-jigyō, 1974), cf. also Burt, "Psychology," pp. 107, 120–21.

13. Hornell Hart, "The Psychic Fifth Dimension," in JASPR 47 (1953): 7–10ff. Hart's conception is ambiguous in that it sometimes uses "dimension" as a mathematical construct and sometimes as referring to some other psychic realm. The problem is far from solution, but it is possible that such a dimension-theory approach may eventually find heuristic utility if not validity.

14. J. Gaither Pratt, "Parapsychology, Normal Science and Paradigm Change," JASPR 73, no. 3 (1979): 25–26.

15. Charles C. Tart, "Emergent Interactionism and Consciousness," in Brain/Mind and Parapsychology, ed. Betty Shapin and Lisette Coly (New York: Parapsychology Foundation, Inc., 1979), p. 182.

16. Gardner Murphy, "Psychical Research and the Mind-Body Relation," JASPR 40, no. 4 (1946): 192, 207.

17. John Beloff, "Parapsychology and Its Neighbors," in Philosophical Dimensions of Parapsychology, ed. Hoyt L. Edge and J. M. O. Wheatley (Springfield, Ill.: Charles C. Thomas, 1976), pp. 410–14.

18. Remy Chauvin, "To Reconcile Psi and Physics," in Philosophical Dimensions of Parapsychology, ed. Hoyt L. Edge and J. M. O. Wheatley (Springfield, Ill.: Charles C. Thomas, 1976), pp. 410–14.

19. Cf. Poynton's observation that "despite remarks such as [Heisenberg's] we still have the ridiculous situation that perhaps most biologists and psychologists are still aggressively trying to conform to outdated world-views which in some way constitute their ideas of physics" ("Parapsychology," pp. 118–19). Cf. also Alister Hardy, "Biology and ESP," in Smythies, Science and ESP, p. 149.

20. Antony Flew, "Parapsychology Revisited: Laws, Miracles, and Repeatability," *Humanist* 36, no. 1 (1976): p. 28.

21. Lawrence LeShan, "Parapsychology and the Concept of the Repeatable Experiment," *IJPP* 7, no. 1 (1966): 133.

22. Michael Scriven, "New Frontiers of the Brain," *JPP* 25 (1961): p. 310.

23. Examples from LeShan, "Parapsychology," p. 124.

24. R. G. A. Dolby, "Reflections on Deviant Science," in *On the Margins of Science*, ed. Roy Wallis (Keele: University of Keele, 1979), p. 32.

25. Pratt, "Parapsychology," pp. 25–26.

26. Gardner Murphy, "Are There any Solid Facts in Psychical Research?" in Edge and Wheatley, *Philosophical,* pp. 396–97.

27. Cf. Max Planck's assertion, "I must take exception to the view . . . that a problem in physics merits examination only if it is established in advance that a definite answer can be obtained" (Max Planck, *A Spiritual Autobiography* [New York: Philosophical Library, 1949], p. 139). Planck goes on to show how experiments without definite answers have still had important results for science.

28. Michael Scriven, "Explanations of the Supernatural," in *Philosophy and Psychical Research,* ed. Shivesh C. Thakur (London: George Allen & Unwin, 1976), pp. 188–89.

29. For an additional discussion of the nature of explanations, see Michael Scriven, "Explanations, Predictions, and Laws," in Baruch A. Brody, ed., *Readings in the Philosophy of Science* (Englewood Cliffs, N.J.: Prentice-Hall, Inc., 1970), pp. 102–3.

30. Scriven, "Explanations of the Supernatural," pp. 192–93.

31. George R. Price, "Science and the Supernatural," *Science* 122, no. 3165 (1955): p. 362.

32. J. B. Rhine, "Comments on 'Science and the Supernatural,' " in *Science* 123, no. 3184 (1956): 12.

33. This argument is used by George Price in "Science and the Supernatural." It is originally found in David Hume, "Of Miracles," in *An Enquiry Concerning Human Understanding* (Chicago: Open Court, 1912), pp. 120–21.

34. Cf. the section headings in Paul Feyerabend, "How to be a Good Empiricist—A Plea for Tolerance in Matters Epistemological," in Baruch A. Brody, *Readings in the Philosophy of Science* (Englewood Cliffs, N.J.: Prentice-Hall, 1970), pp. 328–34.

35. C. J. Ducasse, *A Critical Examination of the Belief in a Life After Death* (Springfield, Ill.: Charles C. Thomas, 1961), pp. 149ff.

36. Cf. J. B. Rhine, "Comments."

37. Lawrence LeShan and Henry Margenau, "An Approach to a Science of Psychical Research," *JSPR* 50, no. 783 (March, 1980): 274–75.

38. Cf. Thomas S. Kuhn, "The Function of Dogma in Scientific Research," in Brody, *Readings,* pp. 357ff.

39. Marcello Truzzi, "Paul Kurtz's Analysis of the Scientific Status of Parapsychology," *JPP* 44, no. 1 (1980): 39–41, 89–90.

40. R. A. McConnell, "The Resolution of Conflicting Beliefs About the ESP Evidence," *JPP* 41, no. 1 (1977): 199ff.

41. Quoted by Rosalind Heywood, "Notes on Changing Mental Climates and Research into ESP," in J. R. Smythies, *Science and ESP,* p. 48.

42. J. Bruner and L. Postman, "On the Perception of Incongruity: A Paradigm," in D. C. Beardsley and M. Wertheimer, *Readings in Perception* (New York: D. Van Nostrand, 1958), pp. 654ff.

43. Thomas Kuhn, *The Structure of Scientific Revolutions,* 2d. ed. (Chicago: University of Chicago Press, 1970), p. 135.

44. Quoted in Rosalind Heywood, "Notes," p. 57.

45. Gardner Murphy and Robert Ballou, eds., *William James on Psychical Research* (New York: Viking Press, 1960), p. 92; originally in *JASPR* 3, no. 2 (Feb. 1909).

46. Ernst Rodin, "The Reality of Death Experiences," *JNMD* 168, no. 5 (May, 1980): 259–62.

47. Cf. D. Bramel and L. Festinger, "The Reactions of Humans to Cognitive Dissonance," in A. J. Bachrach, ed., *Experimental Foundations of Clinical Psychology* (New York: Basic Books, 1962), p. 256; cf. also McConnell, "Resolution," p. 212.

48. Cf. Paul Feyerabend, *Science in a Free Society* (London: NLB, 1978), pp. 1–4, which particularly stresses this idea.

49. Kuhn, "Function of Dogma," p. 357; these same ideas are also found in his *Structure of Scientific Revolutions.*

50. J. W. Brehm, "Post-Decision Changes in Desirability of Alternatives," *Journal of Abnormal Social Psychology* 52 (1956): 378–84.

51. Charles C. Tart, "States of Consciousness and State-Specific Sciences," in Edge and Wheatley, *Philosophical,* p. 444.

52. Thomas Kuhn, *Structure,* pp. 114, 151.

53. In Rosalind Heywood, "Notes," p. 50.

54. Lawrence LeShan, "Some Psychological Hypotheses on the Non-Acceptance of Parapsychology as a Science," *IJPP* 7, no. 3 (1966): 378.

55. Whately Carington, *Telepathy,* 3d ed. (London: Methuen, 1946), p. 45.

56. I. Bernard Cohen, quoted in *JASPR* 46 (1952): 159.

57. Brian MacKenzie and S. L. MacKenzie, "Whence the Enchanted Boundary?" *JPP* 44, no. 2 (1980): 127.

58. Ibid., pp. 149–52.

59. William McDougall, "President's Address to the Society for Psychical Research," in *PSPR* 27 (1914–15): 157–75.

60. W. F. Prince, *The Enchanted Boundary* (Boston: Boston SPR., 1930), esp. pp. 200-220.

61. Cf. Ernst Rodin, "A Reply to Commentaries," *Anabiosis* 2, no. 3 (Feb. 1981): 15.

62. Burt, "Psychology," p. 64.

63. J. M. 0. Wheatley, "Reincarnation, Astral Bodies, and Psi Components," *JASPR* 73, no. 2 (1979): 109.

64. Heywood, "Notes," p. 48.

65. George F. Kneller, *Science as a Human Endeavor* (New York: Columbia University Press, 1978), p. 108.

66. Murphy and Ballou, *William James,* p. 64.

67. Cf. George Mandler, "An Ancient Conundrum" (review of *The Self and Its Brain,* by Sir John Eccles and Karl Popper), *Science,* 200 (June 1978): 1040.

68. Cf. David Boadella, *Wilhelm Reich* (London: Vision Press, 1973) and Michel Cattier, *The Life and Works of Wilheim Reich,* trans. G. Boulanger (New York: Horizon Press, 1971), p. 211.

69. Cf. Harold I. Lief, "Commentary on Dr. Stevenson's 'The Evidence of Man's Survival After Death,' " *JNMD* 165, no. 3 (1977): 171.

Chapter 5: A Model of Resistance and Change in the Sciences

1. In Rosalind Heywood, "Notes on Changing Mental Climates and Research into ESP," in J. R. Smythies, *Science and ESP* (London: Routledge and Kegan Paul, 1967), p. 57.

2. Antony Flew, "Is There a Case for Disembodied Survival?" *JASPR* 66, no. 2 (April 1972): 129.

3. George Price, "Science and the Supernatural," *Science* 123, no. 3184 (1956): 12.

4. C. E. M. Hansel, *ESP: A Scientific Evaluation* (New York: Charles Scribner's Sons, 1966); H. B. Gibson, "The Royal Nonesuch of Parapsychology," *Bulletin of the British Psychological Society* 32 (1979): 65–67.

5. H. M. Collins and T. J. Pinch, "The Construction of the Paranormal," in Roy Wallis, ed., *On the Margins of Science: The Social*

Construction of Rejected Knowledge (Keele, England: Keele University Press, 1979), p. 251.

6. Ruth Reyna, *Reincarnation and Science* (New Delhi: Sterling Publications, 1973).

7. R. A. McDonnell, "The Resolutions of Conflicting Beliefs about the ESP Evidence," *JPP* 41, no. 1 (Sept. 1977): 212.

8. Paul Allison, "Experimental Parapsychology as a Rejected Science," in Wallis, *On the Margins,* pp. 286–87.

9. Marcello Truzzi, "A Skeptical Look at Paul Kurtz's Analysis of the Scientific Status of Parapsychology," *JPP* 44, no. 1 (1980): 90ff.

10. This might explain the relative infrequency of reporting such memories in the West.

11. Eileen J. Garrett, *Adventures in the Supernormal: A Personal Memoir* (New York: Garrett, 1949), p. 441.

12. E. U. Condon, "UFOs I Have Loved and Lost," *Bulletin of the Atomic Scientists,* 25 December 1969, pp. 6–8.

13. Collins and Pinch, "Construction," pp. 257–58.

14. Allison, "Experimental Psychology," p. 278.

15. R. A. McConnell, "Experimenter Effects in ESP," *JASPR* 69 (1975): 144–45.

16. The 1970s and 1980s have seen an increase in the number of death-related journals such as *Theta, Omega,* and *Death Education,* but the majority of these concentrate on social and psychological aspects of bereavement, suicide, and terminal care, rather than on the issue of survival after death. There is also an increase on the survival-related literature within the journals of parapsychology, and a journal devoted exclusively to survival research, *The Journal for Near-Death Studies* (previously *Anabiosis*). However, few of these are listed in the major indexing and computer services, and their subscriptions are quite limited.

17. R. A. McConnell, "Resolution," p. 212.

18. Cf. Collins and Pinch, "Construction," pp. 258–59.

19. George F. Kneller, *Science as a Human Endeavor* (New York: Columbia University Press, 1978), pp. 191–92; cf. Kuhn, *Structure,* p. 168.

20. Allison, "Experimental Parapsychology," p. 279.

21. Raymond Moody, preface to *Life After Life* (Harrisburg, Pa.: Stackpole Books, 1976).

22. See, for example: Brent A. Barlow, ed., *Understanding Death* (Salt Lake City: Desert Books, 1989); Raymond Bayless, *Apparitions and Survival of Death* (New York: Carol Publishing, 1989); Arthur Berger and Joyce Berger, eds. *Perspectives on Death and Dying* (Philadelphia: Charles Press, 1989); David Childster, *Patterns of Transcendence: Religion, Death,*

and Dying (Belmont, Calif.: Wadsworth, 1989); Philip Kapleau, *The Wheel of Life and Death: A Practical and Spiritual Guide to Death, Dying and Beyond* (Garden City, N.Y.: Doubleday, 1989); Robert and Beatrice Kastenbaum, *Encyclopedia of Death* (New York: Oxford University Press, 1989); David Lund, *Death and Consciousness: The Case for Life after Death* (New York: Ballantine Books, 1989); Melvin Morse and Paul Perry, *Closer to the Light: Learning from Children's Near-Death Experiences* (New York: Villard, 1990); Lois B. Murphy, ed. *There is More Beyond: Selected Papers of Gardner Murphy* (Jefferson, N.C.: McFarland, 1989); Mary Murphy, *New Images of the Last Things: Karl Rahner on Death and Life After Death* (Mahwah, N.J.: Paulist Press, 1989); Carol W. Parrish-Harra, *The New Age Handbook on Death and Dying* (San Bernardino, Calif.: Borgo Press, 1989); Robert C. Smith, *You Can Remember Your Past Lives* (New York: Warner, 1989); Chet Snow and Helen Wambach, *Mass Dreams of the Future* (New York: McGraw-Hill, 1989); Joel Whitton and Joe Fisher, *Life Between Life: Scientific Explorations into the Void Separating One Incarnation from the Next* (New York: Warner, 1989); and Ian Wilson, *The After Death Experience* (New York: Morrow, 1989).

23. For the dangers of lay affiliation, see Allison, "Experimental Parapsychology," pp. 238ff.

24. Collins and Pinch, "Construction," p. 253.

25. Apparently Paul Allison's dissertation, in Sociology at the University of Wisconsin at Madison in 1973, was among the first. Jeff Mishlove's dissertation at Berkeley in 1978 has since raised serious questions about the rights of the university to grant such degrees. Stevenson's chair at the University of Virginia Medical School was founded and funded by Chester Carlson, the legendary founder of the Xerox Corporation.

26. Cf. John Grant Fuller, *The Great Soul Trial* (New York: Macmillan, 1969).

27. Collins and Pinch, "Construction," p. 255.

28. Ibid., p. 254.

29. Kuhn, *Structure*, pp. 202–3.

30. Truzzi, "Skeptical," pp. 49, 89.

31. Cf. the excellent coverage in John Grant Fuller, *The Airmen Who Would Not Die* (New York: G. P Putnam's Sons, 1979).

32. Cf. Kuhn, *Structure*.

33. Max Planck, *A Spiritual Autobiography* (New York: Philosophical Library, 1949), pp. 33–34.

34. Tart, "Emergent Interactionism," p. 182.

35. Paul Feyerabend, *Science in a Free Society* (London: NLB, 1978),

pp. 60–90 passim.

36. Paul Feyerabend, quoted in "News and Comment," *Science* 206 (2 Nov. 1979): 537.

37. Kneller, *Science as a Human Endeavor,* pp. 226–32.

38. Cf. Sandra Mertman, "Communicating with the Dead," in Robert Kastenbaum, ed., *Between Life and Death* (New York: Springer, 1979), esp. pp. 124–32.

Chapter 6: What Will the Next World Be Like?

1. Kenneth Ring, *Life at Death* (New York: Coward, McCann & Geoghegan, 1980), pp. 23–33

2. Robert Kastenbaum, *Between Life and Death* (New York: Springer, 1979), esp. pp. 16, 20, 22. Kastenbaum argues for a much-needed antidote to the presentation that might imply death is "fun," or merely an easy release from suffering.

3. Ibid., p. 180.

4. John Hick, *Death and Eternal Life* (New York: Harper & Row, 1976), pp. 414–16.

5. Yogi Ramacharaka, *The Life Beyond Death* (Chicago: Yogi Publication Society, 1940), p. 80.

6. Nils O. Jacobson, *Life Without Death?* trans. Sheila La Farge (New York: Delacorte Press, 1974), p. 266.

7. Cf. Maurice Rawlings, *Beyond Death's Door* (Nashville, Tenn.: Thomas Nelson, 1978), who shows even good Christians occasionally undergoing "hellish" type experiences.

8. This thesis is further developed by Michael Grosso, "Possible Nature of Post-Mortem States," *JASPR* 74, no. 4 (1980): 422.

9. Hick, *Death and Eternal Life,* p. 392.

10. Ibid., p. 457.

11. J. M. O. Wheatley, "Reincarnation, Astral Bodies, and Psi Components," *JASPR* 72, no. 2 (1979): 111, 118.

12. J. B. Rhine, "Research on Spirit Survival Reexamined," *JPP* 20, no. 2 (June 1956): 127.

13. J. B. Rhine, "The Science of Nonphysical Nature," in Jan Ludwig, ed., *Philosophy and Parapsychology* (Buffalo, N.Y.: Prometheus, 1978), p. 125.

14. Hick, *Death and Eternal Life,* p. 344.

15. R. Binkley, "Philosophy and the Survival Hypothesis," *JASPR* 60, no. 1 (1966): 28.

16. John Beloff, "Parapsychology and its Neighbors," in Hoyt L.

Edge and J. M. O. Wheatley, *Philosophical Dimensions of Parapsychology* (Springfield, Ill.: Charles C. Thomas, 1976), p. 383.

17. F. W. H. Myers, *Personality and Its Survival of Bodily Death* (London: Longman's, Green, 1903), pp. xix–xxi.

18. Gardner Murphy, "Are There Any Solid Facts in Psychical Research?" in Edge and Wheatley, *Philosophical Dimensions,* pp. 391–92.

19. Ibid., p. 402.

20. Adrian Dobbs, "Time and Extrasensory Perception," in *PSPR* 54 (1965): 249ff.; cf. also Adrian Dobbs, "Feasibility of a Physical Theory of Psi," in J. R. Smythies, ed., *Brain and Mind,* pp. 241–53.

21. Whately Carington, *Thought Transference* (New York: Creative Age, 1946).

22. Charlie Dunbar Broad, *Lectures on Psychical Research* (New York: Humanities Press, 1962), p. 416.

23. William G. Roll, "A Critical Examination of the Survival Hypothesis," in Angoff and Shapin, *A Century of Psychical Research: The Continuing Doubts and Affirmations* (New York: Parapsychology Foundation, 1971), p. 125.

24. R. H. Thouless and B. P Weiner, "The Psi Processes in Normal and Paranormal Psychology," *PSPR* 48, no. 174 (Dec. 1947).

25. Cf. Stevenson, "Carington's Psychon Theory," *JASPR* 67, no. 2 (1973): 138.

26. J. L. Randall, "Psi Phenomena and Biological Theory," *JSPR* 46 (1971): 151–65.

27. J. B. Rhine, "The Science of Nonphysical Nature," p. 125.

28. Ring, *Life at Death,* pp. 234–37.

29. Karl Pribram, "Holographic Memory," interviewed by Daniel Goleman, *Psychology Today,* February 1979, p. 84.

30. Ring, *Life at Death,* p. 236.

31. Ibid., p. 237.

32. Pribram, "Holographic Memory," p. 84.

33. Quoted in Jacobson, *Life Without Death?* p. 226.

34. Cf. Peter D. Ouspensky, *A New Model of the Universe* (New York: Alfred A. Knopf, 1943).

35. Hornell Hart, "The Psychic Fifth Dimension," *JASPR* 47 (1953): 3–11.

36. C. J. Ducasse, "Letter to Hornell Hart," *JASPR* 47 (1953): 52ff.

37. Herbert Benson, "Physical Aspects of Psi," in Alan Angoff and Betty Shapin, eds., *A Century of Psychical Research: The Continuing Doubts and Affirmations* (New York: Parapsychology Foundation, 1971), pp. 147, 152.

38. Cyril Burt, "Psychology and Parapsychology," in J. R. Smythies, ed., *Science and ESP* (London: Routledge and Kegan Paul, 1967), pp. 106, 120.

39. This suggestion (of reaching other dimensions through tunnels) is Ken Ring's; see *Life at Death*, p. 234.

40. Hart, "Psychic Fifth Dimension," pp. 6–7.

41. Immanuel Kant, *Kritik der Reinen Vernunft*, 2d. ed. (Leipzig: F. Meiner 1906), p. 809.

42. "Human Immortality," in Murphy and Ballou, eds., *William James on Psychical Research* (New York: Viking Press, 1960), p. 292. (Originally written in 1898.)

43. Malcolm M. Moncrieff, *The Clairvoyant Theory of Perception* (London: Faber & Faber, 1951), p. 7.

44. Gilbert Ryle, *The Concept of Mind* (New York: Barnes & Noble, 1949).

45. Charles C. Tart, "States of Consciousness and the State-Specific Sciences," *Science* 176 (12 June 1972): 1203–10.

46. Sir John Eccles, *The Neurophysiological Basis of Mind* (London: Oxford University Press, 1953), pp. 278ff.

47. Lawrence LeShan, *Towards a General Theory of the Paranormal*, Parapsychological Monographs no. 9 (New York:xx Parapsychology Foundation, 1969), and "Human Survival of Biological Death," *Main Currents of Modern Thought* 26, no. 2 (Nov. 1969): 36–57.

48. Jonathan Harrison, "Religion and Psychical Research," in Shivesh C. Thakur, ed., *Philosophy and Psychical Research* (London: George Allen and Unwin, 1976), p. 111.

49. Charlie Dunbar Broad, *Ethics and the History of Philosophy* (New York: Humanities Press, 1952), p. x.

50. H. D. Lewis, *The Self and Immortality* (New York: Seabury Press, 1973), pp. 155–63.

51. Tyrrell, quoted by David Ellis in "The Chemistry of Psi," in Angoff and Shapin, *Parapsychology and the Sciences* (New York: Parapsychology Foundation, 1974), p. 214.

52. C. W. K. Mundle, "The Explanation of ESP," in Smythies, *Science and ESP,* pp. 205–6; cf. John Beloff, "Parapsychology," in Edge and Wheatley, *Philosophical Dimensions,* p. 384.

53. Gardner Murphy, "Psychical Research and the Mind-Body Relationship," *JASPR* 40 (1946): 192.

54. Lawrence LeShan, "Physicists and Mystics, Similarities in World-View," *Journal of Transpersonal Psychology* 1, no. 2 (1969): 1–15.

55. Ring, *Life at Death,* pp. 247–48.

56. Hick, *Death and Eternal Life*, p. 275.

57. Cf. Emilio Servadio, "Mind-Body, Reality, and Psi," in Betty Shapin and Lisette Coly, eds., *Brain/Mind and Parapsychology* (New York: Parapsychology Foundation), pp. 234–38.

58. Charles C. Tart, "States of Consciousness and the State-Specific Sciences," *Science* 176 (12 June 1972): 1203–10.

59. Price's theory is analysed into these two (solipsistic and inter-subjective) levels by Michael Grosso, "The Survival of Personality in a Mind-Dependent World?" *JASPR* 73, no. 4 (1979): 369. Pure Land sutras are cited in Becker, "The Pure Land Revisited," *Journal of Near-Death Studies* 4, no. 1 (1984): 51–68.

60. Werner Heisenberg, *Philosophical Problems of Nuclear Science* (Greenwich, Conn.: Fawcett, 1966), p. 82.

61. H. D. Aiken, *The Age of Ideology* (New York: New American Library, 1956), p. 14.

62. H. H. Price, "Survival and the Idea of Another World," in Terence Penelhum, ed., *Immortality* (Belmont, Calif.: Wadsworth, 1973), esp. pp. 40–46.

63. A. J. Ayer, *The Central Questions of Philosophy* (New York: Holt, Rinehart & Winston, 1974), pp. 124–25.

64. Gardner Murphy, "Field Theory and Survival," *JASPR* 39, no. 4 (1945): 200–201.

65. Hick, *Death and Eternal Life*, p. 464.

66. Ducasse, *Critical Examination*, p. 203.

BIBLIOGRAPHY

Abramovitch, Henry. "An Israeli Account of a Near-Death Experience: A Case Study of Cultural Dissonance." *Journal of Near-Death Studies* 6 (1987): 175–83.

Aiken, H. D. *The Age of Ideology.* New York: New American Library, 1956.

Alcock, James E. *Science and Supernature: Critiques of Parapsychology.* Buffalo, N.Y.: Prometheus Books, 1989.

Al-Issa, Ihsan. "Socio-cultural Factors in Hallucinations." *International Journal of Social Psychiatry* 24, no. 3 (1978): 167–76.

Almeder, Robert. *Beyond Death: Evidence for Life after Death.* Springfield, Ill.: Charles C. Thomas, 1987.

Angoff, Alan, and Betty Shapin, eds. *A Century of Psychical Research: The Continuing Doubts and Affirmations.* New York: Parapsychology Foundation, 1971.

————. *Parapsychology and the Sciences.* New York: Parapsychology Foundation, 1974.

Atwater, P. M. *Coming Back to Life: The Aftereffects of the Near-Death Experience.* New York: Dodd, Mead, 1988.

Ayer, A. J. *The Central Questions of Philosophy.* New York: Holt, Rinehart and Winston, 1974.

Bachrach, A. J., ed. *Experimental Foundations of Clinical Psychology.* New York: Basic Books, 1962.

Badham, Paul, and Linda Badham. *Death and Immortality in the Religions of the World.* New York: Paragon House, 1987.

Baird, A. T., ed. *One Hundred Cases for Survival After Death.* New York: Bernard Ackerman, 1944.

Baldwin, Maitland. "Hallucinations in Neurologic Syndromes." In *Hallucinations,* ed. Louis J. West. New York: Grune and Stratton, 1962.

Banerjee, H. N., and Will Oursler. *Lives Unlimited: Reincarnation East and West.* New York: Doubleday, 1974.

Bardens, Dennis. *Mysterious Worlds.* London: W. H. Allen, 1970.

Barnett, Linda. "Hospice Nurses' Knowledge of and Attitudes toward the Near-Death Experience." *Journal of Near-Death Studies* 9, no. 4 (1989): 225–32.

Barrett, William. *Death-bed Visions: The Psychical Experiences of the Dying.* London: Methuen, 1926.

Bayless, Raymond. *Apparitions and Survival of Death.* New York: Carol Publishing Group, 1989.

Beard, George Miller. *Nature and Phenomena of Trance.* New York: Putnam, 1881.

Beardsley, D. C., and M. Wertheimer. *Readings in Perception.* New York: D. Van Nostrand, 1958.

Becker, Carl B. "ESP, NDEs, and the Limits of Scientific Knowledge." *Journal of Near-Death Studies* 9, no. 1 (1990): 11–20.

———. "The Pure Land Revisited: Sino-Japanese Meditations and Near-Death Experiences of the Next World." *Journal of Near-Death Studies* 4, no. 1 (1984): 51–68.

Becker, Ernest. *The Denial of Death.* New York: Free Press, 1973.

Bede. *A History of the English Church and People.* Harmondsworth, U.K.: Penguin, 1955.

Beloff, John. *The Importance of Psychical Research.* London: Society for Psychical Research, 1988.

———. "Parapsychology and Its Neighbors." In *Philosophical Dimensions of Parapsychology,* ed. Hoyt L. Edge and J. M. O. Wheatley. Springfield Ill.: Charles C. Thomas, 1976.

Benson, Herbert. "Physical Aspects of Psi." In *A Century of Psychical Research,* ed. Alan Angoff and Betty Shapin. New York: Parapsychology Foundation, 1971.

Berger, Arthur S. *Aristocracy of the Dead.* Jefferson, N.C.: McFarland, 1987.

————. *Evidence of Life after Death: A Casebook for the Tough-Minded.* Springfield, Ill.: Charles C. Thomas, 1988.

Berger, Arthur S., Joyce Berger, et al., eds. *Perspectives on Death and Dying.* Philadelphia, Pa.: Charles Press, 1989.

Bergson, Henri. *Mind-Energy.* Translated by H. Wilson Carr. New York: Henry Holt, 1920.

Berkeley, George, Bishop. *Principles of Human Knowledge.* London: Routledge, 1893.

————. *Three Dialogues Between Hylas and Philonous.* Chicago: Open Court, 1947.

Bernstein, Morey. *The Search for Bridey Murphy.* New York: Doubleday, 1956.

Bettelheim, Bruno. *The Empty Fortress: Infantile Autism and the Birth of the Self.* New York: Free Press, 1972.

Binkley, R. "Philosophy and the Survival Hypothesis." *JASPR* 60, no. 1 (1966): 28.

Bishop, G. *The Apparition.* New York: Bantam Books, 1979.

Black, Peter, M. "Brain Death." *New England Journal of Medicine* 299, no. 7 (17 August 1978): 342–44.

————. "Criteria of Brain Death." *Postgraduate Medicine* 57, no. 2 (February 1975): 69–73.

Blacker, R. S. "To Sleep, Perchance to Dream." *JAMA* 242, no. 21 (23 November 1979): 2291.

Blackmore, Susan J., and T. S. Troscianko. "The Physiology of the Tunnel." *Journal of Near-Death Studies* 8, no. 1 (1989): 15–28.

Bliss, Eugene L., and Lincoln D. Clark. "Visual Hallucinations." In *Hallucinations,* ed. Louis J. West. New York: Grune and Stratton, 1962.

Bozzano, E. *Phénomenes psychiques au moment de la mort.* Paris: Nicholas Renault, 1923.

Braddock, Oliver, and Janette Atkinson. "Accommodation and Acuity in the Human Infant." In *Developmental Neurobiology of Vision,* ed. Ralph D. Freeman. New York: Plenum Press, 1979.

Bradley, Francis Herbert. *Appearance and Reality.* Oxford: Clarendon Press, 1897.

Bramel, D., and L. Festinger. "The Reactions of Humans to Cognitive Dissonance." In *Experimental Foundations of Clinical Psychology,* ed. A. J. Bachrach. New York: Basic Books, 1962.

Brehm, J. W. "Post-Decision Changes in Desirability of Alternatives." *Journal of Abnormal Social Psychology* 52 (1956): 378–84.

Brennan, Robert E. *Thomistic Psychology.* New York: Macmillan, 1941.

Brian, D. *The Enchanted Voyager: The Life of J. B. Rhine.* Englewood Cliffs, N.J.: Prentice-Hall, 1982.

Broad, Charlie Dunbar. "Dreaming and Some of Its Implications." *PSPR,* 1958, pp. 57–78.

———. *Ethics and the History of Philosophy.* New York: Humanities Press, 1952.

———. *Lectures in Psychical Research.* London: Routledge and Kegan Paul, 1962.

Brody, Baruch A., ed. *Readings in the Philosophy of Science.* Englewood Cliffs, N.J.: Prentice-Hall, 1970.

Bruner, Jerome. *Beyond the Information Given.* New York: Norton, 1973.

———. *On Knowing, Essays for the Left Hand.* Cambridge: Harvard University Press, 1979.

Bruner, Jerome, and L. Postman. "On the Perception of Incongruity: A Paradigm." In *Readings in Perception,* ed. D. C. Beardsley and M. Wertheimer. New York: Van Nostrand, 1958.

Burt, Cyril. "Psychology and Parapsychology." In *Science and ESP,* ed. J. R. Smythies. London: Routledge and Kegan Paul, 1967.

Campbell, A. B. *Bring Yourself to Anchor.* London: Rider, 1947.

Carington, Whately. *Matter, Mind, and Meaning.* New Haven: Yale University Press, 1949.

———. *Telepathy.* 3d ed. London: Methuen, 1943.

———. *A Theory of the Mechanism of Survival: The Fourth Dimension.* New York: E. P. Dutton, 1920.

———. *Thought Transference.* New York: Creative Age Press, 1946.

Carrington, Hereward H. *Death, Its Causes and Phenomena.* London: Rider, 1911.

———. *Modern Psychical Phenomena.* London: Kegan Paul, Trench, Trubner, 1919.

Case, Charles J. *Beyond Time: Ideas of the Great Philosophers on Eternal Existence and Immortality.* Lanham, Md.: University Press of America, 1985.

"Cases," *JASPR* 18 (1924): 37; 31 (1937): 103.

Castaneda, Carlos. *The Teachings of Don Juan.* New York: Ballantine, 1969.

Cattier, Michel. *The Life and Works of Wilhelm Reich.* Translated by G. Boulanger. New York: Horizon Press, 1971.

Chari, C. T. K. "'Buried Memories' in Survivalist Research." *IJPP* 4, no. 3 (1962): 40.

———. "Paranormal Cognition, Survival, and Reincarnation." *JASPR* 56, no. 4 (1962): 160.

———. "Parapsychological Studies and Literature in India." *IJPP* 2, no. 1 (1960): 24–36.

Charles, R. H. *Eschatology.* New York: Schocken, 1963.

Chauvin, Remy. "To Reconcile Psi and Physics." In *Philosophical Dimensions of Parapsychology,* ed. Hoyt L. Edge and J. M. O. Wheatley. Springfield, Ill.: Charles C. Thomas, 1976.

Child, I. L. "The Question of ESP in Dreams." *American Psychologist* 40, no. 11 (1985): 1219–30.

Childster, David. *Patterns of Transcendence: Religion, Death, and Dying.* Belmont, Calif.: Wadsworth, 1989.

Ciner, E. B., E. Schancl-Klitsch, and M. Schieman. "Stereoacuity Development in Young Children." *Optometry and Vision Science* 68, no. 7 (July 1991): 533–36.

Cohen, Leslie, and Eric R. Gelber. "Infant Visual Memory." In *Infant Perception,* ed. Cohen and Salapatek. New York: Academic Press, 1975.

Cohen, Leslie, and Salapatek, Philip, eds. *Infant Perception.* New York: Academic Press, 1975.

Collins, B. Abdy. "Is Proof of Survival Possible?" *PSPR* 46 (1941): 361–76.

Collins, H. M., and Pinch, T. J. "The Construction of the Paranormal: Nothing Unscientific is Happening." In *On the Margins of Science: The Social Construction of Rejected Knowledge,* ed. R. Wallis. Keele, U.K.: Keele University Press, 1979.

Courage, M. L., and R. J. Adams. "Visual Acuity Assessment from Birth to Three Years Using the Acuity Card Procedure." *Optometry and Vision Science* 67, no. 9 (Sept. 1990): 713–18.

Crabtree, A. *Multiple Man: Explorations in Possession and Multiple Personality.* New York: Praeger, 1985.

Crick, F. H. C. "Thinking About the Brain." *Scientific American* 241, no. 3 (September 1979): 185.

Crookall, Robert. *Events on the Threshold of the Afterlife.* Moradabad, India: Darshana International, 1967.

———. *Intimations of Immortality.* Exeter, U.K.: James Clarke, 1965.

———. *The Mechanism of Astral Projection.* Moradabad, India: Darshana International, 1968.

———. *More Astral Projections.* London: Aquarian Press, 1964.

———. *The Study and Practice of Astral Projection.* London: Aquarian Press, 1960.

———. *The Supreme Adventure: Analyses of Psychic Communication.* Greenwood, S.C.: Attic Press, 1975.

Cummings, Abraham. *Immortality Proved by Testimony of the Sense.* Bath, Me.: J. C. Tobbley, 1826.

Curnock, D. A. "The Senses of the Newborn." *British Medical Journal* 299, no. 6714 (16 Dec. 1992): 1478–79.

Dale, Laura. "Spontaneous Experiences Reported by a Group of Experimental Subjects." *JASPR* 40, no. 2 (1946): 59–69.

Dale, Laura, et al. "Recent Survey of Spontaneous ESP Phenomena." *JASPR* 56, no. 1 (1962): 26–46.

Dallas, Helen. "Bilocation." *JASPR* 40, no. 2 (1946): 59–69.

David-Neel, Alexandra. *Magic and Mystery in Tibet.* New York: University Books, 1958.

Davis, Lorraine. "A Comparison of UFO and Near-Death Experiences as Vehicles for the Evolution of Human Consciousness." *Journal of Near-Death Studies* 7 (1988): 240–56.

Dayton, G. "Analysis of Characteristics of Fixations Reflex in Infants by Use of dc Electro-oculography." *Neurology* 14 (1964): 1152–56.

Dayton, G., M. H. Jones, P. Aiu, R. A. Rawson, B. Steele, and M. Rose. "Developmental Study of Coordinated Eye Movements in the Human Infant." *Archives of Ophthalmology* 71 (1964): 865–75.

de Quincey, Thomas. *Suspiria de Profundis.* London: MacDonald, 1956.

de Rochas, A. *Les vies successives.* Paris, Chacorna, 1911.

Delacour, Jean-Baptiste. *Glimpses of the Beyond.* Translated by E. B. Garside. New York: Delacorte Press, 1973.

Dewhurst, Kenneth. "Autoscopic Hallucinations." *Irish Journal of Medical Science* 342 (1954): 266–68.

Dewhurst, Kenneth, and John Pearson. "Visual Hallucinations of the Self in Organic Disease." *Journal of Neurological and Neurosurgical Psychiatry* 18 (1955): 53.

Dewhurst, Kenneth, and John Todd. "The Double: Its Psychopathology and Psychophysiology." *JNMD* 122 (1955): 47.

Dobbs, Adrian. "Feasibility of a Physical Theory of Psi." In *Science and ESP*, ed. R. Smythies, 241–53. London: Routledge and Kegan Paul, 1967.

————. "Time and Extrasensory Perception." *PSPR* 54 (1965): 249ff.

Dobervich, Carolyn. "Kirlian Photography Revealed." *Psychic* 6, no. 1 (November 1974): 34–39.

Dodds, E. R. "Why I Do Not Believe in Survival." *PSPR* 42 (1934): 147–72.

Dolby, R. G. A. "Reflections on Deviant Science." In *On the Margins of Science*, ed. Roy Wallis. Keele, U.K.: Keele University Press, 1979.

Ducasse, Curt J. *A Critical Examination of the Belief in a Life After Death.* Springfield, Ill.: Charles C. Thomas, 1961.

————. "How Good is the Evidence for Survival After Death?" *JASPR* 53, no. 3 (1959): 97.

————. *Is Life After Death Possible?* Berkeley: University of California Press, 1948.

————. *Nature Mind and Death.* LaSalle, Ill.: Open Court, 1951.

————. *Paranormal Phenomena, Science, and Life After Death.* New York: Parapsychology Foundation, 1969.

Ebon, Martin. *The Evidence for Life After Death.* New York: New American Library, 1977.

Eccles, Sir John C. *Facing Reality.* New York: Longmans/Springer, 1970.

————. *The Neurophysiological Basis of Mind.* London: Oxford University Press, 1953.

Eccles, Sir John C., and Karl Popper. *The Self and Its Brain.* Berlin and New York: Springer Verlag, 1977.

Edge, Hoyt L., and J. M. O. Wheatley. *Philosophical Dimensions of Parapsychology.* Springfield, Ill.: Charles C. Thomas, 1976.

Edge, Hoyt L., R. L. Morris, J. Palmer, and J. Rush. *Foundations of Parapsychology: Exploring the Boundaries of Human Capability.* New York: Routledge, Chapman & Hall, 1986.

Ehrenwald, J. *The ESP Experience.* New York: Basic Books. 1978.

Eisenbud, Jule. *Parapsychology and the Unconscious.* Berkeley, Calif:: North Atlantic, 1984.

Eliade, Mircea. "Mythologies of Death: An Introduction." In *Religious Encounters with Death*, ed. F. E. Reynolds and E. H. Waugh. University Park: Pennsylvania State University Press, 1977.

Elliot, F. A. *Clinical Neurology.* Philadelphia: Saunders, 1966.

Ellis, David. "The Chemistry of Psi." In *Parapsychology and the Sciences,* ed. Alan Angoff and Betty Shapin. New York: Parapsychology Foundation, 1974.

Enright, D. J., ed. *The Oxford Book of Death.* New York: Oxford University Press, 1987.

Erlandson, Douglas. "Timelessness, Immutability and Eschatology." *IJPR,* 9, no. 3 (1978): 130–32.

Ermendrout, G. B. "A Mathematical Theory of Visual Hallucination Patterns." *Biological Cybernetics* 34, no. 3 (October 1979): 137.

Fantz, R. L., and Miranda, S. B. "Newborn Infant Attention in Form of Contour." *Child Development* 44 (1975): 224–28.

Feyerabend, Paul. *Against Method.* London: Verso, 1975.

————. "How to Be a Good Empiricist—A Plea for Tolerance in Matters Epistemological." In *Readings in the Philosophy of Science,* ed. Baruch A. Brody. Englewood Cliffs, N.J.: Prentice-Hall, 1970.

Fiore, E. *The Unquiet Dead.* New York: Dolphin/Doubleday, 1987.

Fisher, Seymour. "Body Image Boundaries and Hallucinations." In *Hallucinations,* ed. Louis J. West. New York: Grune & Stratton, 1962.

Flew, Antony. ed. *Body, Mind and Death.* New York: Macmillan, 1964.

————. "Is There a Case for Disembodied Survival?" *JASPR* 66, no. 2 (April 1972): 129.

————. *The Logic of Mortality.* Oxford: Blackwell, 1987.

————. "Parapsychology Revisited: Laws, Miracles, and Repeatability." *Humanist* 36, no. 1 (1976): 28.

————. "Parapsychology: Science or Pseudo-Science?" *Pacific Philosophical Quarterly* 61 (1980): 100–114.

Flynn, Charles C. *After the Beyond: Human Transformation and the NDE.* Englewood Cliffs, N.J.: Prentice-Hall, 1986.

Ford, Arthur. *Unknown But Known.* New York: Signet, 1969.

Fox, Oliver. *Astral Projection.* London: Rider, 1939.

Freeman, Hilary. "The Case for Immortality." *Pacific Philosophy Forum* 3, no. 2 (December 1964): 4–44.

Freeman, Ralph D., ed. *Developmental Neurobiology of Vision.* New York: Plenum Press, 1979.

Fromer, Jacob. *Ghetto-Dämmerung.* Leipzig: Schuster and Loeffler, 1911.

Fuller, John Grant. *The Airmen Who Would Not Die.* New York: G. P. Putnam's Sons, 1979.

————. *The Great Soul Trial.* New York: Macmillan, 1969.

Furn, Bette G. "Adjustment and the Near-Death Experience: A Conceptual and Therapeutic Model." *Journal of Near-Death Studies* 6 (1987): 4–18, 37–40.

Gabbard, Glen O., and Stuart W. Twemlow. *With the Eyes of the Mind: An Empirical Analysis of Out-of-Body States.* New York: Praeger, 1984.

Gallup, George Jr., with W. Proctor. *Adventures in Immortality: A Look Beyond the Threshold of Death.* New York: McGraw-Hill, 1982.

Garfield, Charles A. "The Dying Patient's Concern with Life After Death." In *Between Life and Death,* ed. Robert Kastenbaum. New York: Springer, 1979.

———. *Psychosocial Care of the Dying Patient.* New York: McGraw-Hill, 1978.

Garrett, Eileen J. *Adventures in the Supernormal: A Personal Memoir.* New York: Garrett, 1949.

———. *My Life as a Search for the Meaning of Mediumship.* London: Rider, 1938.

Geddes, Sir Auckland. "A Voice from the Grandstand." *Edinburgh Medical Journal,* n.s. 44 (1937): 367.

Gettings, Fred. *Ghosts in Photographs.* New York: Harmony Books, 1978.

Ghosh, M. K. *Life Beyond Death.* Flushing, N.Y.: Asia Book Corp. of America, 1985.

Gibson, E. P. "An Examination of Motivation as Found in Selective Cases." *JASPR* 38, no. 2 (1944): 83–103.

Gibson, H. B. "The Royal Nonesuch of Parapsychology." *Bulletin of the British Psychological Society* 32 (1979): 65–67.

Giovetta, Paula. "NDEs in Other Cultures." *Luce y Ombra* 87, no. 3 (1987): 209–13.

Goldstein, Eleanor C., ed. *Death and Dying.* Boca Raton, Fla.: Social Issues, 1987.

Gordon, Henry. *Channeling into the New Age: The "Teachings" of Shirley MacLaine and Other Such Gurus: An Unauthorized Edition.* Buffalo, N.Y.: Prometheus Books, 1988.

Gray, T. "Changing Unsubstantiated Belief: Testing the Ignorance Hypothesis." *Canadian Journal of Behavioral Science* 17 (1985): 263–70.

Greeley, A. M. "The Impossible: It's Happening." *American Health,* Jan.–Feb. 1987, 32–33.

Green, Celia. *Lucid Dreams.* London: Hamish Hamilton, 1968.

————. *Out-of-the-Body Experiences.* London: Institute of Psychophysical Research, 1968.

Green, Celia, and C. McCreery. *Apparitions.* London: Hamish Hamilton, Ltd., 1975.

Greyson, Bruce. "Can Science Explain the Near-Death Experience?" *Journal of Near-Death Studies* 8, no. 2 (1989): 77–91.

————. "Near-Death Encounters with and without Near-Death Experiences." *Journal of Near-Death Studies* 8, no. 3 (1989): 151–62.

————. "Near-Death Experiences Precipitated by Suicide Attempt: Lack of Influence of Psychopathology, Religion, and Expectations." *Journal of Near-Death Studies* 9, no. 3 (1991): 183–88.

————. "The NDE Scale: Construction, Reliability, and Validity." *JNMD* 171 (1983): 369–75.

Greyson, Bruce, and Charles P. Flynn, eds. *The Near-Death Experience: Problems, Prospects, Perspectives.* Springfield, Ill.: Charles C. Thomas, 1984.

Greyson, Bruce, and Barbara Harris. "Clinical Approaches to the Near-Death Experiencer." *Journal of Near-Death Studies* 6 (1987): 41–52.

Grof, Stanislav. *Realms of the Human Unconscious.* New York: Viking, 1975.

Grof, Stanislav, and Christina Grof. *Beyond Death.* New York: Thames and Hudson, 1980.

Grof, Stanislav, and J. Halifax. *The Human Encounter with Death.* New York: Dutton, 1977.

Grosso, Michael. "Plato and Out-of-Body Experiences." *JASPR* 69, no. 1 (1975): 61–73.

————. "Possible Nature of Post-Mortem States." *JASPR* 74, no. 4 (1980): 422.

————. "Some Varieties of OBE." *JASPR* 70, no. 2 (1976): 179–92.

————. "The Survival of Personality in a Mind-Dependent World?" *JASPR* 73, no. 4 (1979): 369.

————. "Toward an Explanation for Near-Death Phenomena." *JASPR* 75, no. 1 (1981): 37–60.

Guirdham, Arthur. *The Cathars and Reincarnation.* London: Spearman, 1970.

Gupta, L. D., and N. R. Sharma. *Inquiry into the Reincarnation of Shanti Devi.* Delhi: Baluja Press, 1936.

Gurney, Edmund, F. W. H. Myers, and Frank Podmore. *Phantasms of the*

Living. London: Trubner, 1894.

Haber, R. N., ed. *Contemporary Theory and Research in Visual Perception*. New York: Holt, 1968.

Hansel, C. E. M. *ESP: A Scientific Evaluation*. New York: Charles Scribner's Sons, 1966.

———. *The Search for Psychic Power*. Buffalo, N.Y.: Prometheus Books, 1989.

Haraldsson, Erlendur. *Modern Miracles: An Investigative Report on Psychic Phenomena Associated with Sathya Sai Baba*. Buffalo, N.Y.: Prometheus Books, 1987.

Haraldsson, Erlendur, and Ian Stevenson. "A Communicator of the Drop-In Type in Iceland." *JASPR* 69, no. 1 (1975): 33ff.

Harary, Keith, and P. Weintraub. *The Free Flight Program*. New York: St. Martin's Press, 1989.

Hardy, Alister. "Biology and ESP." In *Science and ESP*, ed. J. R. Smythies. London: Routledge and Kegan Paul, 1967.

Harlow, S. R. A. *A Life After Death*. New York: Manor Books, 1968.

Harner, Michael J., ed. *Hallucinogens and Shamanism*. New York: Oxford University Press, 1973.

Harrison, Jonathan. "Religion and Psychical Research." In *Philosophy and Psychical Research*, ed. Shivesh C. Thakur. London: George Allen & Unwin, 1976.

Hart, Hornell. *The Enigma of Survival*. Springfield, Ill.: Charles C. Thomas, 1959.

———. "ESP Projection: Spontaneous Cases and the Experimental Method." *JASPR* 48, no. 2 (1954): 121–46.

———. "The Psychic Fifth Dimension." *JASPR* 47 (1953): 3–11.

———. "Rejoinder [to Louisa Rhine]." *JPP* 22 (1958): 59–62.

———. "Scientific Survival Research." *IJPP* 9, no. 1 (1967): 45.

Hart, Hornell, et al. "Six Theories About Apparitions." *PSPR* 50 (1956): 179.

Hartwell, John. "A Study of the Physiological Variables Associated with OOBEs." In *Research in Parapsychology, 1974,* ed. William G. Roll, 127–29. Metuchen, N.J.: Scarecrow Press, 1975.

Haynes, Renee. *The Seeing Eye, The Seeing I*. New York: St. Martin's, 1976.

Head, Joseph, and S. L. Cranston. *Reincarnation: The Phoenix Fire Mystery*. New York: Julian Press, 1977.

IIcarn, Lafcadio. *Gleanings in Buddha Fields*. Boston: Houghton Mifflin, 1897.

Heersema, D. J., and J. vanHof vanDuin. "Gedragsmatige bepaling van de gezichtsscherpte bij kinderen van 1 tot 4 jaar [Behavioral determination of visual acuity in 1- to-4-year-old children]." *Tijdschrift voor Kindergeneeskunde* 57, no. 6 (Dec. 1989): 210–14.

Heisenberg, Werner. *Philosophic Problems of Nuclear Science*. Greenwich, Conn.: Fawcett, 1966.

Henkel, Linda A., and Rick E. Berger, eds. *Research in Parapsychology, 1987*. Metuchen, N.J.: Scarecrow, 1988.

Henshaw, G. *The Proofs of the Truths of Spiritualism*. London: Kegan Paul, Trench, Trubner, 1919.

Heywood, Rosalind. *Beyond the Reach of Sense*. New York: E. P. Dutton, 1961.

———. "Notes on Changing Mental Climates and Research into ESP." In *Science and ESP*, ed. J. R. Smythies. London: Routledge and Kegan Paul, 1967.

Hick, John. *Death and Eternal Life*. New York: Harper and Row, 1976.

———. "Eschatological Verification Reconsidered." *Religious Studies* 12 (June 1977): 191–93.

———. *Evil and the God of Love*. London: Macmillan, 1966.

Hocking, William E. *The Meaning of Immortality in Human Experience, Including Thoughts on Death and Life*. Reprint. Westport, Conn.: Greenwood, 1973.

Holden, C. "Academy Helps Army Be All That It Can Be." *Science* 238 (1988): 1501–2.

Holden, Janice Miner. "Visual Perception during Naturalistic Near-Death Out-of-Body Experiences." *Journal of Near-Death Studies* 7 (1988): 107–20.

Hume, David. "Of Miracles." In *An Enquiry Concerning Human Understanding*. Chicago: Open Court, 1912.

Hyman, Ray. *The Elusive Quarry: A Scientific Appraisal of Psychical Research*. Buffalo, N.Y.: Prometheus Books, 1988.

Hyslop, Gerald P. *Psychical Research and Phenomena of Spiritual Intercourse*. Albuquerque, N.M.: American Institute for Psychological Research, 1988.

Hyslop, James H. *Life After Death: Problems of the Future Life and Its Nature*. New York: Dutton, 1918.

Inglis, B. *Science and Parascience: A History of the Paranormal,*

1914–1939. London: Hodder and Stoughton, 1984.

Insinger, Mori. "The Impact of a Near-Death Experience on Family Relationships." *Journal of Near-Death Studies* 9, no. 3 (1991): 141–80.

Irwin, Harvey J. *Flight of the Mind: A Psychological Study of the Out-of-Body Experience*. Metuchen N.J.: Scarecrow Press, 1985.

———. "Out of the Body Down Under." *JSPR* 50 (1980): 453.

———. "Out-of-Body Experiences in the Blind." *Journal of Near-Death Studies* 6 (1987): 53–59.

Jacobson, Nils O. *Life Without Death?* Translated by Sheila La Farge. New York: Delacorte Press, 1974.

Jahn, R. G. "On the Representation of Psychic Research to the Community of Established Science." In *Research in Parapsychology, 1983*, ed. R. A. White and R. S. Broughton. Metuchen, N.J.: Scarecrow Press, 1984.

James, William. *Essays in Psychical Research*. Cambridge: Harvard University Press, 1986.

———. *Principles of Psychology*. New York: Henry Holt, 1890.

———. *Varieties of Religious Experience*. New York: Longmans, Green, 1902.

Jasper, Herbert H. *Epilepsy and the Functional Anatomy of the Human Brain*. Boston: Little, Brown, 1954.

Jastrow, Robert. Review of *Broca's Brain*, by Carl Sagan. *New York Times Book Review*, 10 June 1979, p. 6.

Jayatilleke, K. N. *The Message of the Buddha*. New York: Free Press, 1974.

———. *Survival and Karma in Buddhist Perspective*. Kandy, Sri Lanka: Buddhist Publishing Society, 1969.

Joad, C. E. M. *The Recovery of Belief*. London: Faber and Faber, 1952.

Johnson, Ralph C., Jr. *Confronting Death: Psychoreligious Responses*. Edited by Margaret Miles. Ann Arbor: University of Michigan Research Press, 1988.

Jones, M. "The Development of Early Behaviour Patterns in Young Children." *Pedagogical Seminary and Journal of Genetic Psychology* 33 (1926): 537–85.

Jung, C. G. *Memories, Dreams, Reflections*. London: Collins and Routledge & Kegan Paul, 1963.

Kalish, Richard A. *The Final Transition*. Amityville, N.Y.: Baywood, 1987.

Kant, Immanuel. *Dreams of a Spirit-Seer.* Translated by E. F. Goerwitz. London: New-Church Press, 1915. (Origally published in 1766.)

———. *Kritik der Reinen Vernunft.* 2d ed. Leipzig: F. Miner, 1906.

Kapleau, Philip. *The Wheel of Life and Death: A Practical and Spiritual Guide to Death, Dying and Beyond.* Garden City, N.Y.: Doubleday, 1989.

Karmel, B. Z., and E. B. Maisel, "A Neuronal Activity Model for Infant Visual Attention." In Leslie Cohen and Philip Salapatek, eds., *Infant Perception.* New York: Academic Press, 1975.

Kastenbaum, Robert. *Between Life and Death.* New York: Springer, 1979.

———, ed. *Is There Life After Death?* London: Rider, 1984.

Kastenbaum, Robert, and Ruth Aisenberg. *The Psychology of Death.* New York: Springer, 1972.

Kastenbaum, Robert, and Beatrice Kastenbaum. *Encyclopedia of Death.* New York: Oxford University Press, 1989.

Kellehear, Allan. "Community Attitudes Toward Near-Death Experiences: A Chinese Study." *Journal of Near-Death Studies* 8, no. 3 (1989): 163–73.

Kellehear, Allan, and Michael D. Gliksman. "Near-Death Experiences and the Measurement of Blood Gases." *Journal of Near-Death Studies* 9, no. 1 (1990): 41–44.

Kilner, Walter J. *The Human Atmosphere.* New York: S. Weiser, 1973.

Kirlian, Semyon, and Valentina Kirlian. "Photography and Visual Observations by Means of High Frequency Currents." *Journal of Scientific and Applied Photography* 6 (1961): 397–403.

Klimo, Jon. *Channeling: Investigation on Receiving Information from Paranormal Sources.* Los Angeles: Jeremy Tarcher Press, 1988.

Kneller, George F. *Science as a Human Endeavor.* New York: Columbia University Press, 1978.

Knight, David C., ed. *The ESP Reader.* New York: Grosset and Dunlap, 1969.

Koestler, Arthur. "The Perversity of Physics." In *Parapsychology and the Sciences,* ed. Alan Angoff and Betty Shapin. New York: Parapsychology Foundation, 1974.

———. *The Roots of Coincidence.* New York: Random House, 1974.

Kolb, Lawrence C. "Phantom Sensations, Hallucinations, and the Body Image." In *Hallucinations*, ed. Louis J. West. New York: Grune and Stratton, 1962.

Kramer, Kenneth P. *The Sacred Art of Dying: How the World Religions Understand Death.* Mahwah, N.J.: Paulist Press, 1988.

Kramer, Scott, and Wu Kuan-ming. *Thinking Through Death.* Melbourne: Krieger, 1988.

Krippner, Stanley, ed. *Advances in Parapsychological Research, 5.* Jefferson, N.C.: McFarland, 1987.

Kübler-Ross, E. *Death: The Final Stage of Growth.* Englewood Cliffs, N.J.: Prentice-Hall, 1975.

————. *Living with Death and Dying.* New York: Macmillan, 1982.

————. *On Death and Dying.* New York: Macmillan, 1969.

Kuhn, Thomas. *The Structure of Scientific Revolutions.* 2d ed. Chicago: University of Chicago Press, 1970.

Kurtz, Paul, ed. *A Skeptic's Handbook of Parapsychology.* Buffalo, N.Y.: Prometheus Books, 1985.

————. *The Transcendental Temptation: A Critique of Religion and the Paranormal.* Buffalo, N.Y.: Prometheus Books, 1986.

Kutscher, Austin, and M. Kutscher, eds. *A Bibliography of Books on Death, Bereavement, Loss and Grief: 1896–1972.* New York: Health Sciences, 1974.

LaBerge, Stephen, ed. *Lucid Dreaming.* New York: Plenum Press, 1988.

Lancelin, Charles. *La vie posthume.* Paris: Henri Durville, 1920.

Landau, Lucian. "An Unusual OBE." *JSPR* 42, no. 717 (1963): 125–28.

Laubscher, B. J. F. *Beyond Life's Curtain.* Capetown, South Africa: Howard Timmins, 1967.

Lauf, Detlef I. *Secret Doctrines of the Tibetan Books of the Dead.* Boston: Shambhala, 1989.

Lavater, Ludwig. *Of Ghostes and Spirites Walking by Nyght.* Edited and translated by J. Dover Wilson. London: Oxford University Press (for the Shakespeare Association), 1929. (Originally published in 1573.)

Leadbeater, C. W. *The Life After Death.* London: Theosophical Publishing House, 1912.

————. *Man Visible and Invisible.* London: Theosophical Publishing House, 1907.

Lean, Florence Marryat. *There Is No Death.* London: Kegan Paul, Trench, Trubner, 1891.

Lemaître, A. "Fritz Algar." *Archives de Psychologie* 5 (1906): 85ff.

Lenz, F. *Life-times: True Accounts of Reincarnation.* Indianapolis: Bobbs-Merrill, 1979.

LeShan, Lawrence. *Alternate Realities.* New York: M. Evans, 1967.

———. *From Newton to ESP.* New York: Sterling, 1985.

———. "Human Survival of Biological Death." *Main Currents of Modern Thought* 26, no. 2 (November 1969): 36–57.

———. "Physicists and Mystics, Similarities on World-View." *Journal of Transpersonal Psychology* 1, no. 2 (1969): 1–15.

———. *The Science of the Paranormal: The Last Frontier.* New York: Sterling, 1987.

———. "Some Psychological Hypotheses on the Non-acceptance of Parapsychology as a Science." *IJPP* 8 (1966): 367–85.

———. *Towards a General Theory of the Paranormal.* Parapsychological monographs no. 9. New York: Parapsychology Foundation, 1969.

LeShan, Lawrence, and Henry Margenau. "An Approach to a Science of Psychical Research." *JSPR* 50, no. 783 (March 1980): 274–75.

Lewis, H. D., ed. *Persons and Life After Death.* New York: Barnes & Noble, 1978.

———. *The Self and Immortality.* New York: Seabury Press, 1973.

Lewis, L. M. *"Ecstatic Religion": An Anthropological Study of Spirit Possession and Shamanism.* Harmondsworth, U.K.: Penguin Books, 1971.

Lief, Harold I. "Commentary on Dr. Ian Stevenson's 'The Evidence of Man's Survival After Death.'" *JNMD* 165, no. 3 (1977): 171.

Liverziani, F. *Reincarnation and its Phenomena—"Who" or "What" Becomes Reincarnated.* London and New York: Regency Press, 1988.

Locher, T. *Parapsychologie in der Schweiz.* Biel, Switzerland: Schweizerischen Vereinigung für Parapsychologie, 1986.

Lombroso, Cesare. *After Death—What?* New York: Sterling, 1988.

Lorimer, David. *Survival? Body, Mind and Death in the Light of Psychic Experience.* London: Routledge and Kegan Paul, 1984.

Lowe, Gordon R. "The Phenomenology of Hallucinations as an Aid to Differential Diagnosis." *British Journal of Psychiatry* 123 (1973): 630.

Lund, David H. *Death and Consciousness: The Case for Life after Death.* New York: Ballantine, 1989.

Lundahl, Craig, ed. *A Collection of Near-Death Research Readings.* Chicago: Nelson-Hall, 1985.

Mach, Ernst. *The Analysis of Sensations and the Relation of the Physical to the Psychical.* Chicago: Open Court, 1914.

MacKenzie, Andrew. *Hauntings and Apparitions: An Investigation of the*

Evidence. Chicago: Academy Chicago, 1988.

Malitz, Brian, and S. L. MacKenzie. "Whence the Enchanted Boundary?" *JPP* 44, no. 2 (1980): 125–66.

Mandler, George. "An Ancient Conundrum." Review of *The Self and Its Brain,* by Karl Popper and Sir John Eccles. *Science* 200 (June 1978): 1040.

Margenau, Henry. "ESP in the Framework of Modern Science." In *Science and ESP,* ed. R. Smythies. London: Routledge and Kegan Paul, 1967.

Marvin, Fred R. *Last Words of Distinguished Men and Women.* New York: F. H. Revell, 1901.

Maslow, A. H. *Religions, Values and Peak Experiences.* New York: Viking Press, 1970.

Matson, A. *Afterlife: Reports from the Threshold of Death.* New York: Harper and Row, 1975.

Maurer, Daphne. "Infant Visual Perception: Methods of Study." In *Infant Perception,* vol. 1, ed. Leslie Cohen and Philip Salapatek, 5–34. New York: Academic Press, 1975.

Maxwell, Nicholas. "The Rationality of Scientific Discovery, Part II." *Philosophy of Science* 41 (September 1974): 275–95.

McAdams, Elizabeth, and Raymond Bayless. *The Case for Life after Death: Parapsychologists Look at the Evidence.* Chicago, Ill.: Nelson-Hall, 1981.

McClenon, J. *Deviant Science: The Case of Parapsychology.* Philadelphia, Pa.: University of Pennsylvania Press, 1984.

McConnell, R. A. *ESP Curriculum Guide.* New York: Simon and Schuster, 1971.

———. "The Resolution of Conflicting Beliefs About the ESP Evidence." *JPP* 41, no. 1 (September 1977): 199–212.

McCormick, D. L., ed. *Courses and Other Study Opportunities in Parapsychology.* New York: American Society for Psychical Research, 1987.

McDougall, William. "President's Address to the Society for Psychical Research." *PSPR* 27 (1914–15): 157–75.

McGill, Arthur. *Death and Life: An American Theology.* Edited by Charles A. Wilson and Peter M. Anderson. Minneapolis: Augsburg Fortress, 1987.

McHarg, J. F. Review of *At the Hour of Death,* by Haraldsson and Osis. *JSPR* 49 (1978): 886.

Meek, George W. *After We Die, What Then?* Rev. ed. Canal Winchester,

Ohio: Ariel Press, 1987.

Mertman, Sandra. "Communicating with the Dead." In *Between Life and Death,* ed. Robert Kastenbaum. New York: Springer, 1979.

Miller-McLemore, Bonnie J. *Death, Sin and the Moral Life.* Atlanta: Scholars Press, 1988.

Mitchell, J. L. *Out-of-body Experiences: A Handbook.* Jefferson, N.C.: McFarland, 1981.

———. "Out of the Body Experience." *Psychic* 2 (March 1973): 44–47.

———. "A Psychic Probe of the Planet Mercury." *Psychic* 4, no. 4 (June 1975): 17–21.

Mitchell, Weir. "The Case of Mary Reynolds." *Transactions of the College of Physicians of Philadelphia,* 4 April 1888.

Moncrieff, M. *The Clairvoyant Theory of Perception.* London: Faber and Faber, 1951.

Monroe, R. A. *Far Journeys.* Garden City, NY: Doubleday, 1985.

Moody, Raymond A. Jr. "Commentary on Rodin." *JNMD* 168, no. 5 (May 1980): 264.

———. *Life After Life.* Harrisburg, Pa.: Stackpole Books, 1976.

———. *The Light Beyond.* New York: Bantam Books, 1988.

———. *Reflections on Life After Life.* Atlanta, Ga.: Mockingbird, 1977.

Morris, J. D., and R. L. Morris, eds. *Research in Parapsychology.* Metuchen, N.J.: Scarecrow Press, 1976.

———. *Research in Parapsychology.* Metuchen, N.J.: Scarecrow Press, 1977.

Morse, Melvin, and Paul Perry. *Closer to the Light: Learning from Children's Near-Death Experiences.* New York: Villard Books, 1990.

Moss, Thelma. *The Probability of the Impossible.* Los Angeles: J. P. Tarcher, 1974.

Moss, Thelma, and Gertrude Schmeidler. "Quantitative Investigation of a Haunted House." *JASPR* 62, no. 4 (1968): 399–409.

———. "Quantitative Investigation of a Haunted House." *JASPR* 69 (1975): 341–51.

Mostofsky, D., ed. *Attention: Contemporary Theory and Analysis.* New York: Appleton, 1970.

Muldoon, Sylvan and H. Carrington. *The Case for Astral Projection.* London: Aries, 1936.

———. *Projection of the Astral Body.* London: Rider, 1929.

Muller, Karl. *Reincarnation Based on Facts.* London: Psychic Press, 1971.

Murphy, Gardner. "Are There Any Solid Facts in Psychical Research?" In *Philosophical Dimensions of Parapsychology,* ed. Hoyt L. Edge and J. M. O. Wheatley. Springfield, Ill.: Charles C. Thomas, 1976.

———. "A Caringtonian Approach to Ian Stevenson's *Twenty Cases Suggestive of Reincarnation." JASPR* 67, no. 2 (1973): 120.

———. "Difficulties Confronting the Survival Hypothesis." *JASPR* 39, no. 2 (1945): 67–94.

———. "Field Theory and Survival." *JASPR* 39, no. 4, pp. 200–201.

———. "Hornell Hart's Analysis of the Evidence for Survival." *JASPR,* 65, no. 1 (1961): 9–18.

———. "Outline of Survival Evidence." *JASPR* 38, no. 1 (1944): 2–4.

———. "Psychical Research and the Mind-Body Relation." *JASPR* 40, no. 4 (1946): 191–209.

Murphy, Gardner, with Laura Dale. *Challenge of Psychical Research: A Primer of Parapsychology.* New York: Harper and Row, Harper Colophon Books, 1970.

Murphy, Lois B., ed. *There is More Beyond: Selected Papers of Gardner Murphy.* Jefferson, N.C.: McFarland, 1989.

Murphy, Mary. *New Images of the Last Things: Karl Rahner on Death and Life After Death.* Mahwah, N.J.: Paulist Press, 1989.

Myers, F. W. H. "A Defence of Phantasms of the Dead." In *PSPR* 6 (1890): app. 1.

———. *Human Personality and Its Survival of Bodily Death.* London: Longmans, Green & Co., 1903.

———. "On Recognized Apparitions Occurring More than a Year After Death." *PSPR* 6 (1890): 29.

Naegeli-Osjord, Hans. *Possession and Exorcism.* Gerrards Cross, U.K.: Colin Smythe, 1988.

Nash, C. B. *Parapsychology: The Science of Psiology.* Springfield, Ill.: Charles C. Thomas, 1986.

Nicol, J. Fraser. "Old Light on New Phenomena." *Psychic* 2, no. 6 (May 1971): 26–28.

Noyes, Russell Jr. "Attitude Change Following Near-Death Experiences." *Psychiatry* 43 (1980): 234–32.

———. "The Experience of Dying." *Psychiatry* 35 (1972): 174–84.

———. "The Human Experience of Death; or, What Can We Learn from Near-Death Experiences?" *Omega* 13 (1983): 251–59.

———. "Near-Death Experiences: Their Investigation and Significance."

In *Between Life and Death,* ed. Robert Kastenbaum. New York: Springer, 1979.

Noyes, Russell Jr. and D. Slymen. "Subjective Response to Life-Threatening Danger." *Omega* 9 (1979): 313–21.

Oaten, E. W. *That Reminds Me.* London: Two Worlds, 1938.

Oesterreich, T. K. *Possession, Demoniacal and Other.* Translated by D. Ibberson. New York: University Books, 1966.

Olson, Melodie. "Incidence of Out-of-Body Experiences in Hospitalized Patients." *Journal of Near-Death Studies* 6 (1987): 169–174.

Oppenheim, Janet. *The Other World: Spiritualism and Psychical Research in England, 1850–1914.* New York: Cambridge University Press, 1988.

O'Roark, M. A. "Life After Death: The Growing Evidence." *McCall's,* March 1981, p. 28.

Osborn, Arthur W. *The Expansion of Awareness.* Wheaton, Ill.: Quest Books, 1967.

Osis, Karlis. "Deathbed Visions and the Afterlife Hypothesis." *Journal of Indian Psychology* 2, no. 1 (1979): 15.

———. "Kinetic Effects at the Ostensible Location of an Out-of-Body Projection During Perceptual Testing." *JASPR,* 74, no. 3 (1980): 319–28.

———. "Perceptual Experiments on OOBEs." In *Research in Parapsychology, 1974,* ed. William G. Roll, 53. Metuchen, N.J.: Scarecrow Press, 1975.

———. "Perspectives for Out-of-Body Research." In *Research in Parapsychology, 1972,* ed. William G. Roll, 113–16. Metuchen, N.J.: Scarecrow Press, 1973.

———. "Toward a Methodology for Experiments on OOBEs." In *Research in Parapsychology, 1972,* ed. William G. Roll, 78. Metuchen, N.J.: Scarecrow Press, 1973.

———. "Correspondence: Reply to Dr. McHarg." *JSPR* 50 (1979): 126–28.

Osis, Karlis, and Donna McCormick. "Kinetic Effects at the Ostensible Location of an OB Projection during Perceptual Testing." In *Research in Parapsychology, 1979,* ed. William G. Roll, 142–45. Metuchen, N.J.: Scarecrow Press, 1980.

Osis, Karlis, and Erlendur Haraldsson. *At the Hour of Death.* New York: Avon, 1977.

Osis, Karlis, and Erlendur Haraldsson. "Out-of-Body Experiences in Indian Swamis Sai Baba and Dadaji." In *Research in Parapsychology, 1975,* ed. J. D. Morris and R. L. Morris, 147–50. Metuchen, N.J.: Scarecrow

Press, 1976.

Ouspensky, Peter D. *A New Model of the Universe.* New York: Alfred A. Knopf, 1943.

Owen, Robert. *Footfalls on the Boundary of Another World.* London: Trubner, 1860.

Palmer, John. "Deathbed Apparitions and the Survival Hypothesis." *JASPR* 72 (1978): 392–95.

———. "ESP and Out-of-Body Experiences: EEG Correlates." *JASPR* 68, no. 3 (1974): 257–75.

———. "ESP Scoring from Four Definitions of the Sheep-Goat Variable." In *Research in Parapsychology, 1971,* ed. William G. Roll, 135–38. Metuchen: Scarecrow, 1972.

———. "Influence of Psychological Set on ESP and OBE's." *JASPR* 69, no. 3 (1975): 193–212.

Parker, Adrian. *States of Mind.* New York: Taplinger, 1975.

Parrish-Harra, Carol W. *The New Age Handbook on Death and Dying.* San Bernardino, Calif.: Borgo Press, 1989.

Pasricha, Satwant, and Ian Stevenson. "NDEs in India." *JNMD* 174, no. 3 (1986): 165–70.

Patterson, Robert L. "The Case for Immortality." *IJPR* 6, no. 2 (Summer 1975): 91.

Payne, Phoebe. *Man's Latent Powers.* London: Faber and Faber, 1938.

Penelhum, Terence, ed. *Immortality.* Belmont, Calif.: Wadsworth, 1973.

———. *Survival and Disembodied Existence.* London: Routledge & Kegan Paul, 1970.

Penfield, Wilder. *The Mystery of the Mind.* Princeton: Princeton University Press, 1975.

Pennachio, John. "Near-Death Experiences and Self-Transformations." *Journal of Near-Death Studies* 6 (1987): 162–68.

Piaget, Jean. *The Child's Conception of the World.* Lanham, Md.: Littlefield, Adams, 1975.

———. *Judgment and Reasoning in the Child.* Lanham, Md.: Littlefield, Adams, 1976.

Pierson, Jocelyn. "Externalized Images." *JASPR* 35, no. 2 (1941): 49.

———. "Old Books on Psychical Phenomena." *JASPR* 35, no. 3 (1941): 74–80, 98–104.

Planck, Max. *A Spiritual Autobiography.* New York: Philosophical Library, 1949.

Plato. *The Republic.* Bk. 10. Translated by A. D. Lindsay. London: J. M. Dent, 1925.

Playfair, Guy Lyon. *The Indefinite Boundary.* New York: St. Martin's, 1976.

Polanyi, Michael. *Tacit Knowing.* London: Routledge and Kegan Paul, 1967.

———. "Tacit Knowing: Its Bearing on Some Problems of Philosophy." *Review of Modern Physics* 34 (1962): 601–16.

Pole, Wellesley T. *Private Dowding.* London: J. M. Watkins, 1917.

Popper, K. R., and J. C. Eccles. *The Self and Its Brain.* New York: Springer, 1977.

Powell, A. E. *The Etheric Double.* London: Quest Books, 1969.

Poynton, John C. "Parapsychology and the Biological Sciences." In *Parapsychology and the Sciences,* ed. Alan Angoff and Betty Shapin. New York: Parapsychology Foundation, 1974.

Pratt, J. Gaither. *ESP Research Today: A Study of Development Since 1960.* Metuchen, N.J.: Scarecrow, 1973.

———. "Parapsychology, Normal Science and Paradigm Change." *JASPR* 73, no. 3 (1979): 25–26.

———. *The Psychic Realm: What Can You Believe?* New York: Random House, 1975.

Pribram, Karl. "Holographic Memory." Interview by Daniel Goleman. *Psychology Today,* February 1979, p. 84.

———. "The Cognitive Revolution in Mind/Brain Issues." *American Psychologist* 41 (1986): 507–20.

Price, George R. "Science and the Supernatural." *Science* 122, no. 3165 (1955): 362.

———. "Survival and the Idea of Another World." *PSPR* 50 (January 1953): 182.

Prince, Walter F. *The Enchanted Boundary.* Boston: Boston Society for Psychical Research, 1930.

———. *Noted Witnesses for Psychic Occurrences.* Boston: Boston Society for Psychical Research, 1928.

Puccetti, R. "Sperry on Consciousness." *Journal of Medicine and Philosophy* 2, no. 2 (June 1977), 130–37.

Punzak, Dan. "The Use of Near-Death Phenomena in Therapy." *Journal of Near-Death Studies* 7 (1988): 173–82.

Randall, J. L. "Psi Phenomena and Biological Theory." *JSPR* 46 (1971): 151–65.

Rao, K. R., and J. Palmer. "The Anomaly Called Psi: Recent Research and Criticism." *Behavioural and Brain Sciences* 10 (1988): 538–51.

Rauscher, William V., and Allen Spraggett. *The Spiritual Frontier.* New York: Doubleday, 1975.

Rawlings, Maurice. *Beyond Death's Door.* Nashville, Tenn.: Thomas Nelson, 1979.

Rees, W. Dewi. "The Hallucinations of Widows." *British Medical Journal,* 4 (1971): 37–41.

Reeves, M. P. "A Review: Tyrell's Study of Apparitions." *JPP* 8, 1 (1944): 64–83.

Reid, Thomas. *Essays on the Intellectual Powers of Man.* Cambridge: M.I.T. Press, 1969.

Reim, M., C. Teping, and J. Silny. "Vision stereoscopique: Etude objective et developpement pendant les premiers mois de la vie." *Journal Francais d'Opthalmologie* 12, no. 10, pp. 623–27.

Restok, Richard. Review of *Broca's Brain,* by Carl Sagan. *New York Times Book Review,* 29 May 1977, p. 8.

Reyes, Benito F. *Conscious Dying: Psychology of Death and Guidebook to Liberation.* Ojai, Calif.: World University of America, 1987.

Reyna, Ruth. *Reincarnation and Science.* New Delhi: Sterling, 1973.

Reynolds, F. E., and E. H. Waugh, eds. *Religious Encounters with Death.* University Park: Pennsylvania State University Press, 1977.

Rhine, J. B. "Comments on 'Science and the Supernatural.' " *Science* 123, no. 3184 (1956): 12.

———. "Research on Spirit Survival Reexamined." *JPP* 20, no. 2 (June 1956): 127.

Rhine, Louisa E. "Auditory Psi Experience: Hallucination or Physical?" *JPP* 27, no. 3 (1963): 182–97.

———. "Case Study Review." *JPP* 33, no. 3 (1969): 260.

———. "Hallucinatory Psi Experiences." *JPP* 21, no. 1 (1957): 33–35.

———. "Reply to Dr. Stevenson." *JPP* 32, no. 2 (1970): 161–62.

———. Review of *Twenty Cases Suggestive of Reincarnation,* by Ian Stevenson. *JPP* 30, no. 4 (1966): 263–72.

Rhodes, Leon, "Are Out-of-Body Experiences Evidence for Survival?" *Journal of Near-Death Studies* 7 (1988): 57–61.

Richards, Hubert J. *Death and After: What Will Really Happen?* Mystic, Conn.: Twenty-Third, 1987.

Richet, Claude. *Thirty Years of Psychical Research.* Translated by Stanley deBrath. New York: Macmillan, 1923.

Ring, Kenneth. "Commentary on 'The Reality of Death Experiences' by Rodin," *JNMD* 168, no. 5 (May 1980): 273–74.

———. "Further Studies of the Near-Death Experience." *Theta* 7 (1979): 1.

———. *Heading Toward Omega.* New York: Morrow, 1984.

———. *Life at Death.* New York: Coward, McCann & Geoghegan, 1980.

———. "Precognitive and Prophetic Visions in Near-Death Experiences." *Anabiosis* 2 (1982): 47–74.

Ring, Kenneth, and Christopher J. Rosing. "The Omega Project: An Empirical Study of the NDE-Prone Personality." *Journal of Near-Death Studies* 8, no. 4 (1989): 211–39.

Ritchie, G. G. *Return from Tomorrow.* Waco, Tex.: Chosen Books, 1978.

Robb, James H. *Man as Infinite Spirit.* Milwaukee, Wis.: Marquette University, 1974.

Rodin, Ernst A. "The Reality of Death Experiences." *JNMD* 158, no. 5 (May 1980): 262.

———. "A Reply to Commentaries." *Anabiosis* 2, no. 3 (February 1981): 15.

Rogo, D. Scott. "Astral Projection in Tibetan Buddhist Literature." *IJPP* 10, no. 3 (1968): 278–83.

———. *The Evidence for Life after Death.* Wellingborough, U.K.: Aquarian Press, 1985.

———. *The Welcoming Silence.* New Hyde Park, N.Y.: University Books, 1973.

Roll, William G. "A Critical Examination of the Survival Hypothesis." In *A Century of Psychical Research,* ed. Alan Angoff and Betty Shapin. New York: Parapsychology Foundation, 1971.

———. "OBE Experiments with a Cat as Detector." In *Research in Parapsychology, 1974,* ed. William G. Roll, 55–56. Metuchen, N.J.: Scarecrow Press, 1975.

———, ed. *Research in Parapsychology, 1974.* Metuchen, N.J.: Scarecrow Press, 1975.

———, ed. *Research in Parapsychology, 1979.* Metuchen, N.J.: Scarecrow Press, 1980.

———. "A New Look at the Survival Problem." In *New Directions in*

Parapsychology, ed. John Beloff. London: Elek Science, 1974.

———. "Pagenstecher's Contribution to Parapsychology." *JASPR* 61, no. 3 (1967): 219–40.

———. "Poltergeists and Hauntings." *Papers from the 19th Annual Convention of the Parapsychology Association.* Metuchen, N.J.: Scarecrow Press, 1977.

Rugh, Robert S., and Landrum B. Shettles. *From Conception to Birth.* New York: Harper and Row, 1971.

Ryall, Edward. *Born Twice: Total Recall of a Seventeenth-Century Life.* New York: Harper and Row, 1975.

Ryle, Gilbert. *The Concept of Mind.* New York: Barnes and Noble, 1949.

Saavedra-Aguilar, Juan C. "A Neurobiological Model for Near-Death Experiences." *Journal of Near-Death Studies* 7 (1988): 205–22.

Sabom, Michael. *Recollections of Death.* New York: Harper and Row, 1982.

Sabom, Michael, and S. Kreutzinger. "The Experience of Near-Death." *Death Education* 1 (1977): 195–203.

Sagan, Carl. *Broca's Brain.* New York: Random House, 1979.

Salapatek, Philip. "Pattern Perception in Early Infancy." In *Infant Perception,* ed. Leslie Cohen and Philip Salapatek. New York: Academic Press, 1975.

———. "Visual Scanning of Geometric Figures by the Human Newborn." *Journal of Comparative Physiological Psychology* 66 (1968): 247–57.

Salter, W. H. *Ghosts and Apparitions.* London: G. Bell and Sons, 1938.

———. *Zoar; or, The Evidence of Psychical Research Concerning Survival.* London: Sidgwick and Jackson, 1961.

Scheler, Max. "Tod und Fortleben" [Death and survival]. *Schriften aus dem Nachlass.* Bern, Switzerland: Franke, 1933.

Schmeidler, Gertrude. "Investigation of a Haunted House." *JASPR* 60, no. 2 (1966): 139–49.

———. *Parapsychology and Psychology: Matches and Mismatches.* Jefferson, N.C.: McFarland, 1988.

———. "Predicting Good and Bad Scores in a Clairvoyance Experiment." *JASPR* 37, no. 4 (1943): 210–21.

Schoenbeck, S. B. and G. D. Hocutt. "Near-Death Experiences in Patients Undergoing Cardiopulmonary Resuscitation." *Journal of Near-Death Studies* 9, no. 4 (1990): 211–18.

Schopenhauer, Arthur. *Death and the Indestructibility of Our Inner Nature.*

Albuquerque, N.M.: Foundation for Classical Reprints, 1986.

———. *Parerga und Paralipomena.* Translated by E. J. F. Payne. Oxford: Clarendon Press, 1974.

Schulman, C. "Eye Movements in Infants Using dc Recording." *Neuropediatrie* 4 (1973): 76–86.

Schwarz, Berthold E. *Psychic Nexus: Psychic Phenomena in Psychiatry and Everyday Life.* New York: Van Nostrand Reinhold, 1980.

———. "Telepathic Events in a Child Between One and 3 1/2 Years." *IJPP* 3, no. 4 (1961): 5–46.

Scriven, Michael. "Explanations of the Supernatural." In *Philosophy and Psychical Research,* ed. Shivesh C. Thakur. London: George Allen & Unwin, 1976.

———. "Explanations, Predictions, and Laws." In *Readings in the Philosophy of Science,* ed. Baruch A. Brody. Englewood Cliffs, N.J.: Prentice-Hall, 1970.

———. "New Frontiers of the Brain." *JPP* 25 (1961): 309–11.

———. "Personal Identity and Parapsychology." *JASPR* 69, no. 4 (1965): 312.

Seki, Hideo. *Five Dimensional World.* Tokyo: Chūo-kōron-jigyō, 1974.

Serdahely, William J. "A Comparison of Retrospective Accounts of Childhood Near-Death Experiences with Contemporary Pediatric Near-Death Experience Accounts." *Journal of Near-Death Studies* 9, no. 4 (1991): 219–24.

Serdahely, William J., and Barbara A. Walker. "Near-Death Experiences of a Nonverbal Person with Congenital Quadriplegia." *Journal of Near-Death Studies* 9, no. 2 (1990): 91–96.

Servadio, Emilio. "Mind-Body, Reality, and Psi." In *Brain/Mind and Parapsychology,* ed. Betty Shapin and Lisette Coly. New York: Parapsychology Foundation, 1979.

Shaffer, Jerome A. "Personal Identity: The Implications of Brain Bisection and Brain Transplants." *Journal of Medicine and Philosophy* 2, no. 2 (June 1977): 147–60.

Shapin, Betty, and Lisette Coly. *Brain/Mind and Parapsychology.* New York: Parapsychology Foundation, 1979.

———, eds. *Communication and Parapsychology.* New York: Parapsychology Foundation, 1980.

———. *Parapsychology, Philosophy, and Religious Concepts.* New York: Parapsychology Foundation, 1985.

———. *The Repeatability Problem in Parapsychology.* New York: Parapsychology Foundation, 1985.

Shira, Indre. "The Raynham Hall Ghost." *Country Life,* 16 December 1936, pp. 673–75.

Shirley, R. *The Mystery of the Human Double.* New York: University Books, 1965.

Shneidman, Edwin S. *Death: Current Perspectives.* Mountain View, Calif.: Mayfield, 1984.

Sidgwick, Henry, et al. "Phantasms of the Dead." *PSPR* 10 (1894): 394.

———. "Report on the Census of Hallucinations." *PSPR* 10 (1894): 36–44.

Siegel, Ronald K. "The Psychology of Life After Life." *American Psychologist* 35, no. 10 (October 1980): 923.

Siegel, Ronald K., and L. J. West., eds. *Hallucinations: Behavior, Experience and Theory.* New York: John Wiley and Sons, 1975.

Slawinski, Janusz. "Electromagnetic Radiation and the Afterlife." *Journal of Near-Death Studies* 6 (1987): 127–45.

Smith, Robert C. *You Can Remember Your Past Lives.* New York: Warner Books, 1989.

Smith, S. *The Enigma of Out-of-Body Travel.* New York: Garrett Publications, 1965.

Smythies, J. R., ed. *Brain and Mind.* London: Routledge and Kegan Paul, 1965.

———, ed. *Science and ESP.* London: Routledge and Kegan Paul, 1967.

Snow, Chet B., and Helen Wambach. *Mass Dreams of the Future.* New York: McGraw-Hill, 1989.

Snyder, R. D., S. K. Hata, B. S. Brann, and R. M. Mills. "Subcortical Visual Function in the Newborn." *Pediatric Neurology* 6, no. 5 (Sept.-Oct. 1990): 333–36.

Stearn, J. *A Matter of Immortality: Dramatic Evidence of Survival.* New York: Atheneum, 1976.

Steiner, Rudolf. *Life Between Death and Rebirth.* New York: Anthroposophic Press, 1975.

Stevens, E. W. *The Watseka Wonder.* Chicago: Religio-Philosophical Publishing House, 1887.

Stevenson, Ian. "Carington's Psychon Theory . . . " *JASPR* 67, no. 2 (1973): 132.

———. *Cases of the Reincarnation Type.* Vol. 1: *Ten Cases in India.* Charlottesville: University Press of Virginia, 1975.

————. *Cases of the Reincarnation Type.* Vol. 2: *Ten Cases in Sri Lanka.* Charlottesville: University Press of Virginia, 1977.

————. "Comments on 'The Reality of Death Experiences' by Rodin." *JNMD* 168, no. 5 (May 1980): 271–72.

————. "A New Case of Responsive Xenoglossy: The Case of Gretchen." *JASPR* 70, no. 1 (1976): 65–77.

————. "A Reply to Gardner Murphy." *JASPR* 67, no. 2 (1973): 132–34.

————. Review of *The Cathars and Reincarnation,* by Arthur Guirdham. *JASPR* 66, no. 1 (1972): 113–19.

————. *Twenty Cases Suggestive of Reincarnation.* 2d ed. Charlottesville: University Press of Virginia, 1974.

————. *Xenoglossy: A Review and Report of a Case.* Charlottesville: University Press of Virginia, 1974.

Stevenson, Ian, et al. "Research into the Evidence of Man's Survival After Death." *JNMD* 165, no. 3 (1977): 153–83.

Story, Francis. *Rebirth as Doctrine and Experience.* Kandy, Sri Lanka: Buddhist Publication Society, 1975.

Sutherland, Cherie. "Changes in Religious Beliefs, Attitudes, and Practices Following Near-Death Experiences: An Australian Study." *Journal of Near-Death Studies* 9, no. 1 (1990): 21–32.

————. "Psychic Phenomena Following Near-Death Experiences: An Australian Study." *Journal of Near-Death Studies* 8, no. 2 (1989): 93–102.

Tabori, Cornelius. "The Case of Iris Farczady." Translated by Paul Tabori. *IJPP* 9, no. 3 (1967): 223–26.

Tart, Charles T. "Altered States of Consciousness and the Possibility of Survival of Death." In *Consciousness and Survival,* ed. J. Spong. Sausalito, Calif.: Institute of Noetic Sciences, 1987.

————. "Emergent Interactionism and Consciousness." In *Brain/Mind and Parapsychology,* ed. Betty Shapin and Lisette Coly. New York: Parapsychology Foundation, 1979.

————. "Out-of-the-Body Experiences." In *Psychic Exploration, A Challenge for Science,* ed. E. D. Mitchell and J. White. New York: G. P. Putnam's Sons, 1974.

————. *Psi.* New York: E. P. Dutton, 1977.

————. "Psychics' Fear of Psychic Powers." *JASPR* 80 (1986): 279–92.

————. "Psychological Resistance in Research on Channeling." *Research in Parapsychology 1986,* ed. D. H. Weiner and R. D. Nelson. Metuchen, N.J.: Scarecrow Press, 1987.

————. "A Psychophysiological Study of Some OBEs." *JASPR* 62, no. 1 (1968): 3–23.

————. "Report to the Parapsychology Association Conventions." *JPP* 29, no. 4 (1965): 281–82.

————. "Report to the Parapsychology Association Conventions." *JPP* 30, no. 4 (1966): 278.

————. "States of Consciousness and State-Specific Sciences." *Science* 176 (12 June 1972): 1203–10.

————. *Waking Up: Overcoming the Obstacles to Human Potential.* Boston: New Science Library, 1986.

Thakur, Shivesh C., ed. *Philosophy and Psychical Research.* London: George Allen and Unwin, 1976.

Thomas, C. D. *Life Beyond Death with Evidence.* London: W. Collins Sons, 1928.

Thouless, R. H., and Betty P. Weiner. "The Psi Processes in Normal and Paranormal Psychology." *PSPR* 48, no. 174 (December 1947).

Tietze, Thomas R. "The Mysterious Wax Gloves." *Psychic* 2, no. 5 (April 1971): 24–25.

Toynbee, Arnold, ed. *Life After Death.* New York: McGraw-Hill, 1976.

————. *Man's Concern With Death.* London: Hodder and Stoughton, 1968.

Tribbe, F. C., ed. *The Ashby Guidebook for the Study of the Paranormal.* York Beach, Me: Samuel Weiser, 1987.

Truzzi, Marcello. "A Skeptical Look at Paul Kurtz's Analysis of the Scientific Status of Parapsychology." *JPP* 44, no. 1 (1980): 89–95.

Twemlow, Stuart. "Clinical Approaches to Out-of-Body Experience." *Journal of Near-Death Studies* 8, no. 1 (1989): 29–44.

Tylor, E. B. *Primitive Culture.* Vol. 2. New York: Harper, 1958.

Tymms, Ralph. *Doubles in Literary Psychology.* Cambridge: Bowes & Bowes, 1949.

Tyrrell, G. N. M. *Apparitions.* London: Duckworth, 1953.

Ullman, Montague. *Dream Telepathy.* Jefferson, N.C.: McFarland, 1989.

Ullman, Montague, et al. "Experimentally-Induced Telepathic Dreams." *IJPP* 8, no. 4 (1968): 577–97.

Vasiliev, Leonid V. *Mysterious Phenomena of the Human Psyche.* Translated by Sonia Volochova. New York: University Books, 1965.

Vaughan, A. *The Edge of Tomorrow.* New York: Dodd, Mead, 1988.

Vital-Durand, F., and A. Hullo. "La mésure de l'acuité visuelle du nourrisson en six minutes." *Journal Francais d'Opthalmologie* 12, no. 3 (1989): 221–25.

Walker, Benjamin. *Beyond the Body*. London: Routledge and Kegan Paul, 1974.

Wallis, Roy, ed. *On the Margins of Science: The Social Construction of Rejected Knowledge*. Keele, U.K.: Keele University Press, 1979.

Wambach, Helen. "Life Before Life." *Psychic* 9 (January 1972): 10–13.

Warburg, M. "Synets udvikling" [Development of sight]. *Ugeskrift for Laeger* 153, no. 22 (27 May 1991): 1571–75.

Watson, Lyall. *The Romeo Error*. New York: Doubleday, 1975.

Weiner, D. H., and Robert L. Morris, eds. *Research in Parapsychology, 1987*. Metuchen, N.J.: Scarecrow Press, 1988.

Weiner, D. H., and Roger D. Nelson, eds. *Research in Parapsychology, 1986*. Metuchen, N.J.: Scarecrow Press, 1987.

Weiner, D. H., and Dean I. Radin, eds. *Research in Parapsychology, 1985*. Metuchen, N.J.: Scarecrow Press, 1986.

West, Donald J. *Psychical Research Today*. London: Duckworth, 1954.

———. Review of "Facts and Fallacies in the Name of Science," by Gardner Murphy. *JSPR* 39 (September 1958): 297.

West, Louis J., "A General Theory of Hallucinations and Dreams." In *Hallucinations*, ed. Louis J. West, 282–88. New York: Grune and Stratton, 1962.

———, ed. *Hallucinations*. New York: Grune and Stratton, 1962.

Westen, Robin. *Channelers: A New Age Directory*. New York: Putnam, 1988.

Westman, A. S. and F. M. Canter. "Fear of Death and the Concept of Extended Self." *Psychological Reports* 56 (1985): 419–25.

Wheatley, J. M. O. "Implications for Religious Studies." In *Advances in Parapsychological Research*, ed. Stanley Krippner. New York: Plenum, 1977.

———. "The Necessity for Bodies." *JASPR* 66, no. 3 (July 1972): 322–27.

———. "The Question of Survival: Some Logical Reflections." *JASPR* 59, no. 1 (1965): 207–9.

———. "Reincarnation, Astral Bodies, and Psi Components." *JASPR* 73, no. 2 (1979): 109.

White, John, and S. Krippner, eds. *Future Science: Life Energies and the Physics of Paranormal Phenomena*. Garden City, N.Y.: Anchor Press, 1977.

White, Rhea A. *Déjà Vu: A Bibliography*. Dix Hills, N.Y.: Parapsychology Sources of Information, 1989.

————. *Parapsychology Almanac*. Dix Hills, N.Y.: Parapsychology Sources of Information, 1989.

White, Rhea A., and Jerry Solfvin, eds. *Research in Parapsychology, 1984*. Metuchen, N.J.: Scarecrow, 1985.

Whitton, Joel L., and Joe Fisher. *Life Between Life: Scientific Explorations into the Void Separating One Incarnation from the Next*. New York: Warner Books, 1989.

Wigan, Arthur Ladbroke. *The Duality of Mind*. London: Brown and Longmans, 1844.

Wilson, Ian. *The After-Death Experience*. New York: Morrow, 1989.

Wolman, Benjamin, ed. *Handbook of Parapsychology*. New York: Van Nostrand, 1976.

Wood, F. H. *This Egyptian Miracle*. London: John Watkins, 1955.

Zalesky, Carol. "Evaluating Near-Death Testimony," *Journal of Near-Death Studies* 5, no. 2 (1986): 17–52.

————. *Otherworld Journeys: Accounts of Near-Death Experience in Medieval and Modern Times*. New York: Oxford University Press, 1987.

INDEX